WHAT IS A WELCOME?

It is the cup of tea an old man offered
me as we crouched together under
a banana tree during a late-afternoon
rainstorm in Malaysia. The bowl of
handmade noodles I was served in
a Japanese farmhouse. The off-key
harmonizing of a group of school
children in Manila who greeted me
with a folk song and fistfuls of
fresh-picked flowers.

All over Asia, tea, food, and music
are the universal signs of welcome.
They bring the promise of sharing,
friendship, and laughter. And it is in
that spirit that I offer this book to you.

Welcome to my home-away-from-
home. My birthplace and my culinary
touchstone. Welcome to my Asia.

Japan

China

India

Taiwan

Hong Kong

The Philippines

Thailand

Malaysia

Singapore

Borneo

Sumatra

Indonesia

Java

MARTIN YAN'S

Asia

— favorite recipes from —

Hong Kong, Singapore, Malaysia, the Philippines, and Japan

by Martin Yan

Companion to the
Public Television Series
YAN CAN COOK

Food Photography
by Geoffrey Nilsen

YAN CAN COOK is made possible
by generous grants from Circulon
Cookware, Lee Kum Kee, Vitasoy,
Azumaya & Nasoya, Cost Plus World
Market, Foster Farms, Elkay
Manufacturing Co., Aroma Housewares,
GE Monogram, and Braun.

KQED
BOOKS &TAPES

San Francisco

Publisher: James Connolly
Editorial Director: Pamela Byers
Art Director: Jeffrey O'Rourke
Project Editor: Tina Salter
Writer: Stephen Siegelman
Book and Cover Design: Traci Shiro
Project Coordinators for Yan Can Cook:
    Maura Devlin & Helen Soehalim
Copy Editor and Glossary: Margaret McKinnon
Food Photography: Geoffrey Nilsen
Art Direction: Traci Shiro
Food Stylist: Pouké
Prop Stylist: Carol Hacker
Food Photography Coordinator: Tina Salter
Photography Chefs: Bernice Chuck Fong & Karen Wang
Travel Photography: Stephanie Jan & Linda Mead
Photographs on pages.62, 63,74,79,83,101, 115, 134, 161, 232-
    240: Keng Lim, Yellow Studios
Photographs on pages 16 and 19: Hong Kong Tourist
    Association
Photograph on page 60: Singapore Tourist Promotion Board
Food and props provided by:
    Genji: San Francisco
    Man-U, Treasures of China: San Mateo, California
    Ethnic Arts: Berkeley, California
    Red and Green Company: San Francisco
    Chef Sonny Lee: Sushi Kinta Restaurant,
        San Francisco
Photography on pages 67 and 218 shot on location at
    Orientations: Asian Antiques, San Francisco
Hand models: Chizuko Shiro, Stella Nilsen, Karen Wang,
    Martin Yan

Text © 1997 by Yan Can Cook
Photos © 1997 by Bay Books & Tapes

Educational and nonprofit groups wishing to order this book
at attractive quantity discounts may contact Bay Books & Tapes,
555 De Haro St., No. 220, San Francisco, CA 94107.

Library of Congress Cataloguing-in-Publication Data

Yan, Martin, 1948- Martin Yan's Asia : favorite recipes from Hong
Kong, Singapore, Malaysia, the Philippines, and Japan / Martin
Yan ; food photography by Geoffrey Nilsen.
p. cm.
"Companion to the Public Television series Yan Can Cook."
Includes index.
ISBN 0-912333-32-4 (pbk.)
1. Cookery, Oriental. I. Yan Can Cook (Television program)
II. Title.
TX724.5.A1Y36 1997   97-36267
641.595--dc21   CIP

KQED Books & Tapes™, an imprint of Bay Books & Tapes,
is a trademark of KQED, Inc.

ISBN 0-912333-32-4

Printed in China
10 9 8 7 6 5 4 3 2

On the cover: Tea Fields on Mount Fuji,
© Travelpix/FPG International LLC

Distributed to the trade by Publishers Group West

ACKNOWLEDGMENTS

This beautiful book and the public television series *Yan Can Cook: The Best of Asia* are the work of many hands. I am so proud to be a part of the team of talented, hardworking people who have joined me in bringing the best of Asia to you.

Let me begin by thanking my publishers at KQED Books: Pam Byers, who is always gracious, charming, and receptive; and James Connolly, a gentleman and a scholar. Thanks also to Bob Manley and Jeffrey O'Rourke.

I am truly grateful to Tina Salter, managing editor, who managed to keep her sanity and good humor while working 25 hours a day, 8 days a week! She is a good friend and a true professional. Special thanks to Steve Siegelman, writer extraordinaire, who once again has eloquently captured the spirit of Asia on these pages as no one else can; Traci Shiro, our unflappable designer and art director, for her sense of style and aesthetic vision; and Margaret McKinnon, our wise and dedicated copy editor.

Geoffrey Nilsen's beautifully evocative photographs bring the flavors of Asia to life. Geoffrey, you are a master and a true magician, and I'm so glad we could work together again.

For helping to create the stunning settings and the mouthwatering food in the photographs that grace this book, my thanks to Pouké, food stylist; Carol Hacker, prop stylist; Karen Wang and Bernice Chuck Fong, chefs; and volunteers Michael Procopio and Carol Odman.

If Yan can cook, so can Jan Nix, Jennifer Yuen Louie, Linda Mead, Winnie Lee, and Julia Lee. I thank you all for your tireless dedication in testing and perfecting my recipes. Thanks also to Soon Har Tan for her helpful advice on the Singapore and Malaysia chapters.

Stephanie Jan has been my indefatigable personal assistant and right hand throughout this remarkable journey. I am deeply indebted to Virginia Bast for her many years of dedicated support in our office, and to Maura Devlin, our multitalented marketing director. As always, Helen Soehalim rose to the occasion, overseeing recipe testing and making herself generally indispensable.

And of course thanks to Sue, for her constant and immense patience and support.

Introduction

In my late teens, I left Hong Kong and went to work for a friend who owned a restaurant in Alberta, Canada. I can remember exactly what I was thinking as the airplane took off: "I wonder if I'll ever come back."

Which just goes to show you that the journey of life is full of surprises. In the last two years alone, I've made 15 trips to Asia. I sometimes feel like I spend more time in the air than on the ground!

Most of those trips had something to do with researching and filming the seventh season of the *Yan Can Cook* show, *Yan Can Cook, The Best of Asia*, and this companion cookbook. My television crew and I filmed hundreds of hours of footage, took reams of notes, collected stacks of recipes, and shot roll after roll of still photos in cities, villages, restaurants, homes, and all kinds of exotic locations all over Asia.

There's a tattered, food-stained map hanging on the wall in my office that charts our odyssey. The crisscrossing lines of colored ink form a long, tall stripe, from the northern tip of Japan to Hong Kong, the Philippines, Malaysia, and Singapore.

These two years have been energizing, exhausting, and entirely unforgettable. At last count, we had covered more than a million miles by plane, car, boat, train, and bus. Oh, and I almost forgot bicycle, pedicab, horseback, and water buffalo.

Whenever we could, we tried to look beyond the five-star hotels and tourist spots, and connect with real people in real places. In the Philippines and Malaysia, we spent a few days living with headhunters—and I don't mean the corporate type. In Hong Kong's Aberdeen Harbour, we slept, ate, and fished for two days on the tiny boat of a Tanka family. We learned how to sleep while bouncing along bumpy backroads.

I awoke one morning in Tokyo to find that I couldn't move my right leg. After three weeks of sitting on the floor with my feet tucked under me while we shot take after take, my kneecap had decided enough was enough. Desperate to stay on schedule and to regain the ability to walk, I visited an acupuncturist. There I was in a room surrounded by men, women, and lots of little kids, all stoically enduring their treatments. I tried to remain calm, but soon tears were streaming down my face. The more

I cried, the more the kids thought I was joking and the harder they laughed.

Then there was the root canal surgery in Singapore. But that's another story.

The View from the Kitchen

Of course, in between all the stress and strain of traveling and filming, there was the thrill of sampling some of the most spectacular food I've ever tasted.

As a chef and cooking teacher, my goal when I travel is not just to eat, but to really get inside the food. Sure, it's wonderful to try restaurants and feast on street foods; but that's just the beginning. The part I love—and I'm very fortunate to be able to experience it wherever I go—is what happens behind the scenes in the kitchen.

In preparing this book, I worked in Asian kitchens of every imaginable kind. Gleaming stainless steel ones that feed thousands of people a night. Tiny home kitchens with a single wood-and-straw burner and chickens running in the yard. The portable kitchen carts of street vendors. The cramped yet miraculously efficient kitchen of a luxury train. The vast commissary of an international airline that fills an entire airplane hangar.

I roasted a suckling pig in an open-pit barbecue at a fiesta in the Philippines, steamed rice in bamboo trunks over glowing embers in a tribal village deep in the jungle of Borneo, and joined in the excitement of preparing a communal dinner for 1,000 in a Hakka village in the New Territories of Hong Kong.

I met master chefs, self-made restaurant millionaires, hardworking street hawkers, spice vendors and fishmongers, experts on local ingredients and seasonings, and home cooks whose food is the product of generations of kitchen lore and know-how.

They are the true authors of this book, and I've tried to capture their inspirations and their infectious enthusiasm about cooking in these pages.

Chronicling the Cuisines of Asia

Of course, there's really no such thing as "Asian cuisine." The region's diverse geography, climates, cultural factors, and religious guidelines have given rise to an enormous range of culinary styles. In the

Riding the rails at a palm oil plantation near Kuala Lumpur, Malaysia.

Bent on trying every kind of bento box lunch in Japan.

hands of a Malaysian cook, prawns might be simmered with a fiery ground spice paste and coconut milk to make a rich curry. In Hong Kong, I imagine them being pulled fresh from a tank in a restaurant, quickly steamed, and served in a light oil, ginger, and scallion sauce. In Japan, they might not even be cooked at all but rather served as sushi with a bit of soy sauce and wasabi for dipping.

So what do the cuisines of Asia have in common? To me the answer comes down to one word: respect. No matter where I travel in Asia, I find that cooks share a respect for food—not just as a fuel for living but as one of life's most important gifts to be appreciated, discussed, prepared, shared, and honored with great love and care.

It is a respect for the traditions of cooking, passed along from one generation to the next. And above all, it is a respect for the integrity and true flavor of ingredients.

The recipes in this book were developed with that sense of respect in mind. Some of the dishes are hundreds—even thousands—of years old. Some are modern inventions. Some are my own interpretations and creations.

I have simplified and adapted some of these recipes to make them easy and enjoyable for a worldwide audience of home cooks. I've tried to strike a balance between readily available ingredients and hard-to-find ones in order to give you as much of a taste of the authentic flavors of Asia as possible. And rather than be a slave to "authenticity," I've added some of my own favorite ingredients here and there because that's the real fun of cooking.

Don't let the exotic ingredients in this book intimidate you. If there's no store that sells lemongrass where you live, maybe there's a Malaysian or Thai restaurant in your city that will. If you can't track down an ingredient, substitute the closest thing you can think of or omit it altogether— you'll still have something wonderful. Keep searching and exploring. Be bold. And most of all, have fun.

Discovering new foods can be one of life's greatest adventures—whether you travel thousands of miles a year or never leave home. The older I get, the more clearly I understand that cooking is not a craft or a set of skills. It's a journey. Follow your nose, cook from your heart, and may all your journeys be filled with joy and wonder.

Tools, Techniques, and Tips

Most Asian kitchens are simple and functional, and most of the Asian cooks I know rely on a very few trusty tools and cooking implements. I've written the recipes in this book with that in mind. Whether you're preparing a classic Hong Kong-style stir-fry or simmering a Malaysian curry, you won't need much more in the way of specialized equipment than a wok or stir-fry pan, a steamer, and a good knife. In Malaysia and Singapore, a mortar and pestle is essential for making spice pastes, but I find that a blender does just as well. I also rely on my trusty electric rice cooker, which frees up the stovetop and makes perfect rice every time.

The Wok

In Malaysia and Singapore, it's called a kuali, in the Philippines, it's a carajay, but most of the world simply calls it by its Chinese name, a wok. In Asia, the wok is probably the most frequently used kitchen implement, and once you discover how versatile it can be, it might just become the most-used piece of cookware you own. You'll find that stir-frying is just the beginning. A wok is great for steaming, deep-frying, braising, stewing, boiling, poaching, and even smoking.

If you don't already own a wok, or if you're thinking of upgrading, you might consider buying one of the many wok kits on the market. Most contain everything you need, including a lid, wok stand, spatula, ladle, strainer, and steaming rack.

Round-bottomed woks work best when used over gas burners. You can set the wok directly over the burner grate or, for greater stability, use a perforated, ring-shaped metal stand to hold the wok in place. Flat-bottomed woks or stir-fry pans are designed for use with electric burners, and can sit right on the heating element without a stand.

For family cooking like the kind presented in this book, a wok measuring 12 to 14 inches in diameter is your best bet. It will hold enough food to serve four to six people.

The time-honored carbon steel wok must be seasoned before using. Wash the wok well, place it over medium heat, and, using paper towels, wipe it with cooking oil until it begins to darken. Keep changing towels until they come away clean. Carbon steel woks should be cleaned with hot water and little or no soap while they're still hot. After cleaning and rinsing, always dry your wok over high heat.

Woks and stir-fry pans made of hard anodized aluminum are becoming quite popular and readily available. They need no seasoning, and many offer a nonstick, scratch-resistant cooking surface. Because they require little or no oil, they're great for healthy cooking. These substantial, durable pans are also excellent conductors of heat, and many kinds—particularly Circulon—can withstand oven temperatures of up to 350°F. Stir-fry pans with flat bottoms work well over both gas and electric stoves.

Electric woks are designed for all-purpose use, and they're ideal for deep-frying, braising, and steaming since they allow you to set and maintain exact cooking temperatures.

Ten Steps to Perfect Stir-Frying

Here are my ten steps to stir-fry success. (Of course, every dish is different, and the recipes in this book will give you exact directions.)

Wokking to work in a Hakka Village in Hong Kong's New Territories.

1. Chop till you drop. To ensure even cooking, chop, slice, dice, or shred each ingredient into uniform pieces.

2. Get ready. Stir-frying is like downhill skiing—once you start, there's no stopping. So, read the recipe and make sure you have everything cut up, marinated, measured, and close at hand. Don't forget the serving plate and the garnish.

3. Seat the guests. No kidding! You don't want your piping hot creation getting cold and soggy while you herd your friends and family to the table.

4. Heat first, oil second. Place the empty wok over high heat for a minute or two. When you can feel the heat by lowering your hand slightly into the wok, you're ready to add the oil. Drizzle the oil (it doesn't usually take more than a few tablespoons) around the sides of the wok, swirling it to coat the surface. Wait until the oil is hot, about 15 seconds, before adding other ingredients.

5. Know your orders. Stir-frying is usually done in batches, and the sequence in which ingredients are added is important. Aromatic seasonings like ginger and garlic usually go in first, followed by meat, seafood, or poultry, which is often removed before vegetables are added; heartier, denser vegetables usually go in before softer or leafier ones.

6. Stir, don't stare. Use your spatula to flip and toss the food vigorously, breaking up any clumps, so everything cooks evenly without sticking to the wok. I like to give the wok a good shake from time to time to keep everything moving.

7. Avoid overcrowding. If you add too big a batch of any ingredient, it becomes hard to stir-fry evenly, and the excess moisture may prevent uniform browning.

8. Get saucy. Many recipes call for returning everything to the wok with a final addition of liquid (such as wine or broth) and/or a prepared sauce (such as soy sauce or oyster sauce). This liquid is sometimes thickened with a mixture of cornstarch and water, depending on the type of sauce desired.

9. Taste. Don't forget to taste the dish before you put it on the serving plate. Then quickly adjust the seasonings, if necessary, and serve.

10. Garnish. This is a little touch that makes a big difference. I like to use a bit of an ingredient that's already in the dish (like an slice of lemon with lemon chicken). Keep it simple. Even a sprig of cilantro or a sprinkling of toasted sesame seeds adds a special finish to the dish.

Deep-Frying

Your wok makes a wonderful deep-fryer that heats evenly and is easy to use. Deep-frying has gotten a bad rap in recent years, and it does require a large amount of oil, but foods that have been properly deep-fried at the right temperature absorb less oil and can be light and crispy without being greasy. When foods are added to oil that has been heated to between 350° and 375°F (check your recipe for exact temperature), the surface of the food is quickly sealed, forming a coating the oil cannot permeate. If the oil is not hot enough, too much of it soaks in. If it's too hot, the outside of the food can burn before the inside is cooked.

Deep-Frying Tips

Getting Ready. Make sure the wok is solidly positioned to avoid tipping. Pour oil into the wok to a depth of 2 to 3 inches. Heat the oil to the temperature called for in the recipe, checking it with a deep-frying thermometer.

Cooking. Be extra-careful when sliding foods into hot oil to avoid splashing and

spattering. Bring the ingredients you're going to deep-fry to room temperature before adding them to the oil. This will minimize the lowering of the oil temperature. Add the ingredients to the oil in small batches to keep the oil temperature consistent and promote even browning. Use a wire strainer or a slotted spoon to turn and separate the food as it cooks and to lift it out and transfer it to paper towels for draining.

Reusing Oil. Oil used for deep-frying can be reused, although after two to three uses, it will begin to break down. To reuse oil, allow it to cool, pour it through a fine mesh strainer to remove particles of food, then store it in an airtight jar in the refrigerator. When, after repeated use, the oil begins to darken, discard it.

The Steamer

Steaming, after stir-frying, is probably the most common cooking method in Asia. Many traditional home kitchens don't have ovens, and the steamer helps fill the void. It's used to cook seafood, meats, poultry, and vegetables; to make silky steamed custards; and to "bake" buns, dumplings, and even cakes over moist heat.

Your trusty wok makes a fine steamer base. To it, you'll need to add some kind of steaming rack, depending on your recipe, and a lid. The rack can be as simple as four chopsticks placed tic-tac-toe-style a few inches above the boiling water and topped with a plate on which the food is set. You can also use a conventional metal vegetable-steaming rack.

My favorite tool for steaming is the one I grew up with: the old-fashioned but ingenious wok steamer. It's a flat round basket made of bamboo that sits right in the wok, an inch or so above the water. These steamers have space between the slats on the bottom to let the steam in, and a lid to keep it there. They can be stacked so you can cook a lot of food at once. For a 14-inch wok, look for steamer baskets 12 to 13 inches in diameter.

Bamboo steamers have latticed lids of woven bamboo which let just the right amount of steam escape so condensed water doesn't drip down onto the food. They're so attractive and unusual-looking that you can serve food right out of them.

Steamer Tips

Getting Ready. Place foods that steam in their own juices—like a whole fish—on a heat-resistant plate inside the steamer. A glass pie dish makes an ideal liner for steaming fish, custard, and other foods. Choose a dish that's slightly smaller than the steamer so the steam can rise around it. To keep dumplings and buns from sticking, line the steamer with a damp cloth, a piece of parchment paper, or with greens, such as napa cabbage or lettuce leaves.

Cooking. Check the water level in the bottom of the steamer occasionally. If it's low, add boiling water to avoid lowering the temperature. Don't get steamed! To avoid burns, open the steamer with care. Wear oven mitts, and lift the lid so that it points away from you.

The Knife

I like to tell my students that the Chinese chef's knife is the original food processor. It can slice, mince, chop, crush, tenderize, and scoop up food—and you can even use the end of the handle to grind spices.

I recommend a high-carbon stainless steel Chinese knife, because it keeps a fine, sharp edge and won't rust or discolor acidic foods like onions or lemons.

Making a Spice Paste

Spice pastes, pounded together and slowly simmered, are a cornerstone of Southeast Asian cooking, and they are the basis of many of the recipes in the Malaysia and Singapore chapters of this book.

Traditionally, dry spices—like turmeric, cumin, star anise, cardamom, and cloves—as well as "wet spices"—from shallots, onions, and garlic to fresh turmeric, chilies, ginger, galangal, basil, and lemongrass—are carefully pounded in a heavy stone mortar to form a paste, or *rempah*, to which *blachan*, a pungent dried shrimp paste, is often added. The rempah is slowly simmered in oil until its flavors bloom and blend. If you don't have a mortar and pestle, a blender or food processor will do the trick.

Hong Kong Flavors of the Fragrant Harbor

When I was 13 years old, I fell in love for the first time. It was a schoolboy's crush—the kind you remember all your life. I fell in love with Hong Kong.

The train trip to Hong Kong from our tiny house in Guangzhou, China, lasted through the night. I remember sitting on top of the battered rattan suitcase my mom had packed with my clothes and food for the trip, trying to stay awake and peering out the window, eager to see the famous city I'd heard about for so long. I was going to be an apprentice at the Sun Wong Kee restaurant, and I could hardly wait.

By the time we finally arrived, I was sound asleep.

I woke up as the train lurched to a stop and looked around, half-convinced I was still dreaming, slowly taking in the spectacle: the enormous concrete buildings, the low, steady rumbling in the humid air, the smell of diesel fuel mixing with the fragrance of cooking food. The sun was just coming up, but already people were rushing by like they had someplace important to be. And I was one of them! My heart pounded wildly as I stepped out onto the street and into a new life.

A City that Rises to the Occasion

My lifelong adventure in food began that morning, and I still think of that first

trip to Hong Kong as a major turning point in my life. My apprenticeship turned out to be every bit as grueling as I had expected it to be. I mopped, scrubbed woks, and cut up mountains of vegetables, working 16-hour days in exchange for room and board. Technically, I should just say "board," because instead of a room with a bed, they gave me a long, thin board to lay across one of the booths in the dining room! No matter—I didn't sleep much. When I wasn't working, I spent every spare moment wandering around the city, devouring it like a banquet.

Hong Kong has changed a lot since those days. But one thing has stayed constant: The pace just never lets up, and the building never stops.

To give you a quick snapshot of the place, Hong Kong is a 410-square-mile metropolis that's made up of several satellite cities. The name Hong Kong means "Fragrant Harbor," and Victoria Harbour is the territory's center point. To the south is Hong Kong Island, with its steeply sloping Victoria Peak. Across the harbor to the north is the booming commercial center of Kowloon, and beyond that the residential "new towns" and industrial developments of the sprawling New Territories that stretch all the way to the Chinese border.

Much of Hong Kong is too steep and rocky for building, so most of its 6.2 million inhabitants are crammed into a fraction of the land. There's nowhere to go but up, but that has never stopped anyone here. Between the mountainous terrain and the skyscrapers, this is truly a city on the rise!

The spirit of urgency, ambition, explosive growth, and 24-hour-a-day commerce is the result, no doubt, of years of living on borrowed time, as the 1997 handover to China drew nearer. The sense of excitement is impossible to resist—I know from personal experience. Believe it or not, I was a pretty mellow little kid when I arrived in Hong Kong. But look at me now!

Food City

The frantic pace of Hong Kong makes eating out a fact of life for most people.

From home-style food stalls and round-the-clock noodle shops to opulent floating food palaces, Hong Kong has more places to eat per capita than any place on earth—more than 50,000 at last count! I once figured out that you could eat at a different restaurant in Hong Kong every day for almost 140 years without ever repeating yourself. And believe me, I've tried. I just hope I live long enough to make it to all of them!

Hong Kong's culinary influences have included the regional cuisines of China, India, Japan, Thailand, Vietnam, and Malaysia as well as those of Great Britain, Italy, France, and, nowadays, even my own adopted home, California. The territory has attracted some of the world's greatest chefs, offering them an overwhelming variety of ingredients from Asia, America, Europe, Australia, and New Zealand. As a result, an exciting new cuisine has emerged that combines the best of Hong Kong with innovative techniques and flavors from all over the world.

Doing drip irrigation the old-fashioned way in Hong Kong's New Territories.

You'll find every imaginable kind of seafood and produce on Hong Kong's menus, alongside all kinds of truly exotic delicacies. Feeling adventurous? Maybe you're ready to try a bit of shark's fin or bird's tongue washed down with a glass of snake bile wine. Order seafood, and you're likely to see it fished live and flopping from a huge tank just for you.

There's scarcely a type of food you can't find in Hong Kong. But I come here to sample the best of regional Chinese cooking. Without ever leaving the city, you can take a mouthwatering culinary tour of China—from Guangzhou (the south), to Shanghai (the east), Beijing (the north), and Sichuan (the west).

Guangzhou—Simply Spectacular

The population of Hong Kong largely comes from the bordering province of Guangdong, famous for its rich agriculture and its bustling capital, the port city of Guangzhou (Canton). So it's no wonder that the majority of restaurants in Hong Kong offer Cantonese cuisine.

The cuisine of Guangzhou is known for its simplicity and delicacy. The full

Shanghai—Where the River Meets the Sea

flavors of the region's fresh ingredients come through in subtle dishes that are often lighter than the more condiment-based cooking of other regions. But don't let that simplicity fool you. The great chefs of Canton are masters of diversity, combining ingredients to achieve a harmonious balance of flavors and colors.

Dim sum—a delightful array of delicate dumplings and small dishes—is a perfect example, and Hong Kong's dim sum houses (known to the locals as teahouses) have become the standard of excellence worldwide.

Cantonese main dishes are equally varied. Southern chefs fry, roast, steam, stir-fry, barbecue, and braise an astounding array of meats, poultry, seafood, and vegetables.

If I had to choose one regional Chinese cuisine—and I hope I never do—I'd have to pick Cantonese. After all, my very first teacher was one of the finest cooks in Guangzhou—my mom!

Shanghai, the sprawling seaport at the mouth of the mighty Yangtze River, is China's largest city. It's also the culinary capital of eastern China, the fertile region known as the "great rice bowl" of China that's also famous for its fresh produce and tea.

In Hong Kong, Shanghainese restaurants are known for their straightforward preparation of freshwater fish, shellfish, and seafood, notably the freshwater hairy crab. Many Shanghainese dishes—especially those made with pork and poultry—derive their rich, sweet, and hearty flavors from slow simmering. Drunken chicken, tender steamed chicken steeped in rice wine, is a popular Shanghainese specialty—not surprising, since Shanghai is famous for its Shaoxing rice wine.

Beijing—Dine Like Royalty

Beijing has been the center of trade and government for much of China's history, and the sophisticated menus of the northern capital find their origin in

For the freshest seafood afloat, check out one of Hong Kong's famous floating restaurants.

19

the lavish banquet food of the Imperial Court.

The food in Hong Kong's northern-style restaurants is hearty and flavorful, drawing heavily on strong-flavored roots and vegetables such as garlic, ginger, leeks, and peppers. In much of northern China, it's too cold to grow rice, so meals are often accompanied by wheat-flour dumplings, noodles, rolls, and breads.

There are plenty of restaurants in Hong Kong where you can try the most famous northern Chinese specialty of them all, Peking duck—slow-cooked and crisp-skinned, served in delicate pancakes with green onions and sweet hoisin sauce.

Dining á la carte in a bustling dim sum teahouse, Hong Kong.

Some northern-style restaurants feature dishes from Mongolia, including Mongolian lamb and the popular Mongolian hot pot, a sort of Asian fondue pot in which meat and vegetables are simmered in steaming broth, heated by a central chamber filled with hot coals.

Sichuan—The Spice Box of China

The central region of Sichuan is China's largest province. Sichuanese food has enjoyed increasing popularity in Hong Kong over the years because of its intriguing combinations of hot, sour, sweet, and salty tastes, a trait shared by neighboring Hunan. These combinations often include generous helpings of aromatic Sichuan peppercorns, star anise, fennel seed, coriander, and, most importantly, fiery hot chilies.

What's Ahead?

As I write these words, the handover to China has just taken place. Hong Kong has entered a new era, and no one can say what changes that era may bring. But I have a hunch: If there's one thing no one will want to change, it's the food.

For me, the flavors of the Fragrant Harbor will always be as fresh and magical as the day I first discovered them. I guess what they say is true: You never forget your first love.

Dim Sum

Savoring the Sum of the Parts

Since the 10th century, southern China has been famous for its teahouses, where family, friends, and business people get together to catch up on the latest news over a pot of tea. Out of this tradition evolved dim sum—an endless array of Cantonese-style dumplings, pastries, noodles, stuffed breads, and other delectable tidbits, all designed to be eaten with tea as a light breakfast or lunch.

Dim sum means "point to the heart" or "heart's delight." They say home is where the heart is, and for me, there's no place better in the world to enjoy dim sum than my second home, Hong Kong.

If you thought the pace in Hong Kong was fast and frenetic, try walking into one of the city's world-famous dim sum houses. It's like the trading floor of the international stock exchange. Only louder and a lot better smelling! First, you squeeze past the crowd jammed into the front entryway to check in with the host. A loudspeaker blares names and table numbers over the din

of laughter and lively conversation and the constant clatter of plates and dishes. When your number finally comes up, you're led into the enormous dining room, where you join the hundreds of diners seated at large round tables. This is a communal affair: the more people in your party, the more you can try.

The teahouse roots of dim sum are reflected in the phrase, *yum cha* (literally "to drink tea"), the common way to refer to eating a dim sum lunch. When I lead culinary tours of Hong Kong, I always tell people: "The *cha* part means tea. The *yum* part refers to the food!" Most places will offer several types of tea to choose from. As you take your first sip and breathe in the intoxicating aromas of the food, your appetite suddenly becomes voracious and uncontrollable!

Good thing there's no menu to order from, and no waiting necessary. The food comes streaming out of the kitchen in a steady parade of carts loaded with little plates and stacks of small steamer baskets filled with dumplings and other delicacies. When they say everything is à la carte, they really mean it!

Baked dim sum: Char Siu Bao (barbequed pork bun), Ga Lei Gog (curry puffs).

There are usually three or four pieces to an order. If you like what you see, you just point and eat! But pace yourself. The individual dishes are small and light, but the "sum" is greater than the parts, and you'll be full sooner than you think. My advice is to take it slow, so you can scope out all the offerings.

Soon you'll have a collection of empty little plates and tiny steamers stacked up at the center of the table. At the end of the meal, your bill is calculated by counting the number of plates in the stack or the number of stamps on your guest check.

One tip: I don't recommend doing what my friends and I once did when we were young and starving. We hid half the plates under the table, somehow imagining that we were the first people ever to have thought of such a clever scheme. But at the end of the meal, the waiter, suspecting foul play, lifted the tablecloth. To our horror, someone else had already left a huge stack of plates, and our bill instantly doubled!

Steamed dim sum (left to right): Siu Mai (pork and shrimp dumplings), Gow Choy Gao (chive dumplings), Noh Mai Gai (glutenous rice in lotus leaf), Har Gau (shimp dumplings).

Summing It Up: A Guide to My Personal Dim Sum Favorites

It's been said that there are more than 1,000 types of dim sum. But most dim sum chefs draw from a repertoire of 75 to 100 house specialties. Authentic dim sum is a time-consuming, labor-intensive culinary art requiring years of practice to perfect. Handmade doughs of wheat starch, rice flour, and wheat flour are rolled out into flat pancakes and stuffed with countless combinations of meat, vegetables, and sweet bean pastes. The fillings are enclosed by carefully folding and pleating the dough, which is shaped it into all sorts of beautiful dumplings.

Steamed

Har gau. Plump dumplings with a filling of tender, fresh shrimp and bamboo shoots, wrapped in a translucent skin of flour-and-water dough, so thin you can see the filling right through it.

Siu mai. Cylindrical dumplings, open on top, filled with ground pork and shrimp.

Fun guor. Half-moon crescents of translucent dough stuffed with ground pork and shrimp.

Char siu bao. Chunks of sweet glazed barbecued pork steamed in a dome-shaped bun of soft, sweet bread dough. (These are sometimes baked.)

Churn fun. Soft rice noodle skins rolled around shrimp, minced beef, or barbecued pork.

Noh mai gai. A little feast in a bundle: glutinous rice, Chinese sausage, mushrooms, and other savory ingredients steamed in a lotus leaf.

Fried

Chun guen. Crispy deep-fried spring rolls filled with meat, shrimp, and bamboo shoots.

Har dor see. Shrimp toast—a Western-inspired item featuring toast points or rounds topped with shrimp purée and deep-fried.

Woo gok. Egg-shaped dumplings made of mashed taro root filled with shrimp, pork, and mushrooms.

Sweet and Savory Specialties

See jup ngau hor. Also known as chow fun: wok-charred fresh rice noodles with beef or chicken.

Jin dui jai. Chewy glutinous rice dough wrapped around a sweet bean paste, rolled in sesame seeds and deep-fried; a nice dessert with tea.

Don tot. The traditional dim sum

dessert: individual egg custard tarts.

To add dimension and flavor to dim sum, you can request all kinds of extra sauces and condiments for dipping, including soy sauce, red or black vinegar, chili oil, hot mustard, sweet and sour sauce, and XO Sauce, made from dried scallops, shrimp, chilies, and spices.

Try Some Dim Sum

Of course, you don't have to go all the way to Hong Kong to find dim sum. If you live near a Chinatown, go between the hours of 10 A.M. and 2 P.M. and look for the crowds. You'll probably find at least one Cantonese restaurant serving dim sum. Plan to arrive on the early side to get the best selection and the freshest items.

If you can't find a dim sum restaurant, don't despair. It's a lot of fun to make your own— especially when you get the whole family involved. And don't stop at lunch: Dim sum dumplings make terrific appetizers and party food! The recipes on the following pages will help you get started.

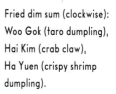

Fried dim sum (clockwise): Woo Gok (taro dumpling), Hai Kim (crab claw), Ha Yuen (crispy shrimp dumpling).

BEAN CURD ROLLS

Let the good times roll! Start the meal with these unusual—and unusually tasty—dim sum dumplings: Deep-fried sheets of bean curd enclose the filling.

AN ASIAN "WRAP-SHEET"

With their chewy texture and mild flavor, bean curd sheets make great wrappers for all kinds of popular dim sum dishes. When fried, their texture is a lot like crispy chicken skin, and Buddhist vegetarian cooks have used them for centuries to create "vegetable goose" and other mock poultry dishes. The sheets are a byproduct of tofu production. You know how milk forms a skin on top when it's heated? The same thing happens with soybean milk. This skin is carefully removed and laid on bamboo mats to dry in golden yellow, semi-transparent sheets. You can buy dried or frozen bean curd sheets in Asian markets. To soften them before using, soak them in water or place them between damp towels.

4 dried bean curd sheets, each about 7 by 21 inches
2 dried black mushrooms
1 tablespoon dried shrimp
1/4 pound boneless, skinless chicken
2 ounces Chinese sausage (optional)
4 tablespoons cooking oil
1 teaspoon minced garlic
1/4 cup finely diced carrot
1/4 cup frozen peas, thawed
1/4 cup chicken broth
1 tablespoon Chinese rice wine or dry sherry
1/4 teaspoon white pepper
1 tablespoon oyster-flavored sauce
2 teaspoons soy sauce
2 cups cooked glutinous rice or medium-grain rice
24 pieces green onion tops
Soy sauce

Getting Ready

1. Soak bean curd sheets in warm water to cover for 30 minutes; drain and cut each sheet into three 7-inch squares.

2. In separate bowls, soak dried mushrooms and dried shrimp in warm water to cover until softened, about 20 minutes. Drain. Discard mushroom stems and finely dice caps. Chop dried shrimp. Cut chicken (and sausage) into 1/4-inch cubes.

3. Heat a wok over high heat until hot. Add 2 tablespoons oil, swirling to coat sides. Add garlic and stir-fry until fragrant, about 10 seconds. Add mushrooms and dried shrimp; stir-fry for 30 seconds. Add chicken, Chinese sausage, carrot, and peas; stir-fry for 30 seconds.

4. Add broth, wine, white pepper, oyster-flavored sauce, and 2 teaspoons soy sauce. Cook 3 to 4 minutes. Turn off heat and stir in rice. Let filling cool.

5. To make each roll, place a bean curd square on work surface with 1 corner facing you. Place 2 rounded tablespoons of filling across wrapper slightly above the corner. Fold corner over filling, then roll over once. Fold in left and right sides, then roll up completely to enclose filling. Tie roll about 1 1/2 inches from each end with a blanched green onion top. Flatten roll slightly with your hand.

Cooking

1. Place a wide frying pan over medium heat until hot. Add remaining 2 tablespoons oil. Place rolls in pan and cook until golden, about 3 minutes on each side. Remove and drain on paper towels.

2. Serve hot with soy sauce for dipping.

Makes 12 rolls.

ZUCCHINI SIU MAI

Anybody can put zucchini in a dumpling. But here's a different approach: The zucchini is the dumpling! A classic pork siu mai filling is stuffed into hollowed-out zucchini rounds, topped with shrimp, and steamed to make a quick and colorful appetizer.

⋟ FILLING ⋞

1 dried black mushroom
1/4 pound ground lean pork or chicken
1 tablespoon minced green onion
1 teaspoon minced ginger
2 tablespoons water
2 teaspoons oyster-flavored sauce
1 teaspoon soy sauce
2 teaspoons cornstarch
1/4 teaspoon white pepper
1 egg white

3 zucchini, each 8 to 9 inches long
    and 1 1/2 inches in diameter
18 small raw shrimp, shelled
1 1/2 tablespoons cooking oil (optional)
1/3 cup water (optional)

Getting Ready

1. Soak mushroom in warm water to cover until softened, about 20 minutes. Discard stem; mince cap. Place mushroom in a bowl with remaining filling ingredients; stir briskly until mixture is very smooth, about 30 seconds.

2. Trim ends of zucchini; cut each crosswise into six 1-inch pieces. With an apple corer, remove cores from zucchini, leaving a shell 1/4 inch thick.

3. Stuff filling into zucchini cases. Top each case with a shrimp.

Cooking

1. Place a wide frying pan over medium heat until hot. Add oil, swirling to coat sides. Stand zucchini in the frying pan and cook until bottoms are lightly browned, about 2 minutes. Add 1/3 cup water; reduce heat to low, cover, and cook until filling is no longer pink, about 5 minutes.

Or prepare a wok for steaming (see page 14). Stand zucchini on a heatproof dish. Steam over high heat until filling is no longer pink, about 10 minutes.

2. Transfer to a serving plate.

Makes 18.

FLOWER POWER

How do you make an onion flower? You water it, of course! But seriously, making a beautiful green onion flower to use as a garnish is really quite easy. Remove the root end and the green leaves from a green onion, leaving only the white part, which should be 3 to 4 inches long. Using a sharp paring knife, slash one end of the onion, starting about two-thirds of the way up, and cutting straight down to the end. Repeat several times until you have a "brush." Chill the brush in ice water for a couple of hours, and it will "bloom" into a beautiful flower.

GOLDEN SHRIMP ROLLS

Hong Kong chefs are always dreaming up new additions to the world of dim sum, made with nontraditional ingredients from all over the world. These quail egg and shrimp rolls are my contribution. Serve them with a high-quality bottled sweet and sour sauce for dipping, or use my recipe (at left) to make your own.

SWEET & SOUR SAUCE

To make a simple homemade sweet and sour dipping sauce: Heat 1 tablespoon cooking oil in a 1-quart saucepan over medium-high heat. Add 1 teaspoon minced fresh ginger, and cook, stirring, until fragrant, about 10 seconds. Add 1/4 cup each orange juice and rice vinegar, 5 tablespoons each brown sugar and catsup, 2 teaspoons soy sauce, and 1/2 teaspoon chili oil or hot pepper sauce. Cook until sugar dissolves. Mix 1 1/2 tablespoons cornstarch with 2 tablespoons water and add to sauce; cook, stirring, until sauce boils and thickens. Makes about 1 1/2 cups.

8 jumbo raw shrimp

⮞ MARINADE ⮜
1 tablespoon cornstarch
1/2 teaspoon salt
1/4 teaspoon white pepper

8 hard-cooked quail eggs, shelled
1 sheet Japanese seaweed (nori), cut into 8 strips 1 inch wide
Cornstarch
1 egg, lightly beaten
1 1/2 cups Japanese bread crumbs (panko)
Toothpicks
Cooking oil for deep-frying
Sweet and sour sauce

Getting Ready

1. Shell and devein shrimp, leaving tails intact. Butterfly them along the inside curve, then flatten with the flat side of a cleaver.

2. Combine marinade ingredients in a bowl. Add shrimp and stir to coat; let stand 10 minutes.

3. To make each roll: Place a quail egg at one end of a strip of nori and roll up. Center wrapped egg on inner side of a butterflied shrimp. Roll shrimp to enclose egg; secure with a wooden pick. Repeat with other eggs, nori strips, and shrimp.

Cooking

1. In a wok, heat oil for deep-frying to 350°F. Dip stuffed shrimp in cornstarch, then egg; coat with crumbs. Deep-fry, turning once, until golden brown, 2 to 3 minutes. Remove and drain on paper towels.

2. Cut stuffed shrimp in half horizontally and place on a serving plate. Serve with sweet and sour sauce for dipping.

Makes 4 servings.

SHRIMP AND SCALLOP AMANDINE

An elegant but easy first course. The crunchy texture and buttery richness of almonds makes a wonderful contrast with meltingly tender shrimp and scallops.

HAPPY LANDINGS

Flying into Hong Kong is a thrill a minute. Kai Tak Airport is in the heart of Kowloon, and you have to fly right through the city to land there. Look out the airplane window, and you can practically see what's on TV in the apartment buildings all around you. I guarantee you've never flown so close to skyscrapers and antennas! Then, the next thing you know, you're hurtling down the airport's single runway, straight out into Victoria Harbour with nothing but water on all sides. I've flown into Hong Kong so many times I've lost count, and I still get goose bumps every time. It's the perfect opener to the exhilarating pace that awaits you the minute you step off the plane and into the most exciting city in the world. I hope the huge new Chek Lap Kok Airport will be half as much fun!

½ **pound medium raw shrimp**
½ **pound sea scallops**

⇒ MARINADE ⇐
1 **tablespoon Chinese rice wine or dry sherry**
2 **teaspoons cornstarch**
½ **teaspoon salt**
¼ **teaspoon white pepper**

⇒ DIPPING SAUCE ⇐
2 **teaspoons dry mustard powder**
2 **teaspoons water**
¼ **cup sweet and sour sauce**

1 **cup finely chopped almonds**
½ **cup sesame seeds**
Cornstarch
1 **egg, lightly beaten**
¼ **cup cooking oil**

Getting Ready

1. Shell and devein shrimp, leaving tails intact. Butterfly them along the inside curve, then flatten with the side of a cleaver. Combine marinade ingredients in a bowl. Add shrimp and scallops; stir to coat. Let stand for 10 minutes.

2. To prepare dipping sauce: In a bowl, blend mustard powder and water; stir in sweet and sour sauce. Place in a dipping sauce bowl.

3. In a shallow bowl, combine almonds and sesame seeds. Dust each shrimp and scallop with cornstarch. Dip in egg and drain briefly, then coat with almond mixture.

Cooking

1. Place a wide frying pan over medium heat until hot. Add oil; when oil is hot, add shrimp and scallops; pan-fry, turning once, until golden brown, about 1½ minutes on each side.

2. Serve hot with dipping sauce.

Makes 6 servings.

SHRIMP TOAST WITH SCALLOPS

May I propose a toast? Here's to the inventive Cantonese chefs who first decided to include Western-style bread in their repertoire and created what was to become one of the most popular dim sum items: crispy fried shrimp toast. My version has a special surprise: a tender sea scallop hidden in the shrimp filling. Cheers!

4 day-old slices sandwich bread
4 sea scallops

⧼ SHRIMP PASTE ⧽
¹/₂ pound medium raw shrimp
¹/₂ teaspoon salt
1 teaspoon rice wine
¹/₂ teaspoon sesame oil
1 tablespoon cornstarch
¹/₈ teaspoon white pepper
1 egg white

Cornstarch
8 cilantro leaves
Cooking oil for deep-frying

Getting Ready

1. Trim crusts from bread; cut each slice in half diagonally. Cut scallops in half horizontally.

2. Shell and devein shrimp. Place in a food processor with remaining shrimp paste ingredients; process until shrimp are finely minced.

3. Spread shrimp mixture equally on bread triangles.

4. Dust each scallop half with cornstarch and press firmly onto shrimp mixture; top with a cilantro leaf.

Cooking

1. In a wok, heat oil for deep-frying to 350°F. Deep-fry triangles, a few at a time and scallop side down, until golden brown, about 45 seconds; turn over and fry 15 seconds longer. Drain on paper towels.

Makes 8.

TOAST POINTS

Speaking of toasts, if you go out to eat with friends in Hong Kong, brace yourself for a barrage of them. A typical dinner will include several rounds of toasts—often no more than a quick, "yam seng" ("down the hatch") or "gam bui" ("bottoms up")—and it's polite to drain your glass after each one. Toasting with your water glass or teacup is considered rude, and you should show respect by clinking your glass below your host's. Don't be surprised if some very fine cognac shows up later in the meal. It's one of Hong Kong's favorite status symbols, and 11 percent of the world's cognac is consumed here—the highest consumption rate per capita of any place on earth! Many people even have their own personal bottles of cognac stored at their favorite restaurants.

Hosting and toasting with friends at an imperial banquet at the Hsin Kuang restaurant.

FILLED CUCUMBER RINGS

I ♥ BROCCOLI

I am on a cruciferous crusade: Save the endangered broccoli stem! So many people cook the florets and toss the stems in the trash. At our house, it's just the opposite. We think of the stems as the vegetable, and the florets as a cute little garnish. Here's the thing: Peeling broccoli stems transforms them from something chewy and fibrous into a tender, tasty delicacy. The easiest way to do this is to make a small cut with a paring knife at the bottom of the stem, about $1/16$ inch under the surface of the peel; grab a bit of peel between the knife and your thumb, and pull toward you. A long ribbon of peel about $1/4$ inch wide will pull right off the stem. Repeat this until you've removed all the peel. Now you have hearts of broccoli that can be sliced or julienned for steaming and stir-frying. Eat your hearts out, floret fans!

A great hors d'oeuvres to make when cucumbers are in season—everyday of the year!

⧽ FILLING ⧼

$1/2$ of a 14-ounce package extra-firm tofu, drained
$1/4$ pound medium raw shrimp, shelled, deveined, and coarsely chopped
$1/2$ egg white
1 tablespoon chopped Sichuan preserved vegetable
1 tablespoon cornstarch
1 teaspoon chopped cilantro
$1/8$ teaspoon white pepper

2 English cucumbers, each about 2 inches in diameter
Cornstarch
2 tablespoons cooking oil
3 tablespoons vegetable broth
1 cup broccoli florets

⧽ SAUCE ⧼

1 cup vegetable broth
1/4 cup oyster-flavored sauce
2 teaspoons sesame oil
$1/2$ teaspoon white pepper
1 teaspoon salted black beans, rinsed (optional); or 2 teaspoons black bean sauce

4 teaspoons cornstarch dissolved in 2 tablespoons water

Getting Ready
1. Mash tofu in a bowl. Place tofu in a clean towel and squeeze to remove excess liquid. In a food processor, blend tofu and remaining filling ingredients until smooth.

2. Peel cucumbers, cut into 1-inch-thick slices, and cut a quarter-size hole in the center of each slice to make rings. Remove and discard centers. Dust each ring inside and out with cornstarch, then stuff with 2 teaspoons of tofu mixture. Dust stuffed rings with cornstarch.

Cooking
1. Place a wide frying pan over medium-high heat until hot. Add oil, swirling to coat sides. Pan-fry cut ends of rings until golden brown, 1 to 2 minutes on each end. Add vegetable broth; cover pan and simmer until filling is no longer pink, about 3 minutes.

2. Meanwhile, bring a pan of water to a boil. Add broccoli and cook until tender-crisp, about 2 minutes; drain and keep warm.

3. Combine sauce ingredients in a pan; bring to a boil. Add cornstarch solution and cook, stirring, until sauce boils and thickens.

4. To serve, place broccoli in center of a serving plate with cucumber rings around it; pour sauce over.

Makes 6 to 8 servings.

TOFU IN SPINACH BROTH

Here's a simple, comforting soup you can make in just a few minutes: chicken, tofu, and puréed spinach simmered in a light chicken broth.

⇒ MARINADE ⇐
1 tablespoon cornstarch
1/2 teaspoon salt
1/4 teaspoon white pepper

1/4 pound boneless chicken, coarsely
    chopped
1 1/2 cups packed spinach leaves,
    coarse stems removed
1/3 cup water
3 cups chicken broth
2 teaspoons shredded ginger
1/2 of a 14-ounce package regular-
    firm or extra-firm tofu, drained
    and cut into 1-inch cubes
2 tablespoons cornstarch dissolved
    in 2 tablespoons water
1 teaspoon sesame oil
Salt and white pepper
Chopped red bell pepper

Getting Ready
1. Combine marinade ingredients in a bowl. Add chicken; stir to coat. Let stand for 10 minutes.

2. Add spinach and water to a food processor; purée.

Cooking
1. Place broth and ginger in a 2-quart pan; bring to a boil over medium heat. Add marinated chicken and simmer until meat is no longer pink, 1 to 2 minutes. Add tofu, spinach, cornstarch solution, and sesame oil, and salt and white pepper to taste. Cook, stirring, until broth boils and thickens slightly.

2. Pour into individual bowls and garnish with chopped bell pepper.

Makes 4 servings.

NO BONES ABOUT IT
Vegetarian cooking was introduced to China by Buddhist monks more than 2,000 years ago, and over the centuries, it has developed into a sophisticated cuisine in its own right. Today, the elite meet to eat no meat in Hong Kong's wonderful vegetarian restaurants. I recently spent a day cooking with the chefs at one of my favorites, the Kung Tak Lam. You'd be amazed at the meatless wonders they can turn out. There's mock chicken made from bean curd sheets; bean curd dumplings filled with spinach and "ham" (made from wheat gluten), topped with vegetarian oyster sauce; and even sweet and sour "pork" made with pineapple, green pepper, and carrot (with chewy monkey's head mushrooms standing in for the pork).

At the Kung Tak Lam vegetarian restaurant, the chef showed me how to prepare all kinds of wonderful meatless specialties.

HAKKA-STYLE EGGPLANT WITH MINT

In this hearty Hakka-style vegetable dish, chunks of eggplant are double-cooked using a classic Chinese technique called oil-blanching. First, they're quickly deep-fried so they're crisp on the outside and moist inside. Then they're stir-fried with bell peppers, whole garlic cloves, chilies, basil, and mint, and finished with a spicy chili-garlic sauce.

A HAKKA FEAST
Centuries ago, the Hakka people fled the central river plains of China to avoid persecution. Their name means "guest" or "nomad," and they have been guests all over China and Southeast Asia ever since. In the 17th century, many settled in what is now the New Territories of Hong Kong. On special occasions, they put on a traditional "farmer's bucket" banquet, and recently I got to help. Twenty chefs worked for days preparing mouth-watering chicken, pork, squid, tofu, eel, and vegetable dishes. More than 100 tables were set up in the village square, and over 1,000 people ate and laughed under the stars all night long. It was a beautiful symbol of the sense of community that has kept the Hakka people together wherever they may wonder.

⇒ SAUCE ⇐
2 tablespoons oyster-flavored sauce
¼ cup chicken broth
½ teaspoon chili garlic sauce
½ teaspoon sesame oil

¼ cup lightly packed mint leaves
¾ pound Asian eggplants
Cooking oil for deep-frying
6 cloves garlic, peeled

2 teaspoons cooking oil
1 fresh red jalapeño chili, thinly sliced
½ small onion, cut into ½-inch cubes
1 small green bell pepper, cut into 1-inch diamond-shaped pieces
½ cup lightly packed Thai basil leaves

Getting Ready
1. Combine sauce ingredients in a small bowl. Wash mint leaves and dry thoroughly. Roll-cut eggplants.

Cooking
1. In a wok, heat oil for deep-frying to 375°F. Deep-fry eggplants and garlic until golden brown, about 2 minutes. Lift out with a slotted spoon and drain well on paper towels.

2. Deep-fry mint leaves until crisp, about 30 seconds. Lift out with a slotted spoon and drain well on paper towels.

3. Place a wok over high heat until hot. Add 2 teaspoons oil, swirling to coat sides. Add chili, onion, and bell pepper; cook, stirring, until fragrant, about 30 seconds. Add eggplants, garlic, basil, and sauce. Reduce heat to medium and cook until eggplant is tender, 5 to 6 minutes. Garnish with mint.

Makes 4 servings.

Table for 1,000, please: Preparing for the great outdoor "farmer's bucket" banquet at a Hakka village in the New Territories.

BRAISED SPICY TOFU

So you think of tofu as bland, eh? This fiery and flavorful Hunanese tofu, braised with chilies, black bean garlic sauce, and ham, will make you think again!

BEAN CURD BASICS

Bean curd (tofu) is fragile stuff, especially the soft or silken kind. To transfer cubes of it from the cutting surface to the pan without breaking them, don't pick them up with your hands. Instead, slide the flat blade of a chef's knife or cleaver under the tofu and gently lift it, holding it in place on the blade with your hand. If you're pan-frying tofu, a nonstick pan is indispensable for keeping the soft cubes intact. Try to resist the temptation to push and prod the cubes, letting them brown nicely on each side before you turn them. To prolong the life of tofu sold in plastic tubs, pour out the liquid in the tub; refill the tub with tap water; cover it with plastic wrap and store it in the refrigerator for several days, changing the water daily. If tofu develops a strong odor, throw it away.

1 package (about 16 oz.) soft tofu or 1 package (about 14 oz.) regular-firm or extra-firm tofu, drained
2 ounces Smithfield ham, sliced 1/8 inch thick

⋟ SAUCE ⋞
1/2 cup chicken broth
1 tablespoon dark soy sauce
1 teaspoon black bean sauce
1 teaspoon sesame oil
2 teaspoons sugar

1 tablespoon cooking oil
6 cloves garlic, thinly sliced
1 small fresh red jalapeño chili, thinly sliced
1 tablespoon salted black beans, rinsed and drained
3 green onions, cut into 2-inch lengths
2 teaspoons cornstarch dissolved in 1 tablespoon water

Getting Ready

1. Cut tofu into pieces about 1/4-inch thick and 1 1/2-inches square. Cut ham slices into 1 1/2-inch squares.

2. Combine sauce ingredients in a bowl.

Cooking

1. Place a nonstick frying pan over high heat until hot. Add oil, swirling to coat sides. Add garlic, chili, and black beans; cook, stirring, until fragrant, about 10 seconds. Add tofu and cook, turning once, until golden brown, about 2 minutes. Add ham and green onions; cook for 1 minute.

2. Add sauce and bring to a boil. Add cornstarch solution and cook until sauce boils and thickens.

Makes 4 servings.

FISH AND SHRIMP BALLS WITH RICE NOODLES

Let the French have their quenelles. My tender fish and shrimp balls poached in a light broth are every bit as tasty. Bon appétit!

⇒ MARINADE ⇐

4 tablespoons cornstarch
1/2 teaspoon salt
1/2 teaspoon white pepper
1 teaspoon sesame oil

1 egg white
1/2 pound firm white fish fillets, such
    as red snapper or cod
1/2 pound medium raw shrimp,
    shelled and deveined
1/2 pound rice stick noodles
Cooking oil for deep-frying
6 wonton wrappers, cut into
    1/4-inch-wide strips
2 cups chicken broth
1 cup water
1/4 cup julienned carrot
1 green onion, julienned
1/2 cup shredded bok choy leaves
3 fresh basil leaves, shredded
1/2 sheet Japanese seaweed (nori),
    halved, then cut into 1/4-inch-
    wide strips
1 tablespoon cornstarch dissolved in
    2 tablespoons water
Salt and white pepper

Getting Ready

1. Combine marinade ingredients in a small bowl. In a food processor, process egg white, fish, and half of marinade until smooth. Process shrimp with other half of marinade until smooth. Let both mixtures stand for 10 minutes.

2. Dip hands into cold water, then shape each fish mixture into 1-inch balls.

3. Soak rice stick noodles in warm water until soft, about 30 minutes; drain.

4. In a wok or 2-quart saucepan, heat oil for deep-frying to 350°F. Deep-fry wonton strips until golden, about 30 seconds. Remove with a slotted spoon and drain well on paper towels.

Cooking

1. Place broth and water in a 2-quart pan; bring to a boil. Add carrot, onion, and bok choy; cook for 1 minute. Add fish balls, basil, nori strips, and noodles. Cook for 2 to 3 minutes.

2. Add cornstarch solution to broth and cook, stirring, until soup boils and thickens. Turn off heat. Season soup to taste with salt and white pepper.

3. Ladle into individual soup bowls and garnish with fried wonton strips.

Makes 4 servings.

SNAKES ALIVE!

When the pace of Hong Kong wears me down, I always stop by the Ser Wong Fun King of Snake restaurant, where the owner, Chef Ng, serves a remarkable Hong Kong style of cooking known as "reinforcement cuisine," designed to restore body and soul. What's the specialty of the house? Snake, of course! For breakfast, Chef Ng makes a thick and creamy snake soup that's said to cleanse and detoxify the system. There's also chicken poached in snake broth. Chef Ng tells me it's just the thing for rheumatism. And that's just the beginning. The chef uses all kinds of rejuvenating herbs and exotic ingredients, like sea snails, medlars, and black-skinned chicken. And to wash it all down, he recommends a glass of snake wine—light and smooth, with a distinct bite!

SIMMERED MUSHROOMS WITH FISH BALLS

These tender fish balls are simmered with earthy mushrooms, squid, and green onion to create a dish that's both delicate and hearty at the same time.

FRESH FISH FROM THE TANKA

Talk about staying afloat! The resourceful Tanka people have lived in houseboat communities in the waters of Hong Kong and along the coast of southern China for centuries. Recently, I stayed with a Tanka family, the Lais, on their fishing boat in Aberdeen Harbour. In the tiny cabin, they have managed to raise five kids and several cats! We put out the nets at 4 A.M., and by noon we were eating the catch of the day for lunch. I watched in amazement as Mrs. Lai turned out a huge feast of steamed fish and prawns, and stir-fried baby bok choy with oyster sauce. The whole family ate together, surrounded by a magnificent view of the harbor. After our hard day's work, the food tasted better than anything you'd get in a fancy floating restaurant.

The Lais' fishing boat in the floating Tanka village on Aberdeen Harbour.

10 dried black mushrooms

≥ FISH BALLS ≤

³/4 pound firm white fish fillets, such as red snapper or cod
1 tablespoon cornstarch

1 tablespoon oyster-flavored sauce
1 teaspoon sherry
2 teaspoons minced ginger
1 egg white
¹/4 teaspoon white pepper

≥ SEASONING INGREDIENTS ≤

³/4 cups chicken stock
1 fresh red jalapeño chili, sliced
1 tablespoon soy sauce
2 teaspoons sesame oil
2 tablespoons sherry
¹/4 teaspoon sugar
¹/8 teaspoon white pepper

2 slices ginger, each the size of a quarter
¹/4 cup canned straw mushrooms, drained
4 small squid, cleaned and sliced in half (optional)
1 green onion, cut into 1-inch pieces

Getting Ready

1. Soak mushrooms in warm water to cover until softened, about 20 minutes; drain. Discard stems; thinly slice caps.

2. In a food processor, combine fish balls ingredients; blend until smooth. Dip hands into cold water, then shape fish mixture into 1-inch balls.

3. Mix seasoning ingredients in a small bowl; set aside.

Cooking

1. Bring a 2-quart pot of water to a boil. Add fish balls and cook for 2 to 3 minutes. Remove with a slotted spoon.

2. In a clay pot or 3-quart saucepan, place ginger, straw and black mushrooms, squid (if used), green onion, and fish balls. Pour seasoning ingredients over. Bring to a simmer, cover, and cook for 10 minutes.

Makes 4 to 6 servings.

PAN-FRIED FISH WITH SWEET CHILI SAUCE

Golden sautéed fish fillets topped with chili sauce are classic Hong Kong fare. For an extra kick of sweet and spicy flavor, I like to serve them with a fresh mango-apple salsa—my tribute to the spirit of international culinary exchange that makes today's Hong Kong cuisine so vibrant and dynamic.

≽ MARINADE ≼

2 tablespoons Chinese rice wine or
    dry sherry
1/4 teaspoon pepper
2 teaspoons cornstarch

1 pound firm white fish fillets,
    such as sea bass, trout, or
    red snapper; or 1 whole fish

≽ SWEET CHILI SAUCE ≼

1 clove garlic, chopped
3 tablespoons brown sugar
1/2 cup orange juice
2 tablespoons rice vinegar
1/4 cup diced apple
1/4 cup diced mango
1/2 teaspoon chili garlic sauce
1/4 teaspoon salt
1/8 teaspoon black pepper

2 teaspoons cornstarch dissolved
    in 1 tablespoon water
2 tablespoons cooking oil
3 green onions, julienned

Getting ready

1. Combine marinade ingredients in a bowl; brush onto fish. Let stand for 10 minutes.

2. Combine sauce ingredients in a small pan and bring to a boil. Add cornstarch solution; cook until sauce thickens.

Cooking

1. Place a wok over medium heat until hot. Add oil, swirling to coat sides. Fry fish until golden brown, 4 to 5 minutes on each side. Reheat sauce.

2. Arrange fish on a serving plate. Pour sauce over fish. Garnish with green onions.

Makes 4 servings.

STIR-FRIED VEGETABLES WITH OYSTER-FLAVORED SAUCE

I enjoyed this classic Cantonese vegetable dish aboard the Lais' fishing boat (see opposite page). Wash and trim 1 pound asparagus, bok choy, chard, or other leafy greens. Place a wok over high heat until hot. Add 2 tablespoons cooking oil, swirling to coat sides. Add 1 teaspoon each minced ginger and minced garlic, and 1/2 teaspoon salt; stir-fry until fragrant, about 10 seconds. Place vegetables in wok; add 2 tablespoons water and 1 tablespoon wine. Cover and cook until vegetables are tender-crisp and pan juices have evaporated, about 3 minutes. Slide vegetables onto serving plate. Drizzle 2 to 3 tablespoons oyster-flavored sauce and 1/2 teaspoon sesame oil over vegetables. Makes 4 servings.

SEAFOOD IN RICE PAPER WRAPS

I have yet to meet anyone who doesn't love these crisp deep-fried spring rolls filled with shrimp, scallops, black mushrooms, Chinese sausage, and garlic chives.

≽ FILLING ≼

½ pound medium raw shrimp, shelled, deveined, and cut in half lengthwise
½ pound bay scallops
¼ pound firm white fish fillet, such as sea bass, chopped
1 egg white
1 tablespoon cornstarch

4 dried black mushrooms
1 tablespoon cooking oil
1 teaspoon minced ginger
1 Chinese sausage, thinly sliced; or 2 ounces ham, julienned
4 garlic chives or 2 green onions, cut into 2-inch lengths
¼ cup chopped water chestnuts
1 tablespoon oyster-flavored sauce
2 teaspoons hoisin sauce
⅛ teaspoon white pepper
1 tablespoon chopped cilantro
2 tablespoons flour
2 tablespoons water
8 sheets dried rice paper, each about 8 inches in diameter
Cooking oil for deep-frying

Getting Ready

1. In a bowl, combine filling ingredients; mix well. Let stand for 30 minutes.

2. Soak mushrooms in warm water to cover until softened, about 20 minutes; drain. Discard stems; slice caps.

Cooking

1. Place a wok over high heat until hot. Add oil, swirling to coat sides. Add ginger and cook, stirring, until fragrant, about 10 seconds. Add sausage and stir-fry for 1 minute. Add seafood and stir-fry for 1 minute. Add mushrooms, garlic chives, and water chestnuts; stir-fry for 1 minute. Stir in oyster-flavored sauce, hoisin sauce, pepper, and cilantro. Let cool.

2. Mix flour and water together until smooth. To make each wrap: Brush each sheet of rice paper lightly with water to soften. Place 2 heaping tablespoons of seafood mixture across center. Fold left, right, and bottom sides over filling, then roll up. Seal edges with flour-water paste.

3. In a wok, heat oil for deep-frying to 350°F. Add half the seafood wraps and deep-fry, turning frequently, until golden brown, 1½ to 2 minutes. Remove and drain on paper towels. Repeat with remaining seafood wraps.

4. Serve seafood wraps whole, or cut in half diagonally.

Makes 8 rolls.

GARLIC CHIVES

In the spring and summer, you can find fresh garlic chives, also known as Chinese chives or gou choy, in Asian produce markets. If you see them, buy them. You won't be sorry. They're a lot like their cousin, the ordinary Western chive, but with a distinctly garlicky flavor and aroma. They're also beautiful to look at and make a wonderful garnish. Green garlic chives look like wide, long blades of grass; yellow garlic chives have shorter, more tender leaves and a mild onion-garlic flavor; and flowering garlic chives have firm stalks with small edible flower buds at the top. Look for buds that have not yet opened: They're younger and more tender.

Garlic chives on display at an open-air market in the New Territories.

WOK-SEARED FISH FILLET WITH ASPARAGUS

This tasty way to serve salmon or other firm-fleshed fish is simple enough to do on a week night yet elegant enough for a fancy dinner party.

FISH TRADITIONS

Fish is more than a staple food in Chinese culture. It symbolizes wholeness and abundance, partly because the word for fish, yu, sounds like the word for plenty or prosperity. Fish is always on the menu at lunar New Year celebrations to bring abundance in the year ahead. Many people believe that on this occasion fish should be presented but not eaten to underscore the idea of surplus and abundance.

So if you're ever at a Chinese New Year banquet, and you find that no one's touching the fish, don't just dig in! And by the way, if the head of a whole fish is pointing your way, congratulations. That means you're the guest of honor.

2 teaspoons black sesame seeds
2 teaspoons white sesame seeds
1 salmon or halibut fillet (1 lb.)
10 asparagus spears, trimmed
2 teaspoons cooking oil

⇒ SAUCE ⇐
1/4 cup chicken broth
2 tablespoons soy sauce
4 teaspoons rice vinegar
1 tablespoon sugar
4 teaspoons black bean sauce

1 teaspoon cornstarch dissolved in
    2 teaspoons water
Silvered green onions
Cilantro sprigs

Getting Ready

1. Toast sesame seeds: Place black and white sesame seeds in a small frying pan over medium heat; cook, shaking pan frequently, until white sesame seeds are lightly browned, 3 to 4 minutes. Immediately remove from pan to cool.

2. Cut fish diagonally crosswise into pieces about 2 by 4 inches.

3. Bring a pan of water to a boil. Add asparagus and cook until tender-crisp, 2 to 3 minutes. Drain. Lay asparagus in a fan shape on a serving plate.

Cooking

1. Place a nonstick frying pan over medium-high heat until hot. Add oil, swirling to coat sides. Add salmon, skin side up, and cook for 4 minutes. Turn and cook until fish turns opaque and begins to flake, about 4 minutes longer.

2. Combine sauce ingredients in a saucepan; bring to a boil. Add cornstarch solution and cook, stirring, until sauce boils and thickens.

3. To serve, spoon sauce over asparagus on serving plate. Place fish on sauce and sprinkle with sesame seeds. Garnish with green onions and cilantro sprigs.

Makes 4 servings.

SEAFOOD AND GARLIC CHIVE LO MEIN

This is my homage to the noodle shops of Hong Kong: chewy egg noodles, tossed with stir-fried shrimp and squid. You can also serve the stir-fried seafood over a crispy noodle pancake (at right).

1 package (16 oz.) fresh thin
   Chinese egg noodles
2 teaspoons sesame oil
6 squid (about 4 oz.), cleaned
³/₄ pound medium raw shrimp,
   shelled and deveined
1 tablespoon cornstarch
¹/₂ teaspoon salt

⇒ SAUCE ⇐
²/₃ cup chicken broth
1 tablespoon soy sauce
1 tablespoon oyster-flavored sauce
1 teaspoon sesame oil

4 dried black mushrooms
1 tablespoon cooking oil
1 tablespoon minced ginger
¹/₄ pound yellow garlic chives, cut
   into 2-inch lengths
4 green onions, cut into 2-inch
   lengths

Getting ready

1. Bring a 4-quart pan of water to a boil. Add noodles and cook according to package directions. Drain, rinse with cold water, and drain again. Add sesame oil and toss to coat.

2. Cut off squid tentacles. Cut squid bodies in half lengthwise; with a knife, score the inside diagonally several times in a cross-hatch pattern. Combine squid tentacles and bodies, shrimp, cornstarch, and salt in a bowl. Stir to coat; let stand for 10 minutes. Combine sauce ingredients in another bowl.

3. Soak dried mushrooms in warm water to cover until softened, about 20 minutes; drain. Discard stems and thinly slice caps.

Cooking

1. Place a wok over medium-high heat until hot. Add oil, swirling to coat sides. Add mushrooms, ginger, garlic chives, and green onions; stir-fry for 2 minutes. Add shrimp and squid; stir-fry for 2 minutes.

2. Add sauce, stirring, until it boils and thickens. Toss in noodles and mix well.

Makes 4 to 6 servings.

BAKED NOODLE PANCAKE

Crispy noodle pancakes are usually browned in a pan. Here's my simple method for making a noodle pancake in the oven. It frees up a burner on the stovetop, and frees you up to concentrate on other things, too. Cook 6 ounces (¹/₂ package) fresh egg noodles according to package directions. Drain, rinse with cold water, and drain again. Place a 12-inch pizza pan in a 500°F oven. When pan is very hot, brush 1 tablespoon cooking oil evenly onto pan. Spread noodles evenly in pan and brush top of noodles with 1 teaspoon cooking oil. Bake, uncovered, on bottom rack of oven until pancake is golden brown on top and bottom, 20 to 25 minutes.

SALT AND PEPPER PRAWNS

These prawns are fried with the shell on for extra flavor and texture, then tossed in a wok with garlic, chilies, and green onion and seasoned at the last minute with one of my favorite spice mixtures, Sichuan pepper salt. This magical mix makes a terrific seasoning for roasted chicken and grilled steaks and chops, too.

SICHUAN PEPPERCORNS

No, they're not related to black peppercorns. In fact, Sichuan peppercorns are actually dried berries of the prickly ash tree that are used as a seasoning throughout China. Along with star anise, they're one of the main ingredients in Chinese five-spice powder. Sichuan peppercorns are sold in Chinese markets in small plastic bags. When toasted, they release their fragrant oils and take on a smoky spiciness that's milder than black pepper. They leave a pleasant, numbing feeling on the tongue, rather than a hot, burning sensation. Toast them in a heavy frying pan over low heat, stirring occasionally, until they become fragrant. Use whole, or crush in a spice grinder into a coarse or fine powder.

1 pound medium to large raw shrimp

⇒ PEPPER SALT ⇐
3/4 teaspoon salt
1/4 teaspoon black pepper
1/4 teaspoon sugar
1/8 teaspoon Chinese five-spice
1/8 teaspoon ground toasted Sichuan peppercorns

1/2 cup cooking oil
1 teaspoon minced garlic
1 teaspoon crushed dried red chilies
1 green onion, chopped
Shredded lettuce
1 fresh red jalapeño chili, sliced

Getting Ready

1. Remove heads from shrimp, keeping shells and legs intact. Rinse shrimp and pat very dry with paper towels.

Cooking

1. Prepare pepper salt: Place a small frying pan over medium-high heat until hot. Add salt and cook, stirring continuously, until slightly gray in color, 2 to 3 minutes. Place in a bowl and add remaining pepper salt ingredients.

2. Heat oil in a wok over high heat until hot. Add shrimp and fry until they turn pink, about 2 minutes. Lift out with a slotted spoon; drain on paper towels.

3. Remove all but 2 teaspoons oil from wok. Add garlic, crushed chilies, and green onion; cook, stirring, until fragrant, about 30 seconds. Return shrimp to wok and stir-fry for 1 to 1 1/2 minutes. Add pepper salt and toss to coat.

4. Line a serving plate with lettuce. Place shrimp on top and garnish with chili rings.

Makes 4 servings.

VELVETED SCALLOPS WITH SUGAR SNAP PEAS

Scallops are sweet and tender. Sugar snap peas are sweet and crunchy. Sounds like a match made in heaven to me! I stir-fry the peas, then the scallops, and top them both with a light wine sauce.

⪈ MARINADE ⪇
2 teaspoons cornstarch
1 egg white
1/2 teaspoon salt
1/4 teaspoon white pepper

3/4 pound sea scallops, butterflied

⪈ SAUCE ⪇
1/3 cup Chinese rice wine or
    dry sherry
2 teaspoons black bean sauce
2 teaspoons oyster sauce
1/2 teaspoon sugar

4 teaspoons cooking oil
1/2 pound sugar snap peas or
    snow peas
1 fresh red jalapeño chili, seeded
    and sliced
1 teaspoon cornstarch dissolved in
    2 teaspoons water

Getting Ready
1. Combine marinade ingredients in a small bowl. Add scallops; stir to coat. Let stand for 10 minutes.

2. Combine sauce ingredients in a bowl; set aside.

Cooking
1. Bring a pan of water to a boil. Add scallops and blanch for 1 minute; drain and pat dry with paper towels.

2. Place a wok over high heat until hot. Add 2 teaspoons oil, swirling to coat sides. Add peas and stir-fry for 2 minutes; add a few drops of water if wok appears dry. Remove peas to center of a serving plate.

3. Add remaining 2 teaspoons oil, swirling to coat sides. Add scallops and stir-fry for 1 minute. Add chili and cook for 30 seconds. Add sauce and bring to a boil. Add cornstarch solution and cook, stirring, until sauce boils and thickens.

4. Arrange scallops around peas. Pour sauce over peas and serve.

Makes 4 servings.

EDIBLE VELVET

Have you ever wondered how Chinese restaurants make their scallops so plump and tender? Allow me to reveal the chef's secret: First, the scallops are marinated in a little cornstarch, egg white, and salt to seal in their juices and make them plumper. Then they're quickly blanched in water or oil, drained, and patted dry. At this point, they're half-cooked and ready to be quickly finished by stir-frying in a wok. This technique, often used on seafood and poultry, is called "velveting" because it gives foods such a soft, smooth texture.

CHICKEN AND SEAFOOD TRIO IN A BASKET

This delicate stir-fry of chicken and seafood is guaranteed to generate "oohs" and "ahs," especially if you serve it in a deep-fried potato, taro, or noodle basket (see sidebar).

BASKET-MAKING 101

Here's how to make an edible basket in which to serve stir-fried dishes: You will need two 6-inch metal strainers that can nest one inside the other. In a wok, heat cooking oil for deep-frying to 350°F. Peel and shred or finely julienne one medium potato (taro root or fresh egg noodles, cooked, rinsed and drained, can also be used). Rinse shredded potato under cold running water; squeeze well to remove as much moisture as possible and pat dry with paper towels. Toss potato with I teaspoon corn-starch. Dip strainers into the hot oil to coat them. Line one strainer with potato to a thickness of about 3/8 inch. Nest second strainer on top of potato shreds and immerse strainers in oil. Deep-fry until golden brown. Remove potato basket from strainers and drain on paper towels. Fill basket with cooked food and serve immediately.

3/4 pound asparagus, trimmed and cut into 2-inch lengths
1/2 pound mixed seafood (choose from firm white fish fillets, scallops, and shrimp)
1/4 pound boneless, skinless chicken breast
I tablespoon cornstarch
I egg white
1/2 teaspoon salt
1/4 teaspoon white pepper
I tablespoon cooking oil
2 teaspoons minced ginger
I green onion, finely chopped
3/4 cup chicken broth
2 tablespoons oyster-flavored sauce
I tablespoon fish sauce
I teaspoon cornstarch dissolved in 2 teaspoons water
Edible basket (recipe at left)

Getting ready

1. Bring a large pan of water to a boil. Add asparagus. Cook until tender-crisp, about 2 minutes. Drain.

2. If using fish or large scallops or shrimp, cut into 1/2-inch cubes. Cut chicken into 1/2-inch cubes. Coat seafood and chicken with cornstarch, egg white, salt, and white pepper.

Cooking

1. Place a wok over high heat until hot. Add oil, swirling to coat sides. Add ginger and cook, stirring, until fragrant, about 10 seconds. Add seafood, chicken, and green onion; stir-fry for 1 minute.

2. Add broth, oyster-flavored sauce, and fish sauce; bring to a boil. Add cornstarch solution and cook, stirring, until sauce boils and thickens. Add asparagus and toss to mix.

3. Spoon seafood mixture into basket.

Makes 4 servings.

GLAZED PLUM-FLAVORED CHICKEN WITH WOLFBERRIES

This dish of chicken thighs quickly braised and glazed with dried fruit makes a great autumn or winter dinner. Wolfberries, also known as dried medlars, are small, deep red, oval fruits with a sweet, spiced-apple flavor. I buy them from an herbalist in San Francisco's Chinatown. If you can't find wolfberries, it's OK to meddle with the recipe and use dried cranberries.

≥ MARINADE ≤

2 tablespoons dark soy sauce
2 teaspoons cornstarch

3/4 pound boneless, skinless chicken thighs, cut into 1-inch pieces
6 small dried figs, halved and stemmed
8 pitted prunes
2 tablespoons dried wolfberries or dried cranberries
1/4 cup plum wine
2 tablespoons cooking oil
2 tablespoons plum sauce
1/4 cup chicken broth
1/2 teaspoon cornstarch dissolved in 1 teaspoon water
1/2 cup roasted cashews

Getting Ready

1. Combine marinade ingredients in a bowl. Add chicken; stir to coat. Let stand for 10 minutes.

2. Soak figs, prunes, and wolfberries in plum wine until softened, about 10 minutes.

Cooking

1. Place a wok over high heat until hot. Add oil, swirling to coat sides. Add chicken and stir-fry for 2 minutes. Add figs, prunes, wolfberries, soaking wine, plum sauce, and broth. Bring to a boil; reduce heat to low, cover, and simmer until chicken is no longer pink, about 5 minutes longer. Add cornstarch solution and cook, stirring, until sauce boils and thickens. Add cashews and mix well.

Makes 4 servings.

STRANGE-FLAVOR CHICKEN

People always ask me for the recipe for this mysteriously delicious salad of poached chicken in a sweet, sour, spicy, nutty dressing. The only strange thing about it is its name: "Strange flavor" is the Chinese way of describing a wonderful combination of tastes that usually include black vinegar and ground peanuts or sesame seeds.

¹/₂ teaspoon salt
3 slices ginger, each the size of
    a quarter, lightly crushed
³/₄ pound boneless chicken breast
    halves or thighs
2 teaspoons sesame seeds

⇒ SAUCE ⇐
3 tablespoons creamy peanut butter
    or peanut-flavored sauce
3 tablespoons Chinese black vinegar
2 tablespoons soy sauce
2 tablespoons Chinese rice wine or
    dry sherry
1 tablespoon chili garlic sauce
1 tablespoon honey or sugar
1 teaspoon ground toasted Sichuan
    peppercorns

2 ounces bean thread noodles
2 teaspoons cooking oil
1 medium onion, cut into ¹/₄-inch-
    thick slices and separated
    into rings
Cilantro sprigs

Getting Ready
1. Bring a 2-quart pan of water to a boil. Add salt, ginger, and chicken; return water to boil. Reduce heat to low and simmer until chicken is tender, about 20 minutes; drain. Discard ginger and chicken skin. Thinly slice meat and place in a bowl.

2. Place sesame seeds in a small frying pan over medium heat; cook, shaking pan frequently, until lightly browned, 3 to 4 minutes. Immediately remove from pan to cool.

3. Combine sauce ingredients in a bowl.

Cooking
1. Cook noodles in boiling water for 1 minute. Drain, rinse in cold water, and drain again.

2. Place a wok over high heat until hot. Add oil, swirling to coat sides. Add onion rings and stir-fry until golden brown, 3 to 4 minutes.

3. Place noodles in the center of a serving plate; arrange onion on top. Add half of sauce to chicken; mix well. Place chicken over noodles and onion; sprinkle with sesame seeds. Garnish with cilantro sprigs. Pass remaining sauce at the table.

Makes 4 servings.

BLACK VINEGAR

I love to use a splash of vinegar in cooking to add sparkle and intensity to a dish. For lighter-colored and flavored dishes, I'll often use distilled white vinegar, but for darker, deeper-tasting ones, Chinese black vinegar is the way to go. It's sold in Asian markets (sometimes under the name "Chinkiang vinegar") and it's really worth tracking down. Black vinegar is made by fermenting a mixture of rice, wheat, and millet or sorghum. Its flavor is smokier, sweeter, and less tart than that of Western white or red vinegars. If you can't find it, don't be sour: Balsamic vinegar is a perfect substitute, though you may want to reduce the amount of sugar in your recipe.

CHICKEN AND TARO ROOT STEW

If you think of a stew as something that needs to simmer all afternoon, check out this quick and hearty stew of chicken, mushrooms, and taro root. Serve it with plenty of rice to soak up all the tasty sauce.

READING THE TARO

What's round, has a brown skin, grows underground and is a staple food for millions of people? If you answered "a potato," you were right, but only partly right. If you also said "taro root," you get extra credit. A round rhizome with a hairy brown skin (which must be peeled), taro root is cultivated throughout tropical Asia and Africa. It can be steamed, boiled, fried, braised, or baked. Once cooked, the white flesh of some kinds of taro root turns grayish purple, and it develops a starchy texture and a sweet, nutty flavor that goes well with duck, pork, and chicken. Wear rubber gloves when you peel taro, as its juices may irritate your skin. If you can't find taro, potato can be substituted in many recipes. Unlike a potato, though, taro has a relatively short shelf life—two to three weeks when it's stored in a cool, dry place.

8 dried black mushrooms
$1/2$ pound boneless chicken
1 tablespoon soy sauce
2 tablespoons cooking oil
$3/4$ pound taro root or potato, peeled and cut into 1-inch cubes
6 cloves garlic
5 slices ginger, each the size of a quarter, lightly crushed
2 shallots, quartered
6 green onions, white part only, cut into 2-inch lengths
$1 1/4$ cups chicken broth
2 tablespoons oyster-flavored sauce
2 tablespoons Chinese rice wine or dry sherry
2 teaspoons cornstarch dissolved in 1 tablespoon water
Cilantro or basil sprigs

Getting Ready

1. Soak mushrooms in warm water to cover until softened, about 20 minutes; drain. Discard stems.

2. Cut chicken into 1-inch cubes; toss with the soy sauce.

Cooking

1. Place a wok or wide frying pan over medium heat until hot. Add 1 tablespoon oil, swirling to coat sides. Pan-fry taro root and garlic until golden brown, 2 to 3 minutes. Remove taro root and garlic from pan with a slotted spoon. Drain on paper towels.

2. Add remaining 1 tablespoon oil to pan; increase heat to high. Add chicken, ginger, shallots, and green onions; stir-fry for 1 minute. Return taro root and garlic to pan; add black mushrooms, broth, oyster-flavored sauce, and rice wine; bring to a boil. Reduce heat to low; cover and simmer until taro root is tender, 12 to 15 minutes.

3. Add cornstarch solution and cook, stirring, until sauce boils and thickens slightly. Place in a shallow bowl and garnish with cilantro sprigs.

Makes 4 servings.

BRAISED CHESTNUT CHICKEN

If you're looking for a great cold-weather dish to warm your spirits, why not wing it? These chicken wings braised with chestnuts and mushrooms in a fragrant spiced sauce are sure to do the trick.

1/4 pound dried chestnuts
1 1/2 pounds chicken wings
2 tablespoons cooking oil
4 slices ginger, each the size of
    a quarter, lightly crushed
2 shallots, quartered
2 cups chicken broth
1/2 cup water
1/2 cup sliced white button mushrooms
1/4 cup canned straw mushrooms,
    drained
1/3 cup Chinese rice wine or dry
    sherry
3 whole star anise
1 stick cinnamon
1/4 cup ginkgo nuts
1/4 cup sliced water chestnuts
3 tablespoons regular soy sauce
3 tablespoons dark soy sauce
2 tablespoons packed brown sugar

Getting Ready

1. Soak chestnuts in warm water to cover. Let stand until softened, about 4 hours; drain.

2. Remove tips from chicken wings; save for stock. Cut wings apart at joint.

Cooking

1. Place a wok over medium-high heat until hot. Add oil, swirling to coat sides. Add chicken, ginger, and shallots. Cook until chicken is browned on all sides, about 4 minutes. Remove from wok.

2. Place remaining ingredients and dried chestnuts in a 3-quart pan; bring to a boil. Reduce heat to low and simmer for 10 minutes. Add chicken, ginger, and shallots; cover and simmer until chicken and chestnuts are tender, about 30 minutes.

Makes 4 to 6 servings.

INVESTING IN STOCK

A good chicken stock is the basis of most Chinese soups and stews. Chinese stocks tend to be simpler and quicker to prepare than Western ones. Here's my basic chicken stock recipe: Place 2 quarts water and 2 1/2 pounds raw chicken bones in a large pot. Bring to a boil. Reduce heat, skim foam from surface of liquid, then cover and simmer for 1 1/2 hours. Add 3 green onions and 8 slices of fresh ginger, each the size of a quarter, and salt and pepper to taste. Simmer for 30 minutes. Strain stock, discarding bones and seasonings. Chill stock, then skim and discard fat. The stock will keep in the refrigerator for a week or more if it is brought to a boil every other day. Freeze it for longer storage.

ROAST DRUNKEN DUCK

Here's my easy home-style version of Cantonese roast duck. It's marinated in wine, filled with an aromatic stuffing, and finished off with a soy and hoisin glaze for a beautifully lacquered look.

⇉ MARINADE ⇇
2 teaspoons soy sauce
2 teaspoons dark soy sauce
1/2 cup white wine or dry sherry
1/2 teaspoon salt
1/2 teaspoon Chinese five-spice

1 whole duck (3 to 3 1/2 lb.), cleaned
8 dried black mushrooms

⇉ STUFFING ⇇
2 tablespoons cooking oil
4 slices ginger, each the size of
   a quarter, julienned
3 cloves garlic, minced
2 medium onions, thinly sliced
1/4 cup shredded bamboo shoots
2 tablespoons thinly sliced Sichuan
   preserved vegetable
1/4 cup white wine
1 teaspoon Chinese five-spice
2 tablespoons dark soy sauce
1 tablespoon hoisin sauce or char
   siu sauce

⇉ GLAZE ⇇
2 tablespoons dark soy sauce
1 tablespoon hoisin sauce

Getting Ready
1. Combine marinade ingredients in a bowl. Rub duck inside and out with marinade. Cover and refrigerate for 2 hours.

2. Soak mushrooms in warm water to cover until softened, about 20 minutes; drain. Discard stems; thinly slice caps.

3. Prepare stuffing: Place a wok over high heat until hot. Add oil, swirling to coat sides. Add ginger and garlic; cook, stirring, until fragrant, about 10 seconds. Add onions and stir-fry for 1 minute. Add mushrooms, bamboo shoots, and preserved vegetable; stir-fry for 2 minutes. Add wine, five-spice, soy sauce, and hoisin sauce; cook for 1 minute. Let cool.

4. Place stuffing inside duck; use skewers to enclose.

Cooking
1. Preheat oven to 400°F. Place duck, breast side up, on a rack in a roasting pan. Bake until meat is no longer pink when cut near bone, 1 to 1 1/2 hours.

2. Increase heat to 475°F. Combine glaze ingredients in a bowl. Brush glaze over chicken. Bake until skin is richly glazed, 5 to 7 minutes.

Makes 4 to 6 servings.

LUCKY DUCK

If you live near a Chinese deli that sells roast ducks, you're in luck: You can enjoy a wonderful treat any time without running up a huge "duck bill"! Roasting duck the Chinese way is a real art. First, the birds are parboiled, melting away some of the fat. Then they're blown up with air and hung up to dry to tighten their skin. Finally, they're lacquered with a sweet glaze of honey, maltose, vinegar, and rice wine that caramelizes during roasting, making the skin crisp and brown. You can eat Cantonese roast duck at room temperature, or warm it in the oven. Serve it with the thin brown cooking sauce that's usually included at no extra charge, or shred the meat and use it to top a salad of greens tossed with a vinaigrette enriched either with a bit of the duck sauce, or with bottled plum sauce.

GAME HENS WITH SUGARCANE

Are you game for something a little different? Try this stove top stew of game hens, sweetened with sugarcane and steamed 'till they are so tender you can cut them with a chopstick.

2 game hens, halved; or ¾ pound chicken drumsticks
½ teaspoon salt
1 medium carrot, roll-cut
½ cup canned sugarcane, cut into 1-inch lengths, each piece quartered lengthwise
⅓ cup whole water chestnuts
4 dates, pitted
4 slices ginger, each the size of a quarter, lightly crushed
1 tablespoon chopped dried longan meat (optional)
2 cups chicken broth
1 cup water
¼ cup Chinese rice wine or dry sherry

Getting Ready

1. Rub poultry with salt; let stand for 30 minutes.

Cooking

1. Bring a 2-quart pan of water to a boil. Add poultry. Parboil for 3 minutes; drain.

2. In the top of a double boiler, place meat, carrot, sugarcane, water chestnuts, dates, ginger, longan meat (if used), broth, water, and wine. Cover and cook over simmering water for 1½ hours.

(If you don't have a double boiler, place ingredients in a heatproof bowl, cover tightly with foil, then place bowl on a rack in a deep pan. Pour boiling water about one-third of the way up sides of bowl. Cover pan and simmer for 1½ hours. Check water level and add water as needed.)

3. Place in a serving bowl.

Makes 4 servings.

SWEET AND TANGY TANGERINE SPARE RIBS

Ribs don't have to be barbecued or baked. These succulent pork ribs are cooked in the classic home-style Chinese way my mother taught me: They're simmered in a wok right on the stovetop and finished with a rich tangerine and plum sauce glaze.

1½ pounds spareribs, cut into
    3-inch lengths

¼ cup soy sauce
2 tablespoons hoisin sauce
2 tablespoons cooking oil
2 teaspoons minced ginger
2 pieces (each about 1½ in. square)
    dried tangerine peel, soaked
    and julienned; or 1 tablespoon
    julienned orange zest
2 star anise
1 cinnamon stick
¾ cup chicken broth
3 tablespoons frozen orange
    or tangerine juice concentrate,
    thawed
2 tablespoons brown sugar
3 tablespoons orange-flavored
    liqueur
1 tablespoon dark soy sauce
Orange zest
1 orange, peeled and cut into
    segments

Getting ready

1. Cut ribs between the bones into individual pieces. Bring a 4-quart pot of water to a boil. Add ribs and simmer for 3 minutes; drain.

2. Mix soy sauce and hoisin sauce. Brush onto meat and let stand for 10 minutes.

Cooking

1. Place a wok over high heat until hot. Add oil, swirling to coat sides. Add ginger and cook, stirring, until fragrant, about 10 seconds. Add ribs and cook until browned on all sides, 4 to 5 minutes.

2. Add tangerine peel, star anise, cinnamon stick, and broth; bring to a boil. Reduce heat to low; cover and simmer until meat is tender, about 45 minutes.

3. Increase heat to high. Add juice concentrate, brown sugar, liqueur, and soy sauce; cook, uncovered, until sauce is reduced and ribs are glazed, 4 to 6 minutes.

4. Place ribs on a serving platter and garnish with orange zest and orange segments.

Makes 4 servings.

AN APPEALING ADDITION

My mom always had a supply of dried tangerine peel on hand in her kitchen for flavoring all kinds of slow-simmered meat and poultry dishes. You can buy it in bags in Chinese markets, but it's easy to make your own. After enjoying a tasty tangerine, cut the peel into pieces that are small enough to spread out flat. Use a paring knife to remove as much of the white pith from the inside of the peel as possible. Cut the pieces into smaller strips and set them out to dry in a sunny spot for a few days until they're firm but still flexible and very dry. Stored in an airtight container, dried tangerine peel will keep for months and even years.

MANGO BEEF

Like many Hong Kong–trained chefs, I love to combine the flavors of meat and fresh fruit. Here, it's a case of meat meets mango in a sizzling sweet-and-savory stir-fry. If you can't find mangoes, you can substitute pears or peaches.

⊱ MARINADE ⊰
1 tablespoon oyster-flavored sauce
1 teaspoon cornstarch

³/4 pound beef sirloin, cut into ¹/2-inch cubes

1 ripe mango (about 1 lb.) or pear
1 large Granny Smith or other tart apple
2 tablespoons cooking oil
1 teaspoon minced ginger
¹/4 cup diced red bell pepper
2 tablespoons plum sauce
1 tablespoon Chinese rice wine or dry sherry
2 teaspoons soy sauce
¹/4 cup whole macadamia nuts or blanched almonds
¹/2 fresh red jalapeño chili, sliced

Getting Ready
1. Combine marinade ingredients in a bowl. Add beef and stir to coat. Let stand for 10 minutes.

2. Peel mango and cut flesh from seed; cut flesh into ³/4-inch cubes. Peel and core apple; cut into ¹/2-inch cubes.

Cooking
1. Place a wok over high heat until hot. Add 1¹/2 tablespoons oil, swirling to coat sides. Add ginger and cook, stirring, until fragrant, about 10 seconds. Add beef and stir-fry until no longer pink, 1¹/2 to 2 minutes. Remove meat and ginger from pan.

2. Add remaining ¹/2 tablespoon oil to wok, swirling to coat sides. Add mango, apple, and bell pepper; stir-fry for 2 minutes. Return meat to wok and add plum sauce, wine, and soy sauce; cook until heated through. Add nuts and mix well.

3. Place on a serving plate and garnish with chili slices.

Makes 4 servings.

TOMATO MUSHROOM BEEF

Ground beef, tomatoes, mushrooms, garlic. Sound like the makings of a classic Italian recipe? Surprise! It's a simple, saucy Chinese stir-fry that's great over rice or noodles.

BEEF TIPS

Here are a few simple tips for buying and preparing beef. In the store, pick it up last so it spends as little time as possible at room temperature, and place it in a plastic bag to keep it from dripping onto other foods. Thaw frozen beef in the refrigerator or the microwave—never at room temperature. Marinate all meat in the refrigerator. Discard the leftover marinade that was in contact with the raw meat, or bring it to a rolling boil for 1 minute before using it on cooked meat. Use a quick-read meat thermometer to take the guesswork out of cooking beef. For burgers, the internal temperature should be 160°F (or until no longer pink). For steaks, medium-rare is 145°F, medium is 160°F and well done is 170°F.

⇒ MARINADE ⇐

2 tablespoons oyster-flavored sauce
2 teaspoons cornstarch

¾ pound lean ground beef

⇒ SAUCE ⇐

⅓ cup beef broth
3 tablespoons catsup
2 tablespoons hoisin sauce

3 tablespoons cooking oil
2 teaspoons minced garlic
1 small onion, cut into 1-inch squares
¼ pound button mushrooms, sliced
2 medium tomatoes, diced
2½ teaspoons cornstarch dissolved in 2 tablespoons water

Getting Ready

1. Combine marinade ingredients in a medium bowl. Add beef, stir to coat, and set aside for 30 minutes. Combine sauce ingredients in a small bowl; set aside.

Cooking

1. Place a wok or wide frying pan over high heat until hot. Add 2 tablespoons oil, swirling to coat sides. Add beef and stir-fry until barely pink, about 2 minutes. Remove beef from wok.

2. Add remaining 1 tablespoon oil to the wok. Add garlic, onion, and mushrooms; cook until onion is soft and translucent, about 2 minutes. Stir in the tomatoes and the sauce mixture; mix well.

3. Return the beef to wok and add the cornstarch solution. Cook, stirring, until the sauce boils and thickens.

Makes 4 servings.

BLACK PEPPER
HONEY-GLAZED OSTRICH

Stuck in a rut when it comes to meat and poultry? Get your head out of the sand, and check out ostrich! It's turning up in more and more supermarket meat cases, and I find this super-lean and tender meat works perfectly in stir-fried dishes. I like to bring out its beefy, gamey flavor with a robust honey-mustard sauce.

> MARINADE <
1/4 teaspoon black pepper
1 teaspoon dark soy sauce
1 teaspoon cornstarch
2 teaspoons rice wine

3/4 pound ostrich breast, cut into
    3/4-inch cubes

> SAUCE <
1/4 cup chicken broth
1 tablespoon dark soy sauce
3 tablespoons honey
1 tablespoon rice vinegar
3/4 teaspoon ground black pepper

3 tablespoons cooking oil
2 cloves garlic, minced
1 fresh red jalapeño chili, seeded
    and sliced
1/2 pound asparagus, cut into 2-inch
    lengths
1/2 medium onion, cut into 1-inch
    squares
1/2 red bell pepper, cut into 1-inch
    squares

Getting Ready

1. Combine marinade ingredients in a bowl. Add ostrich and stir to coat. Let stand for 10 minutes. Combine sauce ingredients in another bowl; whisk until blended.

Cooking

1. Place a wok over high heat until hot. Add 2 tablespoons oil, swirling to coat sides. Add ostrich and stir-fry for 2 minutes. Remove meat from wok.

2. Add remaining 1 tablespoon oil to wok, swirling to coat sides. Add garlic and chili; cook, stirring, until fragrant, about 10 seconds. Add asparagus, onion, and bell pepper; stir-fry for 1 minute.

3. Add sauce and cook until it is reduced and slightly thickened, about 2 minutes. Return meat to wok and toss to coat.

4. Place on a serving plate.

Makes 4 servings.

A DELICATE BALANCE

In cooking and in life, I try to remember that balance is the key. And the ancient philosophy of yin and yang is always there to remind me. Yin represents the feminine, yielding, darker, more mysterious forces, while yang stands for the masculine, harder, brighter, hotter ones. In cooking, balancing yin and yang is all about creating a harmony of flavors, colors, and textures. Yin might be cool, moist, soft foods like winter melon, asparagus, or crab meat. Yang might take the form of chilies, ginger, fried foods, or red meat. Chinese cooks believe that balancing yin and yang not only heightens the eating experience, but also keeps the body in a state of equilibrium and good health. I hope my recipes help you achieve both. If Yan can balance yin and yang, so can you!

HONEY TOFU SMOOTHIE

If you're looking for a quick, energizing drink, this one's a honey! At my house, we make it for breakfast or an afternoon snack. For variety, you can throw in your own creative touches, like orange, pineapple, or cranberry juice and strawberries or other fresh or frozen fruit.

SOFT ON SOFT TOFU

I have a soft spot in my heart for soft tofu! It's one of those chameleon-like ingredients that can be whipped in the blender or food processor and used as a lighter, cholesterol-free stand-in for mayonnaise, or a base for all kinds of creamy dressings, sauces, dips, and whipped desserts. In her new cookbook, "Mollie Katzen's Vegetable Heaven" (Hyperion), my friend and colleague Mollie Katzen, of "Moosewood Cookbook" fame, purées silken tofu with banana and melted chocolate in the blender to create an easy chilled chocolate-banana mousse that tastes every bit as rich as the egg-and-cream variety.

2 medium-size ripe bananas
1 package (16 oz.) soft tofu, drained
3 tablespoons honey
1/4 teaspoon vanilla extract or almond extract
1/2 cup crushed ice
Mint leaves

Getting ready

1. Peel bananas and cut into 1-inch pieces; cover with plastic wrap. Place in freezer until firm, at least 2 hours.

Finishing

1. In a blender, purée bananas, tofu, honey, vanilla extract, and ice. Pour into tall dessert glasses and garnish with mint leaves.

Makes about 3 1/2 cups, 4 servings.

RAINBOW TAPIOCA PUDDING

This is my kind of dessert: easy, beautiful, light, and tasty. Creamy tapioca is tinted with fruit purées and layered to create a rainbow in a bowl. Use glass dessert bowls, parfait glasses, or champagne flutes to heighten the elegant "layered look."

¾ cup small (⅛ in.) pearl tapioca
1 cup cold water
2 cups warm water
¾ cup sugar
⅔ cup each puréed mango;
   honeydew melon or cantaloupe;
   and strawberries or canned
   lychees
¼ cup coconut cream or coconut milk
Mint sprigs

Getting Ready
1. Soak tapioca in cold water for 30 minutes (most of the water will be absorbed); drain.

Cooking
1. Combine warm water and sugar in a heavy 2-quart pan. Cook, stirring, over medium heat until sugar dissolves. Add soaked tapioca and bring to a boil. Reduce heat to medium-low and cook, stirring, until mixture thickens and tapioca becomes translucent, about 15 minutes. Divide mixture equally among 3 bowls and let cool.

2. In a food processor, purée fruits. (You will need ⅔ cup of each purée.) Whisk 1 purée into each bowl of tapioca.

3. In 4 dessert bowls, pour 1 layer of each tapioca mixture; chill until serving time.

4. For coconut cream, open a can of unsweetened coconut milk (do not shake it first), and spoon the thick cream off the top. (For coconut milk, shake the can before opening.)

5. To serve, top each dessert with 1 tablespoon of coconut cream; garnish with a mint sprig.

Makes 4 servings.

LYCHEE

Southern China is lychee territory, and Hong Kong chefs use these delicate fruits in a variety of sweet and sour dishes and desserts. They're also served over ice as a refreshing snack. Nowadays, fresh lychees from Taiwan, Thailand, Florida, California, and Hawaii are available during the summer months—which is great news for me, because ever since I was a little boy, I can't get enough of them. Lychees are covered with a bumpy, crimson skin, which is removed before eating. Their flesh is creamy white with a single shiny brown seed and a texture a bit like that of a grape. Canned lychees are not bad, and they save time, because they're already peeled and pitted.

Singapore *Cooking at the Crossroads*

People often call Singapore the "Crossroads of Asia." All I can say is, you'd better look both ways before you cross, because this is one of the busiest intersections on earth!

Singapore is tiny—a single city-state that covers a 238 square-mile island at the tip of the Malay Peninsula. But what a boom town! It's the second busiest trading port in the world, and its standard of living and literacy rate are among the highest in Asia.

I've been coming here for years, but my first glimpse of Singapore never fails to take my breath away. It's crammed with skyscrapers and teeming with people—2.7 million of them—but careful planning and government regulation have kept urban blight at bay.

The streets are jammed with traffic, but they're clean and safe, and there are so many public gardens and pocket parks filled with lush, tropical greenery nestled amid the steel and concrete that Singapore has earned the name "The Garden City." (You'll also hear it called "The Lion City," a translation of the original Sanskrit name Singa Pura. Whoever coined that name probably saw a tiger, not a lion. But that's another story.)

From Tropics to Metropolis

Singapore has been an important trade-route gateway ever since the 13th century, but its transformation into an international center of trade and commerce didn't begin in earnest until 1819, when Sir Stamford Raffles, an enterprising clerk in the British East India Trading Company, arrived on the scene to find an overgrown malarial swamp populated by a handful of Malay fishermen and pirates.

Raffles saw in Singapore the potential for a major British trading post, so he urged Britain to purchase the territory and became one of the city's founding fathers and urban planners. Before long, Singapore had become Britain's key Southeast Asian outpost, and boatloads of traders and immigrant laborers from China, the Malay Peninsula, Indonesia, and India began to pour into the island in search of prosperity.

This multiethnic mix has defined the country's population —and its food— ever since. Today, more than three-quarters of Singaporeans are ethnic Chinese, with Malays (14 percent), Indians (8 percent), and others making up the rest.

It's Always Time for a Little Something

Singaporeans say that there are three national obsessions that bring all of these diverse ethnic groups together: working, shopping, and eating. Personally, I have a hunch that the working and shopping are just excuses to get out of the house and eat!

When I'm visiting friends in Singapore, they insist on breakfast, a midmorning coffee break, lunch, afternoon tea (with a little something to eat, of course), a serious dinner, and finally a little nibble to sleep on sometime after midnight. And at every meal, they spend half the time debating about where to eat next, with everyone trading opinions about their latest discoveries and where to find the best version of any dish. In other words, these are my kind of people.

To illustrate the many flavors of Singapore's ethnic mix, the chefs at the Mandarin Hotel made me an edible pie chart!

It doesn't take much to convince a Singaporean to eat out. After all, it's always too hot to cook, and always more fun to grab a quick bite cooked for you by someone else.

No problem. At last count, Singapore had more than 20,000 eating places! Many are restaurants and coffee shops, but the vast majority, nearly 19,000, are hawker stalls—simple food stands that turn out some of the most flavorful and satisfying snacks and one-dish meals in the world in a matter of minutes.

Singapore has more than 20,000 eating places. And of those, 19,000 are hawker stalls.

A Visit to Hawker Heaven

All over Asia, you'll find hawkers selling street food. It's often the way immigrants make a start in a new country, carrying their mobile kitchens on their backs or on improvised pushcarts, setting up shop on a street corner and serving up the specialties of their native lands. In Singapore, this tradition has been turned into an institution: the hawker center, a food court with stalls selling noodles, rice dishes, dumplings, grilled foods, beverages, and desserts, all clustered together around communal tables. It's fun, fast, informal, spotlessly clean, and unbelievably inexpensive. It's also the best place to get a cook's tour of the Chinese, Malay-Indonesian, Indian, and Nonya (Malay-Chinese) dishes that make up Singaporean cuisine.

Allow me to be your guide. It's a warm Singapore evening, and we're feeling hungry because we haven't eaten in almost an hour! So we head over to the Satay Club on Clarke Quay by the Singapore River, where colonial-era warehouses have been converted into pastel-colored restaurants and shops. Outdoors, it's one giant open-air barbecue every night.

From a block away, we can already smell the skewers of marinated meats grilling over dozens of charcoal fires. We find a table under a string of light bulbs and watch as the Malay cooks wave palm leaf

A front-row seat at the Newton Circus Hawker Centre, the best cooking show in town.

fans over the flames, deftly flipping and basting the neat bundles of skewers as they brown. We dip our satay in sweet-spicy peanut sauce and eat it with little cubes of pressed rice and cooling cucumber and onion, washing it all down with a bottle of Singapore's world-famous Tiger Beer. OK, now we're working up a real appetite.

Time to move on to another booming open-air hawker center, this one at Newton Circus. As a globe-trotting food lover, this place is my idea of heaven. Only noisier. Between the clanging of spatulas in the enormous *kuali* (woks) and kettles, the roar of the gas jets shooting out flames, and the waiters and vendors yelling out orders, you can hardly think straight. But then, you don't have to. Just wander around and take in the sights and sounds. If you like to watch cooking shows—and something tells me you do—you've come to the right place.

A couple of teenage kids rush up and take our order. Hawker food is often a family affair, with mom and dad running the stand, and the kids doing the hawking. Nothing is written down, but somehow

the right food always shows up at the right table in just a few minutes.

I say we start with a little seafood, the great common denominator of Singaporean cooking. Muslim Malays eat no pork, Indian Hindus avoid beef, and many Chinese cooks find the flavor of beef and mutton to be too strong. But seafood is something everyone can agree on.

We'd better try the unofficial national dish of Singapore, chili crab: chunks of fresh crab in the shell, stir-fried and smothered in a fiery sauce of chili, ginger, garlic, tomato, soy sauce, sugar, and spices. It's not Malay, Chinese, or Indian but borrows flavors from all three cuisines. Which is to say, it's Singaporean.

Now let's pay a visit to the *murtabak* man. You know pizza. You know crêpes. Forget about them. This is the real deal. The cook stretches a ball of oiled dough into an impossibly thin sheet, twirling and tossing it high in the air with the flair of a circus performer. Then he flings the dough onto a sizzling griddle, cracks a raw egg over it, and quickly scrambles it with his bare

My favorite murtabak man at the Newton Circus Hawker Centre.

hands. Next come toppings like cabbage, minced chicken or mutton, chilies, and onion. With a few quick flicks of the spatula, the dough is folded into a square, and served up on a banana leaf.

Still hungry? Good. Because you can't visit a hawker center without trying some noodles. How about *mee goreng*? It's the uniquely Singaporean noodle dish invented by Indian hawkers, made with egg noodles tossed in a quick blur of rapid stir-frying and spicy steam that makes your eyes water as much as your mouth?

Singaporeans have three obsessions: working, shopping, and eating. I think the working and shopping are just excuses to get out of the house and eat!

tea and sweetened condensed milk back and forth from pitcher to cup, pulling his hands apart as he pours in a sweeping arc until the tea is whipped into a foamy brew that I like to call "the cappuccino of the East." You're looking a little dazed. Maybe we'd better call this dessert.

Unless you'd care to try *popiah*, the Nonya version of the spring roll. Or maybe a little fish head curry served on a banana leaf? Hainan chicken rice?

Sorry. With so much to choose from, I always get a little carried away in Singapore. Try some of my recipes in this chapter, many of which are adapted from hawker specialties, and you'll soon see why.

Mee goreng goes perfectly with a cup of Indian *teh tarik*, or "pulled" tea, another showstopper. Without spilling a drop, the tea puller pours a mixture of

Meanwhile, if you'll excuse me, I think I can still squeeze in one last bowlful of rice porridge with meatballs before bedtime.

POPIAH

When you order a soft, fragrant popiah—the Nonya version of a spring roll—at a food stall, it's made to order, just for you. The cook layers a tender crêpe-like wrapper with lettuce, shrimp, bits of omelet, and, straight from the pot, a bubbling filling of Chinese sausage and vegetables. When I serve these, I like to arrange all the components on a platter and let my guests roll their own popiah right at the table.

2 ½ tablespoons cooking oil
2 eggs, lightly beaten

▷ FILLING ◁
1 walnut-size shallot, sliced
2 cloves garlic, minced
2 Chinese sausages, julienned
1 small carrot, shredded
½ cup julienned jicama
¼ cup water
1 tablespoon soy sauce
2 teaspoons chili garlic sauce
1 teaspoon sugar
3 green onions (green part only), julienned

8 lumpia wrappers

▷ GARNISHES ◁
8 butter lettuce leaves
Hoisin sauce
Chili garlic sauce
1 cup bean sprouts
8 shelled cooked shrimp, cut in half lengthwise

Getting Ready
1. Place a nonstick 8- to 9-inch frying pan over medium heat until hot. Add ½ teaspoon oil, swirling to coat sides. Add half the eggs and cook until lightly browned on bottom and set on top, about 1 minute. Turn over and cook for 5 seconds longer; remove from pan. Repeat with ½ teaspoon oil and remaining egg. Roll omelets into cylinders and cut crosswise into ¼-inch-wide strips. Use as garnish.

2. Place a wok over high heat until hot. Add remaining oil, swirling to coat sides. Add shallot and garlic; cook, stirring, until fragrant, about 10 seconds. Add sausages, carrot, and jicama; stir-fry for 2 minutes. Add water, soy sauce, chili garlic sauce, and sugar. Reduce heat to medium and cook, uncovered, until vegetables are tender-crisp and pan juices have evaporated, 4 to 5 minutes. Stir in green onions. Remove from heat and let cool.

Assembling
1. Place filling, wrappers, and garnishes in separate serving dishes. To assemble, place a wrapper on a plate. Top with a lettuce leaf, spread with a little hoisin sauce and chili garlic sauce, and top with filling, shrimp, sprouts, and egg strips. Roll up wrapper, turning in the sides so the filling is completely enclosed.

Makes 8 popiah.

NONYA CUSTOMS
Nonya women believe that sewing a button on clothing while you're wearing it can bring bad luck. (I learned about this the hard way when we were filming on location in the home of a Nonya cook, and our production assistant accidentally stabbed me in the chest while trying to hastily replace a button on my shirt!) When moving into a new house, a Nonya woman sprinkles raw rice, salt, and tea leaves in every room and leaves them there for three days to ward off evil spirits. Bringing a full pot of rice and full jars of soy sauce, oil, and other staples is believed to ensure an abundance of food in the new home.

SPICY VEGETABLE TURNOVERS
(Samosas)

Crispy triangles filled with a spicy filling of curried potatoes and vegetables make a great snack when you're in Singapore—or a great hors d'oeuvre when you're at home. Samosas are traditionally vegetarian, although ground chicken can be added; stir-fry ¼ pound of it with the onion.

**HOW TO
FOLD SAMOSAS**

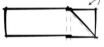

⇒ FILLING ⇐

2 medium potatoes
2 tablespoons cooking oil
2 cloves garlic, minced
4 slices ginger, each the size of a
    quarter, minced
1 fresh red or green jalapeño chili,
    seeded and minced
1 medium onion, finely chopped
¼ cup frozen peas and carrots,
    thawed
2 tablespoons curry powder
2 tablespoons oyster-flavored
    sauce

10 egg roll or spring roll wrappers
2 tablespoons flour
2 tablespoons water
Cooking oil for deep-frying
Plum sauce or sweet and sour sauce

Getting Started

1. In a 2-quart pan, boil potatoes until tender when pierced, about 20 minutes; drain and let cool. Peel potatoes and cut into ¼-inch cubes.

2. Place a wok over high heat until hot. Add the 2 tablespoons oil, swirling to coat sides. Add garlic, ginger, and chili; cook, stirring, until fragrant, about 10 seconds. Add onion and stir-fry until soft, 3 to 4 minutes. Add peas, carrots, potatoes, curry powder, and oyster-flavored sauce. Mix well and cook for 1 minute. Remove from heat and let cool.

Cooking

1. Cut wrappers into thirds. Mix flour and water until smooth.

2. Lay two strips end to end and glue together with flour and water paste. Place 1 tablespoon filling at one end; fold wrapper over filling bringing one corner diagonally across to form a triangle. Continue to fold maintaining a triangle shape, (like folding a flag) until you reach the end. Secure end with flour and water paste.

3. In a wok, heat oil for deep-frying to 350°F. Deep-fry samosas a few at a time, turning occasionally, until golden brown, about 3 minutes. Remove with a slotted spoon; drain on paper towels.

4. Serve warm with plum sauce or sweet and sour sauce.

Makes 20.

SINGAPORE VEGETABLE SALAD
(*Sayur Pecil*)

Have you ever had salade Niçoise? I think of this as the Malay-Indonesian version: green long beans, potatoes, hard-cooked eggs, tofu, and fresh vegetables in a tangy sweet-hot dressing. It's a great choice for a warm-weather meal.

PALM SUGAR
In Southeast Asia, the basic sweetener for cooking is not cane sugar, but palm sugar. It's made by tapping the sap of palm trees and boiling it down to a thick syrup, which is poured into bamboo pipe molds. You can find palm sugar sold in cylindrical blocks in Southeast Asian markets (it's also sometimes sold under the name "coconut sugar"). Its deep, rich, sweetness makes a beautiful complement to the sour, spicy, and salty flavors of Southeast Asian foods. If you can't find it, brown sugar can be substituted, but its flavor is less intense.

¼ pound Chinese long beans, cut into 2-inch lengths
2 medium potatoes
1 package (14 oz.) regular-firm or extra-firm tofu
Cooking oil for deep-frying

⊳ DRESSING ⊲
2 tablespoons tamarind pulp
1 cup hot water
5 walnut-size shallots
2 fresh red or green jalapeño chilies, seeded
1 teaspoon dried shrimp paste (blachan)
¼ cup cold water

2 tablespoons cooking oil
2 tablespoons packed brown sugar
1 tablespoon soy sauce
½ cup roasted peanuts, finely chopped

3 hard-cooked eggs, shelled and cut into quarters
1 cup bean sprouts
1 small red bell pepper, cut into diamond-shaped pieces
½ English cucumber, quartered lengthwise and cut crosswise into ½-inch pieces

Getting Ready
1. Cook beans in boiling water until tender-crisp, 4 to 5 minutes. Drain, rinse with cold water, and drain again. Boil potatoes until tender when pierced, then cut into ¾-inch cubes.

2. Drain tofu; cut into ¾-inch cubes. Place between paper towels and gently press out excess water. In a wok, heat oil for deep-frying to 350°F. Add tofu and deep-fry, turning once, until golden on all sides, 3 to 4 minutes. Drain on paper towels.

3. Soak tamarind pulp in hot water following instructions on page 71. In a blender, process shallots, chilies, dried shrimp paste, and cold water until smooth.

Cooking
1. Place a wide frying pan over medium-low heat until hot. Add oil, swirling to coat sides. Add shallot mixture and cook, stirring, until fragrant, 6 to 8 minutes. Add brown sugar, soy sauce, and tamarind water; simmer for 2 minutes. Add peanuts and simmer for 2 minutes longer. Pour dressing into a serving bowl and let cool.

2. Arrange beans, potatoes, tofu, eggs, bean sprouts, bell pepper, and cucumber in separate piles on a serving platter. Serve dressing alongside.

Makes 6 servings.

NEW YEAR FISH SALAD
(Yu Sheng)

No Chinese New Year feast is complete without yu sheng, the colorful salad of raw fish and crunchy vegetables. It's served in most Singaporean Chinese restaurants throughout the lunar new year celebration. In recent years, the ingredients have become increasingly elaborate and exotic, including jellyfish, preserved papaya, deep-fried yam sticks, pickled shallots, and more. You practically have to start making it a whole lunar year ahead of time! My version is light and flavorful—and a lot easier to prepare. Use very fresh fish. As an alternative to salmon, tuna is also delicious prepared this way.

⇒ SALAD MIXTURE ⇐

1/2 cantaloupe or 1/4 honeydew
 melon
I grapefruit
1/4 cup thinly sliced sweet
 pickled ginger
I medium carrot, shredded
3-inch wedge (1/4 lb.) jicama,
 shredded

⇒ DRESSING ⇐

3 to 4 tablespoons cooking oil
I teaspoon sesame oil
3 tablespoons plum sauce

I tablespoon sesame seeds
6 ounces salmon fillet
6 ounces firm white fish fillet,
 such as sea bass
I tablespoon lime juice
I tablespoon cooking oil
1/2 teaspoon white pepper
1/4 cup chopped roasted peanuts
I green onion, slivered

Getting Ready

1. Peel melon and cut into crescents. Segment grapefruit by cutting away the peel and white pith; cut and lift out segments. In a bowl, combine melon, grapefruit, ginger, carrot, and jicama.

2. Combine dressing ingredients in a small bowl.

3. Place sesame seed in a small frying pan over medium heat; cook, shaking pan continuously, until lightly browned, 3 to 4 minutes. Immediately remove from pan to cook.

4. Remove skin and any bones from fish. Thinly slice fish across the grain to make pieces about 1 by 2 inches. Fan slices on a serving platter, alternating pink and white fish. In a small bowl, combine lime juice, oil, and white pepper.

Assembly

1. Drizzle lime juice mixture over fish. Mound salad mixture in center of fish. Spoon dressing over the salad. Garnish with peanuts, sesame seed, and green onion.

Serves 4 to 6.

A WINNING TOSS
Besides being full of flavors and textures, yu sheng is loaded with symbolic meaning. The raw ingredients signify the renewal of life, and the sound of the word for fish in Cantonese sounds like the word for prosperity. The most important (and fun) part of eating yu sheng is the mixing together of the ingredients. To ensure good luck for the coming year, everyone calls out "Lo hei!"— which means "to mix it up" but also sounds like "to prosper more and more"—while they use their chopsticks to toss the ingredients as high in the air as they can. Now that's what I call a well-tossed salad!

69

PICKLED FRUIT SALAD

Every Nonya cook has a family recipe for this popular, tangy salad. Serve it as a side dish with Braised Duck with Fragrant Sauce (page 90).

COCONUT CHIPS

Toasted coconut chips add a sweet, nutty finishing crunch to all kinds of dishes. You can buy them in Indian markets, and I've seen salted ones packed in cans in some specialty food stores. It's easy to make your own from fresh coconut. Once you've cracked the coconut and separated the shell from the white meat, cut the meat into curls with a vegetable peeler. Toast these in a 300°F oven, stirring once or twice, until they're browned, 6 to 8 minutes. Store in an airtight container.

≥ SPICE PASTE ≤

2 tablespoons dried shrimp
1 teaspoon dried shrimp paste
    (blachan)
1 medium tomato
3 fresh red jalapeño chilies, seeded

1 tablespoon vinegar
3 tablespoons honey or sugar
2 tablespoons plum sauce
1 tablespoon soy sauce or
    ¼ teaspoon salt

½ English cucumber, cut into
    ½-inch cubes
2 medium tomatoes, cut into
    ½-inch cubes
1 small red onion, cut into
    ½-inch cubes
1½ cups pineapple chunks
1 mango, peeled and cut into
    ½-inch cubes (optional)

Toasted coconut chips

Getting Ready

1. Soak dried shrimp in warm water to cover for 20 minutes; drain.

2. Wrap shrimp paste in foil; place in a frying pan over medium heat and toast for 1 minute on each side. Coarsely chop tomato. Place dried shrimp, shrimp paste, tomato, and chilies in a blender; process until smooth.

3. Place spice paste ingredients in a small bowl. Add vinegar, honey, plum sauce, and soy sauce; mix well.

Cooking

1. Place cucumber, tomatoes, onion, pineapple, and mango (if used) in a salad bowl. Add spice paste dressing; stir to coat.

2. Arrange on a serving plate; garnish with coconut chips.

Makes 6 servings.

NOODLES IN
SWEET AND SOUR BROTH
(Asam Laksa)

You can find this spicy soup of seafood and rice noodles at hawker stalls all over Singapore. Some people say it originated in the tiny state of Perlis on the northwest Malay Peninsula. Others say it's from the island of Penang. I say, let them fight it out, and meanwhile, try my easy version. The rice noodles are slippery and fun to slurp, and the fiery-hot broth gets its refreshing, tangy flavor from tamarind (the asam in the name).

⇝ SPICE PASTE ⇜
1 stalk lemongrass
2 walnut-size shallots
1 teaspoon dried shrimp paste
   (blachan)
3 fresh red jalapeño chilies, seeded
1 teaspoon galangal powder
1/4 cup tamarind water
   (see note at right)

1/2 pound dried rice stick noodles
   (1/8 in. wide)
2 tablespoons cooking oil
5 cups water, chicken broth, or
   seafood bouillon
1/2 teaspoon salt
1/4 cup oyster-flavored sauce

⇝ GARNISHES ⇜
1 cup julienned cucumber
1/2 cup pineapple chunks
6 mint leaves
1/4 medium red onion, sliced
1 fresh red jalapeño chili, sliced
3 hard-cooked eggs, quartered
Cilantro sprigs

Getting Ready
1. Thinly slice bottom 6 inches of lemongrass. Place in a blender with remaining spice paste ingredients and process until smooth.

2. Soak rice stick noodles in warm water until soft, about 30 minutes; drain.

Cooking
1. Place a wide 3-quart pan over medium-low heat until hot. Add oil, swirling to coat sides. Add spice paste and cook, stirring, until fragrant, 6 to 8 minutes.

2. Add water, salt, and oyster-flavored sauce to pan; heat to boiling.

3. Add noodles to broth, and cook 1 to 2 minutes.

4. Pour into 6 soup bowls. Scatter garnishes over top.

Makes 6 servings.

TAMARIND TIPS

I like to think of tamarind as the lemon of Southeast Asia. The dusty brown pod of the tamarind tree is filled with seeds and a sticky brown pulp. It's this pulp that gives many Southeast Asian dishes their fruity, sour flavor, and it's one of the "secret ingredients" in Worcestershire sauce. You can buy tamarind pods or tamarind paste (sold in brick form or in jars) in Southeast Asian markets. To make tamarind water, combine 1/2 cup hot water with 2 1/2 tablespoons tamarind pulp (scraped from the pod) or prepared paste. Soak 10 to 15 minutes, then squeeze the pulp to extract all the juices, and strain through a sieve to remove the seeds. You can also buy tamarind in concentrated or powdered form.

Helping a young friend with the tamarind harvest in the countryside.

SPICY CHICKEN NOODLE SOUP
(*Soto Ayam*)

RICE CAKES

Longtong or ketupat is the name for compressed rice cakes, traditionally boiled in small woven palm leaf baskets. The cakes are eaten with satay (see page 132), and a slice or two will often be used to garnish a bowl of soto ayam (at right). Here's my technique for making them at home: Wash and drain 2 cups glutinous rice. Place in a saucepan with 3 cups water; bring to a boil; reduce heat and simmer until all liquid is absorbed, 35 to 40 minutes. Spoon hot rice into a 9-inch square pan lined with lightly oiled foil or banana leaves. Cover with more oiled foil or leaves and a second square pan; weight with large cans or other heavy weight. Let stand 8 hours or overnight. Invert onto a cutting board, remove foil or leaves, and slice into 1½-inch squares with a wet knife. Serve at room temperature.

Older Singaporeans will tell you about the good old days, when the soto ayam man used to come around in the evening with his portable stall and wooden clappers. The mere sound of the clappers was enough to bring people running from their homes, carrying their bowls or tiffin tins into the street.

≽ SPICE PASTE ≼
2 stalks lemongrass
6 cloves garlic
5 walnut-size shallots
2 slices ginger, each the size of a quarter
8 candlenuts or 16 almonds
¼ cup water

2 chicken legs and thighs
6 cups water
2 tablespoons cooking oil
2 teaspoons ground coriander
1 teaspoon galangal powder
1 teaspoon turmeric powder
1 teaspoon chili garlic sauce

3 tablespoons soy sauce
1 package (12 oz.) fresh Chinese egg noodles
½ pound bean sprouts
4 hard-cooked eggs, shelled and halved
Deep-fried shallots (see page 124)
Cilantro sprigs
Sliced fresh red or green jalapeño chili

Getting Ready
1. Thinly slice bottom 6 inches of lemongrass. Place in a blender with remaining spice paste ingredients and process until smooth.

Cooking
1. Place chicken and water in a large pan; bring to a boil. Reduce heat, cover, and simmer for 30 minutes.

2. Place a wok over medium-low heat until hot. Add oil, swirling to coat sides. Add spice paste and cook, stirring, until fragrant, 6 to 8 minutes. Add coriander, galangal, turmeric, and chili garlic sauce; cook for 1 minute. Reserve.

3. Add reserved spice paste to chicken; simmer until chicken is no longer pink near the bone, about 20 minutes longer. Lift out chicken. When it is cool enough to handle, remove and discard skin and bones; shred meat.

4. Pour broth through a wire strainer; discard solids and return broth to the pan. Skim fat from broth and add soy sauce; heat to simmering.

5. In a large pot of boiling water, cook noodles according to package directions; drain, rinse, and drain again. Divide noodles, chicken, and bean sprouts among 4 individual bowls. Pour broth over noodles. Garnish each serving with eggs, shallots, cilantro, and chili.

Makes 4 servings.

BEAN SPROUTS KERABU

Bean sprouts are tossed in a rich and spicy dressing in this refreshing salad from Kelantan on the northeastern Malay Peninsula. Traditionally, the sprouts would be quickly blanched, but I find that their fresh flavor and delicate crunch stand up to the dressing better when you simply leave them raw.

⇒ SPICE PASTE ⇐
2 tablespoons dried shrimp
4 walnut-size shallots
4 cloves garlic
2 fresh red jalapeño chilies, seeded
1/4 cup water

1/4 cup unsweetened desiccated coconut
2 tablespoons cooking oil
1/4 cup unsweetened coconut milk
1/2 teaspoon sugar
2 tablespoons soy sauce
    or 1/2 teaspoon salt
1 teaspoon sesame oil
1 pound bean sprouts
2 green onions, cut into 2-inch lengths
1 fresh red jalapeño chili, seeded and julienned

Getting Ready
1. Soak dried shrimp in warm water to cover for 20 minutes; drain. Place in a blender with remaining spice paste ingredients and process until smooth.

2. Toast coconut in a frying pan over low heat, stirring frequently, until golden brown, 4 to 5 minutes. Remove coconut from pan.

Cooking
1. Return frying pan to medium-low heat. Add cooking oil, swirling to coat sides. Add spice paste and cook, stirring, until fragrant, 6 to 8 minutes. Add coconut milk, sugar, and soy sauce. Cook, stirring, until sauce thickens slightly, about 2 minutes. Stir in sesame oil.

2. Place bean sprouts, green onions, and chili in a salad bowl; pour dressing over, stirring to combine. Garnish with coconut.

Makes 4 to 6 servings.

At the Zhu Jiao "wet market" in Little India, you can find everything from fish and fowl to flowers. Everything is constantly sprayed with water to keep it fresh—even the tourists!

GOLDEN TOFU WITH PEANUT SAUCE

(Tahu Goreng)

In Malaysian and Indonesian cooking, it's not uncommon to find deep-fried tofu used in salads and stir-fried dishes. A popular example is tahu goreng: golden fried tofu, bean sprouts, cucumber, and onion in a warm, spicy-sweet peanut sauce. You can also pan-fry the tofu in a little oil in a nonstick pan, and if you don't want to grind the peanuts, you can substitute ⅓ cup chunky peanut butter. The sauce is so tasty I like to make extra and reheat it the following day to pour over blanched vegetables like long beans, spinach, broccoli, or bok choy.

⇝ SAUCE ⇜

½ cup roasted peanuts
2 walnut-size shallots
2 cloves garlic
2 fresh red jalapeño chilies, seeded
¼ teaspoon dried shrimp paste (blachan)
¼ cup water

2 tablespoons cooking oil
⅓ cup tamarind water (see page 71)
3 tablespoons soy sauce
1 tablespoon plum sauce
1 teaspoon sugar

1 package (14 oz.) regular-firm or extra-firm tofu
Cooking oil for deep-frying
¼ pound bean sprouts
½ small English cucumber, finely shredded
1 green onion, finely shredded

Getting Ready

1. Finely chop peanuts in a food processor.

2. In a blender, combine shallots, garlic, chilies, shrimp paste, and water; process until smooth.

Cooking

1. Place a wok over medium-low heat until hot. Add oil, swirling to coat sides. Add shallot mixture and cook, stirring, until fragrant, 6 to 8 minutes. Add peanuts, tamarind water, soy sauce, plum sauce, and sugar; stir until smooth. Simmer over low heat, stirring, until sauce thickens slightly, 2 to 3 minutes. Remove from heat.

2. Drain tofu; cut in half lengthwise, then into 4 equal slices crosswise; cut each slice in half diagonally. Place between paper towels and gently press out excess water.

3. In a wok, heat oil for deep-frying to 350°F. Add tofu and deep-fry, turning once, until golden on all sides, 3 to 4 minutes. Remove from oil and drain on paper towels.

4. To serve, arrange tofu on a serving plate and garnish with bean sprouts, cucumber, and green onion. Reheat sauce just until warm and pour over tofu.

Makes 4 servings.

SINGAPORE SPEAK

After more than a century of British rule, Singapore became an independent republic in 1965, but many reminders of its colonial days remain. If you're reading these words, you'll have no trouble getting around in Singapore, because English is the lingua franca of business, government, and education, with Malay, Mandarin, and Tamil also recognized as official languages.

SPICED GREEN BEANS WITH SHRIMP
(Kacang Bendi Goreng Rempah)

A spicy Malay sauce tops stir-fried crunchy green beans and shrimp. If you can't find Chinese long-beans you can substitute any kind of green beans, yellow wax beans or any of the new colors or varieties.

⇒ SPICE PASTE ⇐
2 medium onions, coarsely chopped
3 fresh red jalapeño chilies, seeded
3 candlenuts or 6 almonds
½ teaspoon dried shrimp paste (blachan)
¼ cup water

½ pound small raw shrimp
1 pound Chinese long beans or green beans
2 tablespoons cooking oil
¼ cup water
½ teaspoon salt

Getting Ready
1. Place spice paste ingredients in a blender and process until smooth.

2. Shell and devein shrimp. Trim beans and cut into 1½-inch lengths.

Cooking
1. Place a wok over medium-low heat until hot. Add oil, swirling to coat sides. Add spice paste and cook, stirring, until fragrant, 6 to 8 minutes. Add shrimp and stir-fry for 2 minutes.

2. Add green beans; stir-fry for 1 minute. Add water and salt. Cover and simmer over low heat until beans are tender-crisp, 4 to 5 minutes.

Makes 6 servings.

THE LONGEST YARD
I think the beanstalk that Jack grew must have been a stalk of yard-long beans. They can grow up to 12 feet high! The beans themselves actually tend to measure about 18 inches, which is really only half a yard, but "half-a-yard-long beans" just doesn't have the same ring to it. Although green beans are often suggested as an alternative in recipes, they actually bear no relation to yard-long beans, which are drier, denser, and crunchier. Look for thin beans that are flexible but firm, and not limp. Trim the ends (you'll notice there's no string to remove) and cut the beans into 1- to 2-inch pieces. Their compact, crisp texture and mild flavor make them ideal for stir-frying or stewing with bold seasonings like ginger, garlic, chilies, and dried shrimp.

INDIAN FISH CURRY

This is my version of one of Singapore's most famous South Indian-style specialties, fish head curry. It's based on the method that was shown to me by the chefs at Muthu's Curry in Little India. In place of a giant fish head, which can be a bit intimidating to cook and eat, I make this dish with a whole fish simmered on a bed of spicy eggplant and okra.

⮞ SPICE PASTE ⮜
1 stalk lemongrass
8 walnut-size shallots
6 cloves garlic
2 slices ginger, each the size of
   a quarter
2 fresh red jalapeño chilies, seeded
$1/4$ cup water

6 okra pods
3 tablespoons cooking oil
2 tablespoons curry powder
1 teaspoon chili garlic sauce
$1/2$ cup tamarind water
   (see page 71)
1 tablespoon soy sauce
1 tablespoon oyster-flavored sauce
2 teaspoons sugar
$1/2$ teaspoon black pepper

1 Asian eggplant, cut into 6 slices
1 whole fish ($1 1/2$ to 2 lb.), such as
   sea bass or red snapper,
   cleaned
$1 1/2$ cups water
1 tomato, cut into 4 wedges

Getting Ready
1. Thinly slice bottom 6 inches of lemongrass. Place in a blender with remaining spice paste ingredients and process until smooth.

2. Trim okra stems without piercing pods.

Cooking
1. Place a wok over medium-low heat until hot. Add oil, swirling to coat sides. Add spice paste and cook, stirring, until fragrant, 6 to 8 minutes.

2. Stir in curry powder, chili garlic sauce, tamarind water, soy sauce, oyster-flavored sauce, sugar, and black pepper. Place eggplant and okra in pan. Lay fish on top of vegetables and add water. Bring to a boil; reduce heat, cover, and simmer for 10 minutes.

3. Place tomato around fish; cover and simmer until fish just begins to flake, about 20 minutes.

Makes 4 servings.

COCONUT CURRIED FISH
(Ikan Moolie)

Moolie refers to a South Indian style of simmering foods in coconut milk.

⟫ SPICE PASTE ⟪
2 stalks lemongrass
2 walnut-size shallots
4 slices ginger, each the size of a
    quarter
3 cloves garlic
4 candlenuts or 8 almonds
2 fresh red jalapeño chilies, seeded
1/4 cup water

1 1/2 pounds halibut
About 1/2 teaspoon salt
3 tablespoons cooking oil
1/2 medium red onion, thinly sliced
1/4 teaspoon turmeric powder
1 can (13 1/2 oz.) unsweetened
    coconut milk
1/3 cup water
1 fresh red jalapeño chili, seeded
    and cut into thin strips

Getting Ready
1. Thinly slice bottom 6 inches of
lemongrass. Place in blender with
remaining spice paste ingredients and
process until smooth.

2. Remove skin and bones from fish,
then cut fish into 1-inch cubes. Sprinkle
with 1/2 teaspoon salt.

Cooking
1. Place a wok over medium-low heat
until hot. Add oil, swirling to coat sides.
Add spice paste and cook, stirring, until
fragrant, 6 to 8 minutes.

2. Add onion, turmeric, coconut milk,
and water; mix well. Simmer, uncovered,
for 5 minutes.

3. Add fish; simmer, uncovered, until
fish is opaque, 8 to 10 minutes. Season
to taste with salt. Sprinkle with chili.

Makes 6 servings.

MEET ME AT THE RAFFLES
Singapore's most famous
building is not a sky-
scraper, but a rambling,
low-rise, colonial-era
building: the Raffles
Hotel. Dating back to
1866, it wasn't actually
built by Sir Stamford
Raffles (the founder of
modern Singapore), but
merely named after him.
The majestic old Raffles
has played host to the
likes of Rudyard Kipling,
Noël Coward, Joseph
Conrad, and, more
recently, a cooking show
host and his crew!
Happily, the building has
survived Singapore's
massive reconstruction
program, and today
there's no better place to
enjoy a taste of colonial
nostalgia, whether you
visit the hotel museum,
enjoy the elegant Tiffin
Room buffet, take in
a midafternoon cream
tea, or relax over drinks
in the Long Bar.

The Raffles Hotel: an oasis of
colonial splendor amid the
encroaching concrete.

TANGY SPICED PRAWNS
(Udang Asam)

Everything their name implies: plump, fresh prawns quickly cooked in a classic Malaysian spice paste that becomes the base of a tangy honey-tamarind sauce.

DON'T SKIMP ON THE SHRIMP

When is it a shrimp and when is it a prawn? I've searched for an answer to this question for years, and the answer is "No." In other words, there is no one answer. Most people (myself included) use the term "prawn" to refer to large shrimp, but others say prawns are actually a different species. Whatever name they're sold under, I like to buy them with the shells on, because it helps retain their freshness, and I often cook them with the tails intact to add flavor and visual interest. Look for firm shrimp with a clean, oceany aroma. Black spots and an ammonia odor are signs of deterioration. Whatever you call them, buy the best you can find—you'll taste the difference!

1 pound large raw shrimp

➤ SPICE PASTE ◄
4 walnut-size shallots
4 cloves garlic
1 fresh red jalapeño chili, seeded
1 teaspoon galangal powder
1/4 cup water

1/2 cup tamarind water
   (see page 71)
3 tablespoons honey
2 tablespoons soy sauce
2 tablespoons cooking oil
1/2 red onion, sliced
1 tomato, cut into wedges
Cucumber slices

Getting Ready

1. Shell and devein shrimp, leaving tails intact.

2. Place spice paste ingredients in a blender and process until smooth.

3. In a small bowl, combine tamarind water, honey, and soy sauce.

Cooking

1. Place a wok over medium-low heat until hot. Add oil, swirling to coat sides. Add spice paste and cook, stirring, until fragrant, 6 to 8 minutes. Add tamarind-water mixture, onion, and tomato; cook for 1 minute. Add shrimp and cook until they turn pink, 3 to 4 minutes.

2. Place on a serving plate and garnish with cucumber.

Makes 4 servings.

RED CHILI BRAISED PRAWNS

Somewhere between a soup and a curry, these jumbo prawns swimming in a spicy broth with green onion and chunks of pineapple are bursting with flavor and succulent texture. Serve with plenty of steamed rice, noodles, or even Malaysian Roti Jala (page 111) to sop up the broth.

GALANGAL

Galangal (also called "galanga" or "galingale") is a rhizome related to ginger that's used throughout Southeast Asia, especially in Thailand. Fresh galangal is pounded into curry pastes and added in slices to soups and stews (slices are not eaten, but removed from the finished dish). If you can't find fresh galangal, you may have an easier time buying it in dried slices or as a powder (which is sometimes sold under its Indonesian name, "laos," or "laos powder") in Southeast Asian markets. A 1/2-inch piece of fresh galangal is equivalent to about 1 teaspoon of galangal powder.

⋑ SPICE PASTE ⋜

1 stalk lemongrass
2 fresh red jalapeño chilies, seeded
1 walnut-size shallot
3 slices ginger, each the size of a quarter
1 teaspoon dried shrimp paste (blachan)
1 tablespoon curry powder
1 teaspoon galangal powder
1/4 teaspoon salt
1/4 cup water

3/4 pound large raw shrimp
2 green onions
2 tablespoons cooking oil
3/4 cup diced pineapple (3/4-in. cubes)
1 1/2 cups seafood bouillon (from bouillon cube and water)
2 teaspoons tamarind water (see page 71) or lemon juice
Soy sauce
Cilantro sprigs

Getting Ready

1. Thinly slice bottom 6 inches of lemongrass. Place in blender with remaining spice paste ingredients and process until smooth.

2. Shell and devein shrimp, leaving tails intact.

3. Cut green onions into 2-inch lengths.

Cooking

1. Place a wok over medium-low heat until hot. Add oil, swirling to coat sides. Add spice paste and cook, stirring, until fragrant, 6 to 8 minutes.

2. Increase heat to medium-high. Add shrimp and stir-fry for 30 seconds. Add green onions and pineapple; mix well. Add seafood bouillon and tamarind water. Bring to a boil. Reduce heat and simmer, uncovered, until shrimp turn pink, 3 to 4 minutes. Season to taste with soy sauce.

3. Place in a deep serving bowl and garnish with cilantro.

Makes 4 servings.

BLACK PEPPER CRAB

This popular Malaysian dish features chunks of crab, deep-fried in the shell, then quickly simmered in a spicy brown sauce. It's fun to pull the chunks apart and eat the meat with your fingers (though you may want to supply a few finger bowls and towels on the side).

I live Dungeness crab or 4 live blue crabs
2 tablespoons oyster-flavored sauce
I tablespoon soy sauce
I tablespoon sugar
Cooking oil for deep-frying
Cornstarch or flour
I tablespoon butter
4 cloves garlic, minced
2 slices ginger, each the size of a quarter, minced
2 fresh red jalapeño chilies, seeded and minced
2 teaspoons freshly ground black pepper
I green onion, minced

Getting Ready

1. In a pot of boiling water, parboil crab for 2 minutes. Drain, rinse with cold water, and drain again. (If desired, pull off the top shell in one piece and reserve for garnish.) Remove and discard the gills and spongy parts under the shell. Twist off the claws and legs; crack them with a cleaver or mallet. Cut body into 4 pieces (cut blue crabs in half).

2. In a small bowl, combine oyster-flavored sauce, soy sauce, and sugar.

Cooking

1. In a wok, heat oil for deep-frying to 365°F. Dust crab pieces with cornstarch. Deep-fry crab until shells change color, 2 to 3 minutes. Lift out crab and drain. Remove all but 1 tablespoon of oil from wok.

2. Add butter to oil in wok and place over medium heat. Add garlic, ginger, and chilies. Cook, stirring, until fragrant, 1 to 2 minutes. Add pepper and oyster-flavored sauce mixture; mix well. Add crab and stir to coat. Simmer over low heat until crab is cooked, 6 to 7 minutes. (If crab was cooked through when deep-fried, it needs to simmer in sauce only about 3 minutes.)

3. Arrange crab and sauce on a serving plate; garnish with green onion.

Makes 4 servings.

GRAB A CRAB

There's no substitute for the sweet, delicate flavor of crab that has been purchased fresh and live. In the western U.S., Dungeness crab season is during the fall and winter. Summer and fall are the peak seasons for the smaller blue crab, the East Coast's most common variety. When you buy live crabs, refrigerate them as quickly as possible, and cook and eat them within 24 hours. If you're not comfortable with "crab-icide," and you're shopping within an hour or two of cooking time, have your fish seller kill and clean the crabs for you and skip the boiling step in this recipe (and in the other crab recipes in this book). For a dramatic presentation, be sure to retain the whole top shell.

Live blue crabs sell out quickly at Little India's Zhu Jiao Market.

STEAMED CRAB OVER RICE

As this marinated whole crab steams over a bed of seasoned rice, the rice and crab engage in a wonderful exchange of flavors. Glutinous rice is traditional in this recipe, but long-grain rice will also work. If you like, you can substitute walnuts for the peanuts.

2 tablespoons dried shrimp
2 dried black mushrooms
3 water chestnuts
3 tablespoons raw peanuts
2 tablespoons cooking oil
1 teaspoon salt
4 cups cooked rice
1 live Dungeness crab

≽ MARINADE ≼
2 tablespoons oyster-flavored
    sauce
1 tablespoon rice wine or dry sherry
1 tablespoon cornstarch
1 teaspoon minced ginger
$1/2$ teaspoon salt

1 green onion, minced

Getting Ready
1. In separate bowls, soak dried shrimp and mushrooms in warm water to cover until softened, about 20 minutes. Drain shrimp and coarsely chop. Reserve about $1/4$ cup of mushroom-soaking liquid. Discard mushroom stems; dice caps. Dice water chestnuts. Remove skins from peanuts.

Cooking
1. Place a wok over high heat until hot. Add oil, swirling to coat sides. Add dried shrimp, mushrooms, water chestnuts, and peanuts; stir-fry for 1 minute. Add reserved mushroom-soaking liquid and salt; stir-fry for 1 minute. Turn off heat; add rice and mix thoroughly.

2. In a pot of boiling water, parboil crab for 2 minutes. Drain, rinse with cold water, and drain again. Pull off the top shell in one piece and reserve. Remove and discard the gills and spongy parts under the shell. Twist off the claws and legs; crack them with a cleaver or mallet. Cut the body into 6 pieces.

3. Combine marinade ingredients in a large bowl; add crab and stir to coat. Marinate in the refrigerator for 30 minutes.

4. Spread rice mixture in a shallow heatproof dish. Reassemble crab in its original shape over rice; place top shell over body pieces. Sprinkle green onion around crab. Prepare a wok for steaming (see page 14). Cover and steam over high heat for 15 minutes. Serve hot.

Makes 4 to 6 servings.

DINNER AT HOME
When I get together with friends and colleagues in Singapore, we usually eat out. But sometimes I get invited to someone's house for a meal. When cooking for company, a Singaporean host usually prepares as many dishes as there are guests, and generally includes one fish, one fowl, and one meat dish as well as a soup. If the number of guests is small, there will always be one or two extra dishes to round out the menu. These dishes, along with rice and condiments, are served from central bowls, but it's considered rude to pile up portions of more than one dish at a time on your plate. The soup is used as a palate refresher and is sipped throughout the meal between bites of other dishes. Fresh fruit is the customary dessert.

CHILI CRAB

When I ask my Singaporean friends to name their national dish, those who don't say "fish head curry" say "chili crab." And when they say it, their eyes widen and so do their smiles. When you taste this stir-fried crab in its lively chili sauce, based on the recipe of the Red House Restaurant in Singapore's East Coast Seafood Center, you'll understand why.

⇒ S A U C E ⇐

¾ cup chicken broth
½ cup catsup
2 tablespoons soy sauce
1 tablespoon chili garlic sauce
1 tablespoon rice vinegar
1 tablespoon sugar

1 live Dungeness crab
2 tablespoons cooking oil
2 tablespoons minced garlic
1 tablespoon minced ginger
1 fresh red jalapeño chili, seeded and minced
1 egg, lightly beaten
Sliced green onion

Getting Ready

1. Mix sauce ingredients in a small bowl and set aside.

2. In a pot of boiling water, parboil crab for 2 minutes. Drain, rinse with cold water, and drain again. Pull off the top shell in one piece and reserve for garnish. Remove and discard the gills and spongy parts under the shell. Twist off the claws and legs; crack them with a cleaver or mallet. Cut the body into 4 pieces.

Cooking

1. Place a wok over high heat until hot. Add oil, swirling to coat sides. Add garlic, ginger, and chili; cook, stirring, for 1 minute. Add crab and stir-fry for 2 minutes.

2. Add sauce and reduce heat to low; cover and simmer, stirring once or twice, until crab is cooked, 6 to 7 minutes.

3. Stir in egg and cook just until it begins to set, about 1 minute.

4. Arrange crab and top shell on a serving plate. Pour sauce over all and garnish with green onion.

Makes 4 servings.

It's all in the setup: getting ready to make chili crab at the Red House Restaurant.

STEAMED CHICKEN WINGS

These delectably tender Chinese-style steamed chicken wings are boned and stuffed with strips of black mushroom, carrot, bamboo shoot, green onion, and ham. With their wreath of spinach leaves and delicate sauce, they make an elegant first course.

2 dried black mushrooms
2-inch piece carrot
2-inch piece bamboo shoot
2 green onions
2 ounces ham, sliced $1/8$ inch thick
12 chicken wings
$1/2$ teaspoon salt
$1/4$ teaspoon white pepper
$1/2$ teaspoon cornstarch
1 pound spinach

≽ SAUCE ≼
$1/2$ cup chicken broth
1 tablespoon rice wine or dry sherry
2 tablespoons oyster-flavored
    sauce
$1/4$ teaspoon white pepper

2 teaspoons cornstarch dissolved
    in 1 tablespoon water

Getting Ready
1. Soak mushrooms in warm water to cover until softened, about 20 minutes; drain. Discard stems. Cut mushroom caps, carrot, bamboo shoot, green onions, and ham each into 12 matchstick strips.

2. Cut chicken wings between the joints. Chop bone ends off center wing sections; save tips and meaty end pieces for another use. Bone the remaining wing sections by twisting and pushing the two small bones out of each piece.

3. Slide 1 piece of mushroom, carrot, bamboo shoot, green onion, and ham into boned space in each wing section. Place stuffed wings in a single layer in a heatproof dish. Sprinkle with salt, pepper, and cornstarch.

4. Remove coarse spinach stems and wash leaves. Combine sauce ingredients in a pan.

Cooking
1. In a large pot of boiling water, cook spinach for 2 minutes; drain.

2. Prepare a wok for steaming (see page 14). Cover and steam wings over high heat until meat is no longer pink, 6 to 8 minutes. Arrange wings on a serving plate. Pour juices from dish into sauce. Add cornstarch solution and cook, stirring, until sauce boils and thickens. Arrange spinach around wings; pour sauce over chicken.

Makes 6 servings.

CONFESSIONS OF A WING NUT

In Western cultures, the white meat of the chicken breast is considered the choicest part. The French even call it suprême. But in Asia, the opposite is true. It's polite to offer the wings, thighs, and drumsticks to a guest first. On this issue, I'm definitely from the Eastern school—especially when it comes to my favorite chicken part, the wing. To me, it's the bones in the wings, thighs, and drumsticks that give these parts their wonderful flavor and "chickeniness."

SUMATRA CURRIED CHICKEN
(Opor Ayam)

A rich coconut curry chicken, originally from the island of Sumatra, Singapore's Indonesian neighbor.

A CHICKEN CHECKLIST

Here are a few basic food safety tips for storing and preparing chicken: Defrost in the refrigerator, in the sink under cold running water, or in the microwave; never defrost by letting meat sit out on the counter. To avoid cross-contamination, wash your hands, knives, and cutting boards. Cook chicken to an internal temperature of 160°F for boneless, 180°F for bone-in, or until juices are clear and not pink. If you've used a marinade on raw poultry, either discard it or cook it before serving. If you're using the marinade for basting, be sure the last application has enough time to cook completely.

⇒ SPICE PASTE ⇐
1 stalk lemongrass
4 fresh red or green jalapeño chilies, seeded
1 small onion, sliced
4 cloves garlic
2 teaspoons coriander powder
8 candlenuts or 16 almonds
1/4 cup water

6 chicken legs or thighs
1 tablespoon soy sauce
3 tablespoons cooking oil
1 cup unsweetened coconut milk
1 cup water
Cilantro sprigs

Getting Ready
1. Thinly slice bottom 6 inches of lemongrass. Place in a blender with remaining spice paste ingredients and process until smooth.

2. In a bowl, combine chicken and soy sauce; stir to coat. Let stand 10 minutes.

Cooking
1. Place a deep frying pan over medium-high heat until hot. Add 2 tablespoons of the oil, swirling to coat sides. Add chicken and cook, turning as needed, until browned on all sides, 2 to 3 minutes per side. Remove chicken from pan.

2. Reduce heat to medium-low. Return pan to heat and add remaining 1 tablespoon oil. Add spice paste and cook, stirring, until fragrant, 6 to 8 minutes.

3. Return chicken to pan. Add coconut milk and water. Cover and simmer until chicken is no longer pink when cut near bone, 40 to 45 minutes.

4. Place in a serving bowl. Garnish with cilantro.

Makes 3 servings.

CHICKEN BRAISED IN A POTATO SHELL

You've heard of chicken pot pie. Why not chicken potato pie? Boneless chicken, braised in a wok with mushrooms and ginger, then baked in a shell of sliced potatoes and inverted for a showstopping presentation.

8 dried black mushrooms
1 pound boneless, skinless chicken

⇒ MARINADE ⇐
2 tablespoons soy sauce
1 tablespoon oyster-flavored sauce
2 teaspoons cornstarch

⇒ SAUCE ⇐
1/2 cup chicken broth
1/4 cup oyster-flavored sauce
3 tablespoons Chinese rice wine or
    dry sherry
3 cloves garlic, minced
2 whole star anise
1 cinnamon stick

1 large potato
2 tablespoons cooking oil
6 to 8 button mushrooms, sliced
4 slices ginger, each the size of a
    quarter, crushed

2 teaspoons cornstarch mixed
    with 1 tablespoon water

Getting Ready
1. Soak mushrooms in warm water to cover until softened, about 20 minutes. Discard stems; cut caps in half.

2. Cut chicken into pieces 1/2 inch thick and about 1 1/2 inches square. Combine marinade ingredients in a bowl; add chicken and stir to coat. Let stand for 15 minutes.

3. Combine sauce ingredients in a bowl.

4. Peel potato and cut lengthwise into 1/4-inch thick slices. Parboil in boiling water for 1 minute; drain.

Cooking
1. Heat a wok over medium-high heat until hot. Add oil, swirling to coat sides. Add chicken and cook until lightly browned, 2 minutes total. Add black mushrooms, button mushrooms, ginger, and sauce. Bring to a boil; reduce heat and simmer, uncovered, for 5 minutes. Add cornstarch solution and cook, stirring, until sauce boils and thickens slightly. Let mixture cool.

2. Lightly oil a 1-quart ovenproof bowl. Line bowl with potato slices, overlapping them in a concentric pattern. Spoon chicken mixture into bowl.

3. Preheat oven to 425°F. Bake chicken, uncovered, for 15 minutes or until potatoes are tender. To serve, unmold onto a rimmed serving plate.

Makes 4 servings.

AN OPEN-KITCHEN POLICY
At our house, when friends come over for dinner, it's always an informal affair. I find that the best way to keep things light and fun is to tear down the kitchen wall. Well. . .not literally. But I like to keep the kitchen open and friendly, not a frenzied "back-stage." After all, it's where people always seem to congregate, so why not "go with the flow"? I set out food and drinks on the kitchen table and sometimes even give people a task to do, like stuffing dumplings or stirring a sauce. Then, when we all sit down to eat, I get to compliment their cooking!

BRAISED DUCK WITH FRAGRANT SAUCE

"BEARING" GOODWILL

Wherever I travel in the world, I always try to give something back to the communities that welcome me so warmly. One of the most enjoyable charity events I've ever been involved in was a celebrity teddy bear auction to raise funds for the Moral Home for the Disabled, a center for disabled children in Singapore. I'm pleased to report that my contribution, Chef Bearnaise, fetched a handsome bounty. When it comes to charity, it's amazing what the market will "bear!"

This recipe is my tribute to the wonderful Duck Rice stalls you find all over Singapore. Ducks are braised whole in huge bubbling vats of spiced soy sauce broth, then boned, sliced, and served with a bit of the duck gizzard and liver, and hard-cooked duck egg. Add a drizzle of the rich braising liquid, thickened with cornstarch, a sprinkling of cilantro and chopped green onion, a little rice on the side, and voilà: Singapore duck rice, one of the duckiest quick meals on earth.

1 duckling (4 to 5 lb.)
1 stalk lemongrass
4 cloves garlic, crushed
4 slices ginger, each the size of
    quarter, crushed
1/2 onion, sliced
8 cups water
1 cup regular soy sauce
1 cup dark soy sauce
1/2 cup sugar
2 whole star anise
2 cinnamon sticks
2 teaspoons turmeric powder

1 tablespoon dark soy sauce
2 teaspoons cornstarch dissolved in
    1 tablespoon water

Getting Ready

1. Parboil duck in a large pot of boiling water for 3 minutes; drain. Return duck to pot.

2. With the side of a cleaver, lightly crush bottom 6 inches of lemongrass. Place lemongrass, garlic, ginger, and onion in pot with duck. Add the 8 cups water, regular and dark soy sauces, sugar, star anise, cinnamon sticks, and turmeric.

Cooking

1. Bring pot to a boil over high heat; reduce heat, cover, and simmer until duck is tender when pierced, 45 minutes to 1 hour.

2. Lift out duck and place on a cutting board. With kitchen shears, split duck lengthwise and remove backbone. Cut duck crosswise into 1-inch pieces, then reassemble in the original shape on a serving platter.

3. Skim fat from cooking liquid. Place 1/2 cup of the liquid in a small pan with the 1 tablespoon dark soy sauce. Add cornstarch solution and cook, stirring, until sauce boils and thickens. Pour sauce over duck and serve.

Makes 4 to 6 servings.

CRISPY DUCK PÂTÉ

These delicate duck-meat "sausages" are first steamed, then fried in a crispy coating of bread crumbs seasoned with five-spice powder—my version of a remarkable appetizer served at the Drake Restaurant in the Hotel Negara.

¾ pound boneless, skinless duck meat
¼ pound raw shrimp, peeled, deveined, and chopped
¼ cup water chestnuts
½ teaspoon Chinese five-spice
¼ teaspoon black pepper
I tablespoon soy sauce
2 teaspoons sesame oil
I tablespoon hoisin sauce
¼ teaspoon sugar
½ cup ice water
I tablespoon chopped cilantro or green onion
2 teaspoons minced ginger
2 tablespoons chopped carrots

⇒ COATING ⇐
½ cup flour
¼ teaspoon Chinese five-spice
⅛ teaspoon salt
I egg, lightly beaten
½ cup Japanese-style bread crumbs (panko)

2 tablespoons cooking oil
Sweet and sour sauce

Getting Ready
1. In a food processor, whirl duck meat, shrimp, water chestnuts, five-spice, black pepper, soy sauce, sesame oil, hoisin sauce, and sugar until a smooth paste forms. With machine running, pour in ice water in a slow stream.

2. Turn mixture into a bowl; fold in cilantro, ginger, and carrots. Mix well. Divide mixture in half.

3. Shape each portion into a sausage shape about 2 inches in diameter. Wrap each securely in plastic wrap; roll up the wrap, twisting ends as if wrapping a large piece of candy. Holding the two ends, roll the package back and forth on the counter to compress the pâté. Repeat with other roll.

4. Prepare a wok for steaming (see page 14). Steam rolls until no longer pink, about 15 minutes.

5. Mix the flour with five-spice and salt. Coat one roll at a time with the seasoned flour. Dust off excess, then dip in egg, then bread crumbs. Repeat with other roll.

Cooking
1. Heat a wide frying pan over medium heat until hot. Add oil, swirling to coat sides. Fry rolls, turning occasionally, until they are golden brown on all sides, 4 to 6 minutes; drain on paper towels.

2. Cut rolls into ½-inch slices; serve with sweet and sour sauce.

Makes 2 rolls, 6 servings.

A DUCK TALE
On my last visit to Singapore, I ducked into the Drake restaurant in the Hotel Negara, where the whole menu is based on duck! And someone in the kitchen has a sense of humor. I started out with "Seaducktiv," a soup with shredded duck and fish head. Next, I visited "Ducklantis" (braised duckling with sea cucumber), and tried "Wok this Way" (stir-fried duck with black beans). The children's menu even includes "Duck Nuggets." And of course, there are "Eggs in a Pond" for dessert—fluffy clouds of duck egg white floating in a puddle of fruit sauce. Now there's a restaurant that's everything it's quacked up to be!

CURRIED OXTAIL

The deep, rich flavors of a traditional spice paste fortified with curry leaves and curry powder marry beautifully with the hearty taste of slowly stewed oxtails. Serve with rice or longtong (see page 72) and a little Pickled Fruit Salad (see page 70) or Mango Sambal (see page 115) on the side.

CURRY LEAF

Curry doesn't grow on trees. It's a seasoning blended from many spices. So, what, then, is a curry leaf? It's the shiny dark green leaf of a South Asian plant that smells a lot like curry when it's crushed (though the resemblance is purely coincidental, since the plant is not related to any of the curry spices). Curry leaves figure prominently in South Indian and Malaysian cooking. You can some-times find fresh ones in Indian markets, but you're more likely to find them dried. To release their aromatic essence, crush them in a mortar and pestle or grind them in a spice grinder.

⋟ SPICE PASTE ⋞

1-inch piece ginger
1 stalk lemongrass
1 medium onion, coarsely chopped
6 cloves garlic
2 fresh red or green jalapeño chilies, seeded
1 tablespoon chili garlic sauce
1/4 cup water

1 medium potato
1 medium carrot
1/2 small jicama
2 pounds oxtail, cut into segments
2 tablespoons cooking oil
2 tablespoons curry powder
2 cinnamon sticks
10 dried curry leaves (optional)
1 can (13 1/2 oz.) unsweetened coconut milk
3 cups water
1/4 cup soy sauce
1 tablespoon packed brown sugar
Mint leaves

Getting Ready

1. Thinly slice ginger and bottom 6 inches of lemongrass. Place in blender with remaining spice paste ingredients and process until smooth.

2. Peel potato, carrot, and jicama. Cut potato into 1 1/2-inch chunks, carrot and jicama into small cubes.

Cooking

1. In a large pan, parboil oxtail in water to cover for 5 minutes; pour into a colander and let drain.

2. In the same pan, heat oil over medium-low heat until hot. Add spice paste and cook, stirring, until fragrant, 6 to 8 minutes. Add curry powder, cinnamon sticks, and curry leaves.

3. Return oxtail to pan and stir to coat with seasonings. Add coconut milk, water, soy sauce, and brown sugar. Bring to a boil; reduce heat, cover, and simmer until meat is tender, 1 1/2 to 2 hours.

4. Add vegetables to meat; cover and simmer for 30 minutes or until all vegetables are tender when pierced.

5. Ladle into bowls and garnish with mint leaves.

Makes 6 servings.

RICE NOODLES IN TANGY SAUCE
(Mee Siam)

These chewy noodles, topped with a sweet and sour sauce, bean sprouts, and hard-cooked eggs, are a favorite in Singapore's hawker food stalls. Why their name refers to a former name for Thailand remains, as far as I know, a mystery.

DRIED SHRIMP

All over Asia, dried shrimp are used as a flavoring and flavor enhancer, and they're one of my favorite "secret ingredients." They're sold in plastic bags in Asian markets. Before using, soak them in warm water for 20 minutes to soften them. If you're not familiar with them, I suggest you use them sparingly at first. Like shrimp paste (blachan), their flavor is intensified to the point of pungency by the drying process, but once you soak and cook them, they become much less assertive. I think of them not as a main ingredient but as a flavor accent that brings out the taste of other ingredients, especially pork and fresh shrimp. They can add depth to everything from stir-fried dishes to soups and slow-simmered foods.

⋟ SPICE PASTE ⋞
3 tablespoons dried shrimp
1 stalk lemongrass
6 cloves garlic
2 fresh red jalapeño chilies, seeded
1 teaspoon dried shrimp paste (blachan)
1/2 cup tamarind water (see page 71)

3 tablespoons cooking oil
1 teaspoon chili garlic sauce
3 cups water
1/4 cup chunky peanut butter
1/4 cup soy sauce
1 1/2 tablespoons sugar
1 tablespoon hoisin sauce

1/2 of a 14-ounce package regular-firm or extra-firm tofu
Cooking oil for deep-frying
6 ounces dried rice noodles (1/4 in. wide)
2 hard-cooked eggs, shelled and halved
1/4 pound bean sprouts
Cilantro sprigs
Sliced fresh red or green jalapeño chili

Getting Ready
1. Soak dried shrimp in warm water to cover until softened, about 20 minutes; drain. Thinly slice bottom 6 inches of lemongrass. Place in a blender with shrimp, garlic, chilies, shrimp paste, and 1/4 cup tamarind water; process until smooth.

Cooking
1. Place a wok over medium-low heat until hot. Add oil, swirling to coat sides. Add spice paste and cook, stirring, until fragrant, 6 to 8 minutes. Add chili garlic sauce, remaining tamarind water, and water; bring to a boil. Stir about 2 tablespoons of hot liquid into peanut butter; add to wok. Add soy sauce and sugar; simmer for 5 minutes. Stir in hoisin sauce and turn off heat.

2. Drain tofu and cut into domino-size pieces. Place between paper towels and gently press out excess moisture. In a wok, heat oil for deep-frying to 350°F. Add tofu and deep-fry, turning once, until golden on all sides, 3 to 4 minutes. Remove from oil and drain on paper towels.

3. In a large pot of boiling water, cook rice noodles until tender but still slightly firm, 3 to 4 minutes. Drain, rinse, and drain again.

4. Place 1/4 of noodles in each of 4 bowls. Top with eggs, bean sprouts, and sauce. Garnish with cilantro and chili.

Makes 4 servings.

HOKKIEN FRIED NOODLES

Hokkien mee—noodles braised with vegetables and chicken or prawns—is another hawker stall specialty. This recipe is based on a version made famous by my friend Lim Ah Chye, Chinese chef of Singapore Airlines' Catering Service. His special signature touch: using a combination of traditional Hokkien yellow wheat noodles (I've substituted Chinese egg noodles) and rice noodles for doubly intriguing texture and appearance.

⇒ COOKING SAUCE ⇐
I cup chicken broth
2 tablespoons soy sauce
I tablespoon chili garlic sauce
I teaspoon sesame oil
$1/2$ teaspoon white pepper

5 ounces fresh Chinese egg noodles
$1 1/2$ ounces dried rice vermicelli
    (beehoon)
2 tablespoons cooking oil
I tablespoon minced garlic
I teaspoon minced ginger
I green onion, julienned
$1/4$ pound skinless, boneless chicken,
    thinly sliced
$1/4$ pound medium raw shrimp,
    shelled, deveined, and cut in
    half lengthwise
$1/4$ pound firm white fish such as
    sea bass, sliced (optional)
I fresh red jalapeño chili, julienned
$1/4$ cup julienned carrot
3 baby bok choy, sliced
I leaf Chinese cabbage, sliced
I egg, lightly beaten
Chicken broth (optional)
Cilantro sprigs

Getting Ready
1. In a small bowl, combine cooking sauce ingredients.

2. In a large pot of boiling water, cook egg noodles for 2 minutes; drain, rinse with cold water, and drain again. Soak rice vermicelli in warm water for 5 minutes; drain.

Cooking
1. Place a wok over high heat until hot. Add oil, swirling to coat sides. Add garlic, ginger, and green onion; stir for 1 minute. Add chicken, shrimp, and fish (if used); cook 2 minutes longer. Reduce heat to medium.

2. Add chili, carrot, bok choy, cabbage, cooking sauce, noodles, and rice vermicelli. Stir well to coat noodles, then cook until vegetables and noodles are tender, 4 to 5 minutes. Stir in egg. If pan appears dry, add a few spoonfuls of chicken broth. Garnish with cilantro sprigs.

Makes 4 servings.

THE MOTHER OF INVENTION
When it comes to cooking, my mom is the original mother of invention. She's spent a lifetime improvising and creating flavors out of whatever's on hand, and not always out of necessity. She likes it that way—she says the challenge keeps her young. Like most traditional Asian cooks, my mom doesn't work from written recipes, and when I've tried to capture her cooking on paper, I've found that it loses a lot in the translation. You miss all the running commentary and the sudden bursts of inspiration and exasperation. When I teach cooking, I try to preach what my mom practices: Don't be a slave to the recipe. Taste and adjust as you go. Keep an open mind, and don't be afraid to make substitutions. Oh, and call your mother!

Whipping up some Hokkien mee with my pal, Chef Lim Ah Chyer of Singapore Airlines.

STIR-FRIED FRESH RICE NOODLES

Another stellar example of Singapore street fare chow kway teow, is all about contrasts: soft, fresh rice noodles, tender seafood, and crunchy bok choy and bean sprouts—all stir-fried in a deep, dark "secret sauce."

⮞ SAUCE ⮜

1/4 cup chicken broth
2 tablespoons regular soy sauce
1 tablespoon dark soy sauce
1 teaspoon chili garlic sauce
1 teaspoon sesame oil
1/4 teaspoon white pepper

1/3 pound medium raw shrimp
1/3 pound squid, cleaned
2 to 3 baby bok choy
2 tablespoons cooking oil
2 teaspoons minced garlic
1 pound fresh rice noodles, cut
    crosswise into 1/4-inch strips
1 cup bean sprouts
1 egg, lightly beaten

Getting Ready

1. Combine sauce ingredients in a small bowl.

2. Shell and devein shrimp; cut in half lengthwise. Cut squid crosswise into 1/4-inch slices to make rings; leave tentacles whole. Quarter bok choy and slice crosswise into 1-inch pieces.

Cooking

1. Heat a wok over high heat until hot. Add cooking oil and swirl to coat sides. Add garlic and cook, stirring, until fragrant, 10 seconds. Add shrimp and squid; cook, stirring, for 1 minute. Add bok choy and cook, stirring, for 30 seconds.

2. Add sauce; cook for 30 seconds. Add rice noodles and bean sprouts; stir-fry for 1 minute. Add egg and cook until set, about 1 minute.

Makes 4 servings

FRESH RICE NOODLES

If you've ever tried Chinese chow fun, you know that the texture of fresh rice noodles is irresistibly chewy and appealing. Made of water and rice flour, they fry up crispy around the edges and soak up sauces like no other pasta. You can find them in the refrigerated section of Asian markets, where they're sold as folded sheets (left whole so you can roll a filling around them or cut them into whatever width noodles you need) or as precut ribbons or spaghetti-thin strands. It's best to use fresh rice noodles the day you buy them. Once refrigerated, they become stiff; rinse them gently in warm water to soften them up and to remove the oily film added to keep them from sticking together.

SINGAPORE CURRIED EGG NOODLES

(Mee Goreng)

I get cravings all the time. And when I get the uncontrollable urge to fly to Singapore, race to the nearest hawker center, and inhale a big plate of noodles, these are the ones I imagine: curried egg noodles stir-fried with crispy bits of chicken, shrimp, and chewy fried tofu.

NOODLES AT THE READY

I think noodles are among the best emergency resources to have in your kitchen, and I always keep a supply on hand. When you're out of ideas, out of time, or just plain out of food, it doesn't take much to turn fresh or dried noodles into a satisfying, nutritious meal. You can stir-fry them with a little meat or cut-up vegetables and a prepared sauce. Or add them to a simple bowl of broth, along with a bit of something green, like spinach, bok choy, peas, or whatever's around. Throw in a few flavor accents—a drizzle of oyster sauce, soy sauce, or sesame oil; a dash of white pepper or a splash of white vinegar—and you've made something from nothing. Now that's using your noodle!

1 package (12 oz.) fresh Chinese egg noodles
1 package (14 oz.) regular-firm or extra-firm tofu
Cooking oil for deep-frying
1/4 pound boneless, skinless chicken
1/3 pound medium raw shrimp
2 tablespoons cooking oil
2 teaspoons minced garlic
2 fresh red jalapeño chilies, thinly sliced
1/4 pound regular or baby bok choy, thinly sliced
1 cup bean sprouts
2 green onions, cut into 2-inch lengths
2 teaspoons curry powder
3 tablespoons soy sauce
1/4 teaspoon salt
2 eggs, lightly beaten
Lime wedges
Cilantro sprigs

Getting Ready

1. In a large pot of boiling water, cook egg noodles according to package directions. Drain, rinse with cold water, and drain again.

2. Drain tofu; cut into 1/2- by 1-inch rectangles. Place between paper towels and gently press out excess water.

3. In a wok, heat oil for deep-frying to 350°F. Add tofu and deep-fry, turning once, until golden on all sides, 3 to 4 minutes. Remove from oil and drain on paper towels.

4. Thinly slice chicken. Shell and devein shrimp; cut in half lengthwise.

Cooking

1. Place a wok over high heat until hot. Add 2 tablespoons oil, swirling to coat sides. Add garlic and chilies; stir-fry until fragrant, about 10 seconds. Add chicken and shrimp; stir-fry for 2 minutes.

2. Add bok choy, bean sprouts, and green onions; stir-fry for 2 minutes. Add curry powder, soy sauce, and salt; mix well. Add eggs and cook, stirring, for 30 seconds. Add noodles, toss well, and cook for 1 minute. Add tofu and cook until heated through, about 1 minute longer. Serve with lime wedges and garnish with cilantro.

Makes 4 to 6 servings.

HAINANESE CHICKEN RICE

This dish of poached or roasted chicken and fluffy, fragrant rice served with chili sauce, ginger sauce, and other condiments is one of the most popular lunch items in coffee shops and hawker stalls throughout Singapore and Malaysia.

1 pound chicken thighs
4 cups water
1 teaspoon salt

≽ SEASONED RICE ≼
2 tablespoons cooking oil
1 walnut-size shallot, finely chopped
1 teaspoon minced ginger
1/2 teaspoon minced garlic
1 1/2 cups long-grain rice
2 cups chicken broth
1/2 teaspoon sesame oil

≽ GINGER SAUCE ≼
1/3 cup chopped ginger
1/4 cup chicken broth
1 teaspoon salt
1/2 teaspoon sugar
1 teaspoon sesame oil
2 tablespoons cooking oil

≽ CHILI SAUCE ≼
2 fresh red jalapeño chilies, seeded
1/4 cup chicken broth
1 tablespoon minced garlic
2 tablespoons lime juice or tamarind water (see page 71)
1/2 teaspoon sugar
1/2 teaspoon salt
2 tablespoons cooking oil

Thick sweet soy sauce (kecap manis)
Oyster-flavored sauce

Cooking

1. Place chicken, water, and salt in a 2-quart pan and bring to a boil. Reduce heat; cover and simmer until chicken is no longer pink when cut near bone, 30 to 40 minutes. Lift out chicken and let cool; reserve broth for the rice and sauces.

2. To make seasoned rice: Place a 2-quart pan over high heat until hot. Add cooking oil, swirling to coat sides. Add shallot, ginger, and garlic; stir-fry until fragrant, about 30 seconds. Add rice and cook, stirring, for 2 minutes. Add 2 cups broth, and sesame oil. Bring to a boil; cover, reduce heat, and simmer until rice is tender and liquid is absorbed, about 20 minutes.

3. To make ginger sauce: Place all ingredients except cooking oil in a blender and process. Heat oil in a small pan over medium heat. Add purée and cook, until slightly thickened, about 2 minutes.

4. To make chili sauce: Place all ingredients except cooking oil in a blender and process until smooth. Heat oil in a small pan over medium heat. Add purée and cook until slightly thickened, about 2 minutes.

5. To serve, place rice in a wide, shallow serving bowl. Place chicken around rice. Serve with the sauces.

Makes 4 servings.

CHICKEN RICE

Ironically, you won't find Hainanese chicken rice on the island of Hainan in the South China Sea. But you'll find plenty of it in Singapore, where everyone calls it "chicken rice," no matter what language they speak. Singaporeans will drive from one end of the island to the other in pursuit of their favorite version. One of my all-time favorites is prepared by my good friend Han Seng Fong, chef at the Chatterbox Restaurant in the Mandarin Hotel. He buys specially bred chickens from Malaysia, simmers them until they're perfectly tender, and serves them with his famous spicy chili sauce and aromatic ginger rice. Talk about a best-seller: The restaurant serves more than 35,500 chickens a year!

SWEET POTATO AND TARO ROOT PUDDING
(Bubur Cha-Cha)

In Singapore, this rich, home-style pudding made with sweet potatoes, taro root, pearl tapioca, and coconut milk is often served after a light Saturday or Sunday lunch of fried noodles. It's delicious warm or cold.

LET THEM EAT FRUIT

So many people are thrown into a tailspin when they're planning a dinner for friends and it comes time to think about dessert. Why not follow the lead of home cooks all over Southeast Asia, and make dessert a simple array of tropical fruit? Cut up chunks of mango, papaya, pineapple, fresh coconut, banana, and—if you're feeling wild—some passion fruit. Sprinkle a little lime juice and shredded coconut over everything and garnish with a few pineapple leaves. It's a light, refreshing way to finish off a meal, and your friends will think you're exotic. What could be sweeter than that?

$1/2$ cup small ($1/8$ in.) pearl tapioca
I cup cold water
$1/2$ pound sweet potato
$1/2$ pound taro root
6 water chestnuts
I or 2 cans (13$1/2$ oz.) unsweetened coconut milk
I cup warm water
$2/3$ cup sugar
Coconut cream or caramelized sugar

> CARAMELIZED SUGAR ≤
(optional)
I cup sugar
$1/4$ cup water

Getting Ready

1. Soak tapioca in cold water for 30 minutes (most of the water will be absorbed); drain.

2. In a pan of water, boil sweet potato and taro root until tender when pierced, about 20 minutes; drain and let cool. Peel sweet potato and taro root; cut into $1/2$-inch cubes. Cut water chestnuts into $1/4$-inch cubes.

Cooking

1. In a heavy saucepan, combine 1 can coconut milk, warm water, and sugar. Cook, stirring, over medium heat, until sugar dissolves. Add tapioca and bring to a boil. Reduce heat to medium-low and cook, stirring, for 5 minutes.

2. Add sweet potato, taro, and water chestnuts; continue to cook, stirring, until mixture thickens and tapioca becomes translucent, 5 to 7 minutes. Divide pudding among 6 individual bowls and let cool.

3. Garnish each serving with coconut cream or caramelized sugar. For coconut cream: Open a can of unsweetened coconut milk (do not shake it first), and spoon the thick cream off the top. If you like it less rich, blend in a little of the thin coconut milk at the bottom of the can. Caramelized sugar: Place sugar and water in a small heavy pan, and stir to blend. Cook over medium heat, shaking pan continuously, until sugar turns golden and caramelizes. Immediately pour caramel syrup equally over each serving.

4. Refrigerate, loosely covered, for up to 4 hours.

Makes 6 servings.

LIMEADE

If you're a fan of iced tea, try this sparkling refresher made with tea, lime juice, honey, and ginger ale. It's just the thing for washing down a hot and spicy curry on a hot summer day.

10 limes
6 cups water
6 English Breakfast tea bags
$\frac{1}{2}$ cup honey
$\frac{1}{4}$ cup sugar
Ice cubes
Ginger ale (optional)
Mint sprigs

Getting Ready
1. Squeeze juice from 9 limes; thinly slice remaining lime for garnish.

Cooking
1. In a nonreactive pan, heat water to boiling. Turn off heat, add tea bags, and let steep for 10 minutes. Remove tea bags.

2. Add honey and sugar; stir to dissolve sugar. Add lime juice. Let mixture cool, then refrigerate until ready to use.

3. To serve, pour into glasses filled with ice cubes, or fill glasses with equal parts of limeade and ginger ale; stir lightly to mix. Garnish each serving with a slice of lime and a sprig of mint.

Makes 10 to 12 servings.

IN THE SLING OF THINGS

Step into the world-famous Long Bar at the Raffles Hotel and you know you're in the tropics. It's an elegant, colonial-era room complete with white wicker furniture, slowly spinning palm-blade fans, and—my favorite part— all-you-can-eat peanuts (tossing the shells on the floor is encouraged). It was here, around the turn of the century, that a Hainanese bartender, Ngiam Tong Boon, made mixological history by inventing the world-renowned Singapore Sling. A bright pink concoction of gin, cherry brandy, pineapple juice, lime juice, liqueurs, grenadine, and bitters, it tastes like a refreshing punch. But watch out: It packs a punch, too!

Sling for your supper: enjoying a relaxing moment in the Long Bar of the Raffles Hotel.

Malaysia It's All in the Mix

When I think of Malaysia, I get hungry. And sometimes I get a little dizzy. You see, for a small country, Malaysia has one of the most diverse and delightfully complex cuisines I have ever eaten my way through! Rich, spicy, and full of surprises, Malaysian food is easy to love and hard to define, because so many cultures have created it: Muslim Malays, Chinese, Indians, Straits Chinese, and even the Portuguese, not to mention the indigenous tribal people of Borneo.

That's great news for the adventurous eater. On a single street corner in Malaysia, you might find charcoal-grilled satay skewers of chicken, beef, or lamb; fragrant nasi rice dishes served up with fiery sambal chili relishes; a tangy, hot-and-sour Nonya laksa noodle soup; Chinese-style noodles and dumplings; spicy Indian curries and breads to sop them up. And that's

When I think of Malaysia, I get hungry. And sometimes I get a little dizzy.

just on one street corner!

Now, when these cuisines begin to interact and borrow from one another, that's when the real magic of Malaysian cooking begins. Some call this place the melting pot of Asia. Me, I like to think of it as one giant mortar and pestle—the traditional centerpiece of the Malaysian kitchen, where chilies and the herbs and spices of many lands are slowly blended together, offering up their wonderful flavors in an enticing culinary exchange. Are you ready to mix it up? Meet me in Malaysia and let's do lunch!

The "Malay" of the Land

Take a look at a map of Malaysia, and you begin to understand the roots of its diverse cuisine. Close to the equator and rich in tropical vegetation, it is like a huge natural marketplace. Or maybe I should say "hothouse": the temperature here hovers around 80°F almost every day, with only the rains brought by the monsoon at year's end for variation, so fresh ingredients from the sea, the rivers, and farms are abundantly available all year long.

You'll notice that the country is made up of two parts, separated by more than 400 miles of ocean. Peninsular West Malaysia is more populous

Malaysian's claim to have invented satay, the country's national "snack on a stick".

and developed. Here, you'll find the urban centers of Kuala Lumpur, the capital; Georgetown, on the idyllic island of Penang; Ipoh, the town tin mining made rich; and historic Melaka, with its Straits Chinese enclaves. A jungle-covered mountain range runs through the peninsula from north to south, flanked by coconut tree-lined beaches, lush green rice paddies, palm oil plantations, and tropical fruit orchards.

The thing that amazes me about Malaysia is how so many nationalities can come together in the kitchen and at the table.

Across the South China Sea is rugged East Malaysia, on the spectacular island of Borneo. It's home to the mountainous state of Sabah, with its cowboys and lumberjacks, and the dense rain forests of Sarawak, where rivers are still the region's main highways, and if you don't watch your step, you might just wind up sharing your dinner

with a wild orangutan!

A Mix of Many Cultures

The people of Malaysia are as diverse as the landscape. For almost 2,000 years, the region has seen a steady stream of seafaring traders, settlers, and colonists, who came in pursuit of the region's abundant natural resources.

As early as the 15th century, there were Portuguese and Dutch spice traders as well as merchant sailors from the Middle East, India, Indonesia, and China. When early Chinese settlers inter-married with Malay women, they created a new ethnic group: the Straits Chinese or Peranakans. Later, the British came in search of tea, rubber, and tin, recruiting massive migrations of Indians to man their rubber plantations and Chinese to work the tin mines.

Today, Malays, who by law practice

Baking rice in a bamboo trunk with a Daru tribal family in the jungle of Sarawak.

Islam, the official state religion, make up about half of the country's 18 million people. Chinese, primarily Buddhist and Christian, account for another third; and Indians, mainly Hindu, about 10 percent. Eurasians and indigenous ethnic groups, like Ibans, Dayaks, and Kadazans, make up the rest.

That's quite a mix. And, as a cook, the thing that amazes me every time I visit Malaysia is how remarkably these nationalities come together in the kitchen and at the table. Personally, I like to think that food is the essential bond that holds so many ethnic groups together as a single nation. Whenever I cook in the kitchens of Malaysia, it strikes me that this is not a cuisine of chefs, but of the people—a cuisine of home cooks and street hawkers, of storefront restaurants, kerosene burners, and charcoal braziers.

It is a living cuisine. Chinese cooks borrow Indian and Malay curry spices. Indian hawkers use Malay and Southeast Asian ingredients like shrimp paste, bean sprouts, and bean curd to create dishes that never existed in India.

Nonyas spice up traditional Chinese dishes with fiery chilies, and add the mellowing richness of coconut milk. It's all in the mix.

And even with the advances of technology, cooking in the home is still seen by many in Malaysia as a sacred art, to be passed along from one generation to the next. Now that's what I call an "oral tradition"!

In the recipes that follow, I have tried to capture some of the flavors of that tradition so that you can experience them first-hand. I hope you will enjoy them and that you'll be inspired to add a few flavors and touches of your own. After all, that's what the "mortar and pestle" of Malaysian cooking is all about.

High Tea: the Boh Tea Estate in the Cameron Highlands is Malaysia's largest tea plantation.

SHRIMP FRITTERS

These golden fritters are a typical hawker snack sold throughout the day in Malaysia. This recipe was inspired by the method shown to me by my friend Chef Wan Ismail, the culinary ambassador of Malaysia and author of the popular cookbook, "Flavours of Malaysia."

⇒ BATTER ⇐
1 1/2 cups flour
1/2 teaspoon baking powder
1/2 teaspoon ground turmeric
1/4 teaspoon Chinese five-spice
1 egg
1/4 teaspoon salt
3/4 water

3/4 pound medium raw shrimp
1/2 cup finely chopped garlic chives

2 green onions, thinly sliced
Cooking oil for deep-frying
Sweet chili sauce

Getting Ready

1. Prepare batter: Sift together flour, baking powder, turmeric, and five-spice. Add egg and salt. Slowly add enough water to form a thick batter. Do not overmix; batter should be lumpy. Set aside.

2. Shell and devein the shrimp. Save 8 whole ones; finely mince the rest. Fold minced shrimp, garlic chives, and green onions into batter.

Cooking

1. In a wok, heat oil for deep-frying to 350°F. Dip a ladle into the oil for 20 seconds.

2. With a measuring cup, pour 1/4 cup batter into ladle; top with a whole shrimp. Gently lower the ladle into the hot oil and deep-fry until batter is golden, 4 to 5 minutes.

3. With a fork, push the partially cooked fritter out of ladle; fry 2 to 3 minutes longer. Remove fritter and drain on paper towels. Repeat with remaining batter and whole shrimp.

4. Serve with sweet chili sauce.

Makes 8 fritters.

CURRY PUFFS
(Karipap)

Indian cooks brought these flaky, potato-filled turnovers to Malaysia, where chicken, beef, or lamb are sometimes added to the filling. And I am delighted to bring my version to you. Traditionally, they are deep-fried, but I like to brush them with an egg wash, pop them in the oven, and bake them to a golden-brown finish.

⇝ FILLING ⇜
1 small potato
1 tablespoon cooking oil
2 teaspoons minced ginger
1/2 medium onion, finely chopped
2 green onions, thinly sliced
1/2 pound boneless, skinless chicken
    breast, coarsely chopped
2 tablespoons curry powder
    or 1/4 cup curry sauce
1 tablespoon soy sauce

1 egg yolk
1 teaspoon water
Flaky pastry for a double-crust
    deep-dish 9-inch pie

Getting Ready
1. Boil potato in water to cover until tender, then peel and cut into 1/4-inch cubes.

Cooking
1. Place a wok over high heat until hot.

Add oil, swirling to coat sides. Add ginger, onion, green onions, and chicken; stir-fry for 2 minutes. Stir in potato, curry powder, and soy sauce. Remove from heat and let cool.

2. Preheat oven to 375°F. Beat egg yolk with water.

3. On a floured board, roll out pastry, one half at a time, to a thickness of about 1/8 inch; cut into 4-inch circles. Place 1 rounded tablespoon filling on each circle. Brush edges with egg wash, fold dough to make half-moons, and press edges to seal.

4. Place on a lightly oiled baking sheet. Brush tops with egg wash. Bake until golden brown, 25 to 30 minutes. Serve warm.

Makes 20.

WHAT IS CURRY?

I'm glad you asked! The word comes from kari, which simply means "sauce" in southern India, where curry probably originated as a way to preserve food. Curry is not a spice but a blend of spices; not a dish but a method of cooking; and not just Indian but also Malay, Indonesian, Thai, Chinese, Burmese, and more. Curries usually start with turmeric (which makes them yellow), chilies, cumin, and coriander. Other spices might include cardamom, cloves, cinnamon, and fennel. If you've never made a curry from scratch, it's well worth the effort, and many of the recipes in this book show you how. Of course, if you need curry in a hurry, don't worry! There are all kinds of great premixed powders and sauces on the market.

NONYA TOP HATS
(Kueh Pai Ti)

My hat's off to the Nonya cooks of Malaysia, who make these crispy little pastry cups using a top hat-shaped cast-iron mold. The outside of the mold is dipped in hot oil, then in batter, and then again in hot oil. You can find the molds in some Asian markets, or, even easier, use my foolproof baked pastry shells made from store-bought gyoza wrappers.

⟩ **PASTRY SHELLS** ⟨
32 potsticker (gyoza) wrappers or
    wonton wrappers

⟩ **FILLING** ⟨
1 tablespoon cooking oil
2 teaspoons minced garlic
1/4 pound medium raw shrimp,
    shelled, deveined, and chopped
2 cups finely chopped jicama
1 cup finely chopped carrot
2 tablespoons chopped cilantro
2 tablespoons oyster-flavored
    sauce
1 teaspoon sugar
Cilantro leaves
Slivered chilies

Getting Ready
1. If using wonton wrappers, trim corners so they become circles. Coat standard-size muffin pans (2½-in.-diameter cups) with cooking spray. Loosely fit a wrapper into each cup; the edges will be ruffled.

Cooking
1. Preheat oven to 375°F. Bake wrapper cases until edges of shells are golden brown, 6 to 7 minutes. Repeat with remaining wrappers. Let shells cool. Store in an airtight container until ready to fill, up to 3 days.

2. To make filling: Place a wok over high heat until hot. Add oil, swirling to coat sides. Add garlic and stir-fry for 10 seconds. Add shrimp and stir-fry for 1 minute. Add jicama and carrot; reduce heat to medium and cook for 3 minutes, adding a few drops of water if pan appears dry. Add cilantro, oyster-flavored sauce, and sugar. Cook, stirring frequently, until vegetables are tender-crisp, about 2 minutes. Let mixture cool.

3. To serve, fill each pastry cup with 1 tablespoon of filling and garnish each with a cilantro leaf and a sliver of chili.

Makes about 32.

SPICY STUFFED BREAD
(Murtabak)

One of my favorite street treats in Malaysia and Singapore is the "Indian pizza" made by food stall hawkers. Here's how I make it at home.

SMILE WHEN YOU COOK THAT

The best cooks in the world know that cooking is about more than recipes. It's about using all six senses: taste, smell, sight, touch, hearing, and my personal favorite, the sense of humor! There's really no right or wrong in the kitchen, and the more you relax, clown around, and have fun, the more your own style will come through. Like I always tell my students, "If there's one thing my kids have taught me about my profession, it's that cooking is just the grown-up version of playing with your food!"

⇒ DOUGH ⇐
3½ cups flour
1 teaspoon salt
2 tablespoons butter, cut into chunks
1¼ cups warm milk
3 tablespoons cooking oil

⇒ SPICE PASTE ⇐
6 cloves garlic
4 slices ginger, each the size of a quarter
1 onion, thinly sliced
¼ cup water
2 tablespoons chili garlic sauce

4 tablespoons cooking oil

⇒ FILLING ⇐
¾ pound ground chicken or lean ground beef
2 tablespoons curry powder or curry paste
1 tablespoon sugar
½ teaspoon salt or 2 tablespoons soy sauce
1 egg, lightly beaten

Melted butter

Getting Ready

1. To make dough: Place flour and salt in a bowl. With two table knives, cut butter into flour until particles are about the size of peas. Gradually add milk and oil, mixing well. Knead until a smooth dough forms, about 10 minutes. Divide dough into 10 pieces. Roll each piece into ball; cover and let rest for 1 hour.

2. Place spice paste ingredients in a blender and process until smooth.

Cooking

1. Place a wok over medium-low heat until hot. Add 2 tablespoons oil, swirling to coat sides. Add spice paste and cook, stirring, until fragrant, 6 to 8 minutes.

2. Raise heat to medium-high. Add meat, curry powder, sugar, and salt; cook until meat is browned and crumbly, about 2 minutes. Remove from heat; stir in egg.

3. To make each piece of bread: Roll a ball of dough into a circle 8 to 9 inches in diameter. Spread ¼ cup filling in center of circle, leaving 2 inches of dough around the edge. Fold top and bottom edges over filling, overlapping in center by ½ inch; repeat with left and right edges . Brush top with melted butter.

4. Place a wide frying pan over medium heat until hot. Add remaining 2 tablespoons oil, swirling to coat sides. Pan-fry bread, a few pieces at a time, until golden brown, 3 to 5 minutes on each side. Repeat for remaining pieces.

Makes 8.

ROTI JALA

To make these lacy pancakes, Malaysian cooks use a special cup with four funnel-like holes at the bottom. The cup is filled with batter, which is rapidly drizzled through the holes in a circular pattern onto a hot griddle. If you don't have a roti jala cup, don't worry. You can use a plastic squeeze bottle instead. And if you don't have a squeeze bottle, you can try your hand at making handmade roti jala the old-fashioned way: dip your hand right in the batter, and then let it run off your fingers onto the grill as you move your hand in a circle.

1 large egg
1¼ cups water
½ cup unsweetened coconut milk
1 cup flour
1 tablespoon cornstarch
½ teaspoon turmeric powder
½ teaspoon salt
Cooking oil

Getting Ready

1. In a blender, process egg, water, coconut milk, flour, cornstarch, turmeric, and salt until smooth.

Cooking

1. Place a wide nonstick frying pan over medium-high heat until hot. Brush a light coating of oil onto the pan.

2. To use a roti jala cup: Over the hot pan, fill the roti jala cup with about ½ cup batter. Immediately move the cup to drizzle continuous overlapping circles of batter into pan to make a lacy pancake about 8 inches in diameter. When pancake is formed, empty any extra batter back into the bowl.

To use a plastic squeeze bottle: Fill bottle with batter. Over the hot pan, squeeze bottle so batter forms a band of continuous circles from 8 inches in diameter to 1 inch in diameter, leaving ½ inch between each circle. Then squeeze batter in radiating bands so pancake looks like a spiderweb.

3. Cook until top of pancake looks dry and edges begin to curl, 1 to 1½ minutes. With a wide spatula, turn pancake and cook to brown the other side, about 1 minute. Repeat, brushing pan lightly with oil before making each pancake. Serve warm or at room temperature.

Makes 12.

FABULOUS FLATBREADS

Indian flatbreads are like tasty edible silverware, perfect for pushing food around and scooping it up to your mouth. These breads come in so many varieties, it's impossible to count them all. Chapatis are among the best known: simple flour and water flat breads enriched with ghee (clarified butter) and browned on a griddle until they puff up like little balloons. Roti prata is made from a similar dough, but the ghee is incorporated in layers, puff pastry style, by folding and turning the dough, resulting in a lighter, flakier bread. In Malaysia, Indian bakers add their own secret ingredient, condensed milk, to prata dough, to make an even lighter version called roti canai.

In Kuala Lumpur, I tried my hand at making roti jala.

BORNEO-STYLE FISH SALAD

(Ikan Mentah Rempah)

I was served a salad a lot like this one by a family living in a coastal village in Malaysian Borneo. It's a true appetizer—the kind of dish that says to your taste buds "Hey, wake up! It's time for some flavor excitement!" And it's so simple to prepare that I was able to re-create it from memory back in my kitchen in California. Don't be put off by the raw fish. It gets "cooked" by the acid in the lime juice, giving it a delicate, poached texture. Be sure to use only the freshest of fish.

THE RAW FACTS

Cold salads of raw fish show up all over the world. To Western cooks, the Latin American dish seviche, made with lime, onion, and tomato, is probably the most familiar. Filipino cooks have their version, Kinilaw (see page 163), in which the dressing is enriched with coconut milk. And in Singapore, you can find Yu Sheng (see page 69), a fabulous New Year salad made with raw fish, jellyfish, and tropical fruit. Leave it to the Japanese to come up with the simplest and purest of all raw fish dishes, sashimi, which really needs only one ingredient: raw fish!

³/₄ **pound salmon or tuna fillet**
¹/₃ **cup lime juice**

⇒ DRESSING ⇐
2 walnut-size shallots
3 slices ginger, each the size of a quarter
1 fresh red jalapeño chili, seeded
2 tablespoons chopped cilantro
2 tablespoons lime juice
¹/₂ **teaspoon sugar**
¹/₄ **teaspoon salt**

Cilantro leaves

Getting Ready

1. Remove skin and any bones from fish, then cut fish into ¹/₂-inch cubes. Place in a nonreactive bowl; add ¹/₃ cup lime juice and stir to coat. Cover and chill until fish turns opaque, about 4 hours.

Assembly

1. About 30 minutes before serving, finely chop shallots; mince ginger and chili. Place in a medium bowl with cilantro, 2 tablespoons lime juice, sugar, and salt.

2. Drain fish and place in bowl with dressing. Stir gently to mix. Chill for 30 minutes.

3. Place fish in 4 individual bowls; garnish with cilantro leaves.

Makes 4 servings.

FRAGRANT LAMB SOUP

(Sop Kambing)

Here's my recipe for a popular Malaysian food stall snack that's sometimes called "bone soup." Until not long ago, it was often made with goat's tongue and sometimes even eyeballs. I prefer to keep an eye on my soup, not in it, so I make my version with lamb shanks, simmered slowly until they're soft and tender. Aromatic vegetables and spices are added at the very end so their flavors are wonderfully fresh and lively. Served with lots of crusty bread, this makes a great meal in a bowl.

2 pounds lamb shanks, cut through
    bone into 2-inch-thick slices
2 leeks
8 cups water
6 cloves garlic, peeled
4 slices ginger, each the size of a
    quarter
2 whole star anise
1 cinnamon stick
2 tablespoons cooking oil
2 green onions, thinly sliced
1 fresh red jalapeño chili, seeded
    and thinly sliced
2 teaspoons ground coriander
$1/2$ teaspoon ground cumin
$1/2$ teaspoon ground cardamom
2 tablespoons soy sauce
1 medium tomato, cut into 6 wedges
Deep-fried shallots (see page 124)

Getting Ready

1. Trim fat from shanks. Cut leeks, white part only, into $1/4$-inch-thick slices.

Cooking

1. Place shanks in a 5-quart pan with water, garlic, ginger, star anise, and cinnamon stick. Bring to a boil; reduce heat and simmer for 5 minutes. Skim off foam, then cover and simmer until meat is tender, about 2 hours.

2. Place a wok over high heat until hot. Add oil, swirling to coat sides. Add leeks, green onions, and chili; stir-fry for 2 minutes. Add coriander, cumin, and cardamom; stir-fry for 1 minute.

3. Add leek mixture and soy sauce to soup; simmer for 5 minutes. Add tomato and simmer for 2 minutes.

4. Ladle soup into bowls and garnish with deep-fried shallots.

Makes 6 servings.

WHEN IN DOUBT, SELAMAT

Bahasa Malaysia (also known as Malay) is the official language of Malaysia. Allow me to share a few useful Bahasa salutations. There's selamat pagi (good morning), selamat petang (good evening), and selamat malam (good night), as well as the indispensable selamat datang (welcome) and selamat pulang (good-bye). But most important of all, there's the greeting I learned first in Malaysia and used more than any other: selamat makan—good eating!

EGGPLANT SAMBAL
(Sambal Terong)

AN EGGPLANT TIP

How can you distinguish Asian eggplants from their nearly identical, slender, purple Italian cousins? Here's a tip: look at the tip! The stem of an Asian eggplant will generally be black, while those of an Italian eggplant will be green.

You can use Italian eggplants in recipes that call for Asian ones, but they tend to have more delicate skins that don't hold up quite as well during stir-frying. And don't forget to impress your guests with this surprising tidbit: The eggplant is not a vegetable. It's a fruit. In fact, it's a great big berry!

This dish of stir-fried eggplant in chili sauce is like a crash course in Malaysian cooking: A spice paste—dried shrimp and "wet" spices like shallot, garlic and chilies—is slowly simmered in oil until its flavors meld and become wonderfully complex. The addition of coconut milk creates a rich sauce that's the perfect complement to the mild flavor of the eggplant.

➢ SPICE PASTE ◁

2 teaspoons dried shrimp
2 walnut-size shallots
4 cloves garlic
3 fresh red jalapeño chilies, seeded
1/4 cup water

8 fresh basil leaves
3/4 pound Asian eggplants
4 tablespoons cooking oil
1/2 cup unsweetened coconut milk
2 tablespoons hoisin sauce
1 teaspoon sugar
1/4 teaspoons salt
3/4 cup water

Getting Ready
1. Soak dried shrimp in warm water to cover until softened, about 20 minutes; drain. Place in a blender with remaining spice paste ingredients and process until smooth.

2. Cut 6 basil leaves into thin strips; set aside 2 whole leaves for garnish.

3. Cut eggplants into wedges about 1/2 inch wide and 2 1/2 inches long.

Cooking
1. Place a wok over medium-low heat until hot. Add 2 tablespoons oil, swirling to coat sides. Add spice paste and cook, stirring, until fragrant, 6 to 8 minutes. Add basil strips, coconut milk, hoisin sauce, sugar, and salt to taste. Place in a bowl.

2. Place a wok over medium-high heat until hot. Add remaining 2 tablespoons oil and eggplant wedges; stir-fry until pieces are brown on outside, 3 to 4 minutes, then add water. Reduce heat to medium; simmer, covered, until tender-crisp, 5 to 6 minutes.

3. Spoon sauce in center of a serving plate, arrange eggplant pieces on top, and garnish with whole basil leaves.

Makes 4 servings.

An old tribal woman sells eggplants at a pasar tani, or farmers' market, in Kota Belud, Borneo.

MANGO SAMBAL
(Sambal Mangga)

Mexico has its salsas, India its chutneys, and Malaysia its sambals—spicy relishes of fresh fruits and vegetables, flavored with shrimp paste and chilies, and eaten as side dishes with rice and curries.

1 teaspoon dried shrimp paste
   (blachan)
1 or 2 fresh red jalapeño chilies,
   seeded
1 teaspoon sugar
1/2 teaspoon salt
1 tablespoon plum sauce
1 firm-ripe mango (about 1 lb.)

Cooking

1. Wrap shrimp paste in foil; place in a frying pan over medium heat and toast for 1 minute on each side. Let cool.

2. Place shrimp paste in a blender with chilies, sugar, salt, and plum sauce. Process until smooth.

2. Peel mango. Coarsely cut flesh into matchsticks. Add plum sauce mixture and stir until mixed. Cover and chill until ready to serve.

Makes 8 servings.

SAMBAL BLACHAN

Sambal blachan is the quintessential Malaysian condiment that's eaten with just about everything. Serve it on the side in small quantities—it's quite spicy, and a little goes a long way. To make sambal blachan, wrap 3/4 teaspoon dried shrimp paste (blachan) in foil, place in a frying pan over medium heat, and toast for 1 minute on each side. Seed and mince 4 fresh red or green jalapeño chilies. In a blender, finely purée chilies with shrimp paste and 1 1/2 teaspoons sugar, then stir in 2 tablespoon lime juice. Makes about 1/3 cup.

Fresh mangoes.

PENANG SALAD
(Rojak Penang)

SHRIMP PASTE

Like the soy sauces of China and Japan or the fish sauces of Southeast Asia, blachan, or dried shrimp paste, is one of the most common flavor enhancers in Malaysian cooking. Whether you buy it fresh in jars or dried in cakes, the key is to cook it—even when it's used in a cold dish. When raw, its flavor and odor are pungent and off-putting, but it mellows when cooked, adding a salty, mild fish flavor that mingles marvelously with chilies, lime, sugar, and other classic Malaysian seasonings. To prepare blachan for use in uncooked dishes, wrap a small amount in foil and toast it in a skillet for 1 minute on each side.

Originally from Indonesia, by way of the island of Penang, rojak is one of Malaysia's best-know dishes: a sweet and savory salad of tropical fruits and vegetables dressed with palm sugar, shrimp paste, and chilies. This dish is so much a part of Malaysian and Singaporean culture that its name is used to describe mixtures of all kinds. One Malaysian woman I know proudly refers to her Malay-Chinese-Indian-British son as "a real rojak!"

³/₄ pound sweet potatoes or yams
¹/₂ pound bean sprouts
1 mango, cut into ¹/₂-inch cubes
¹/₂ fresh pineapple, peeled and cut into ¹/₂-inch cubes
¹/₂ English cucumber, cut into ¹/₂-inch cubes
¹/₄ small jicama, cut into ¹/₂-inch cubes

⇒ DRESSING ⇐

¹/₂ teaspoon dried shrimp paste (blachan)
2 fresh red jalapeño chilies, seeded
¹/₄ cup tamarind water (see page 71)
2 tablespoons packed brown sugar
2 tablespoons peanut butter or peanut-flavored sauce
2 tablespoons lime juice
2 tablespoons soy sauce or ¹/₂ teaspoon salt

Lettuce leaves
Black and white sesame seeds

Getting Ready

1. In a medium pan, boil sweet potatoes in water to cover until tender when pierced, 20 to 30 minutes; drain and let cool. Peel, cut into ¹/₂-inch cubes, and place in a large bowl; add bean sprouts.

2. To sweet potatoes and bean sprouts, add mango, pineapple, cucumber, and jicama. Cover and chill until ready to serve.

Cooking

1. Wrap shrimp paste in foil; place in a frying pan over medium heat and toast for 1 minute on each side. Place paste in a blender with chilies, tamarind water brown sugar, peanut butter, lime juice, and soy sauce. Process until smooth.

2. Pour dressing over salad and toss. Arrange on a lettuce-lined serving plate and garnish with sesame seeds.

Makes 6 servings.

PINEAPPLE CHUTNEY
(*Paceri Nanas*)

Here's my foolproof
formula for making rice
that sticks together
slightly—perfect for eat-
ing with curries and
stir-fries. For 3 cups of
cooked rice, start with
I cup of raw long-grain
rice. Place it in a medium
saucepan with I¹/₂ cups of
cold water and bring it to
a boil over medium-high
heat. Boil, uncovered, for
10 minutes or until some
water has evaporated
and small holes appear in
the surface of the rice.
Reduce heat to low.
Cover and simmer for
15 minutes or until the
rice is tender. Remove
from heat and let stand,
covered, 5 minutes longer.
Fluff the rice with a fork.
My even more foolproof
formula for perfect
rice: Simply buy a rice
cooker and follow the
manufacturer's directions.

Chutneys are wonderful for the contrasts of flavors and textures they bring to foods. This sweet, tangy, and spicy cooked chutney goes perfectly with my Indian Lamb Curry (page 136), Beef Stew with Onion-Flavored Sauce (page 137), or Venison on Sizzling Hot Plate (page 139).

¹/₂ medium red onion
I fresh red jalapeño chili
I fresh green jalapeño chili
2 tablespoons cooking oil
I¹/₂ cups pineapple cubes (³/₄ in.)
I tablespoon minced ginger
I cinnamon stick
2 whole star anise
I teaspoon turmeric powder
I teaspoon sesame seeds
¹/₂ cup water
2 tablespoons rice vinegar
I tablespoon sugar
Salt

Getting Ready

1. Cut onion into ³/₄-inch cubes. Quarter chilies lengthwise; remove seeds.

Cooking

1. Place a wok over high heat until hot. Add oil, swirling to coat sides. Add onion, chilies, ginger, cinnamon stick, star anise, turmeric, and sesame seeds; stir-fry until fragrant, 10 to 15 seconds. Add pineapple and mix well.

2. Add water, vinegar, and sugar. Reduce heat and simmer until most of liquid has evaporated, 4 to 5 minutes. Add salt to taste; let cool.

3. Cover and chill until ready to serve.

Makes 4 to 6 servings.

SABAH-STYLE GREENS

A Malaysian spice paste can transform any leafy green vegetable into a spectacularly tasty dish. If you make the spice paste ahead of time, you can enjoy this simple stir-fry in just a few minutes.

⇒ SPICE PASTE ⇐
3 walnut-size shallots
2 cloves garlic
2 fresh red jalapeño chilies, seeded
1/2 teaspoon dried shrimp paste
    (blachan)
1/4 water

11/2 pounds spinach or 1 pound
    Swiss chard or bok choy
2 tablespoons cooking oil
1/2 teaspoon sesame oil
Salt
Sesame seeds

Getting Ready
1. Place spice paste ingredients in a blender and process until smooth.

2. If using spinach, discard coarse stems and coarsely chop leaves. If using Swiss chard or bok choy, thinly slice stems and coarsely chop leaves.

Cooking
1. Heat a wok over medium-low heat until hot. Add oil, swirling to coat sides. Add spice paste and cook, stirring, until fragrant, 6 to 8 minutes.

2. Add spinach, increase heat to high, and stir-fry until barely tender, about 2 minutes. Add a few drops of water if pan appears dry.

3. Add sesame oil, and salt to taste. Arrange on a serving plate and garnish with sesame seeds.

Makes 6 servings.

COLOR ME GREEN

Asian greens are showing up in more and more American grocery stores all the time. I'm glad, because they're tasty and nutritious, and now I don't have to grow my own! Let me tell you about three of my favorites: Chinese broccoli (gai lan) looks nothing like regular broccoli. It's got dusty green stems, deep green leaves, and tiny white flowers. With its slightly bitter taste, it's great stir-fried or steamed with oyster sauce. Bok choy, baby bok choy, and the beautiful jade green Shanghai bok choy are delicately crunchy and slightly tangy. Chinese mustard greens (gai choy) have a slightly peppery flavor. Stir-fry them with a little garlic, or add them to soups.

Checking out a field of mustard greens in the Cameron Highlands, the "vegetable garden of Eden."

VEGETABLE CURRY
(*Kari Sayur*)

The next time you feel like a meatless dinner, try this vegetable curry. Served over rice, with a spicy sambal relish on the side, it makes a complete meal.

A NEW LEAF

The leaves and rind of the kaffir lime, a bumpy-skinned, dark green citrus fruit, lend their delicate citrus aroma and flavor to many Southeast Asian dishes. Like bay leaves, kaffir lime leaves are removed after cooking and not eaten. In North America, they're sold dried, and can be found frozen in some Asian markets. Kaffir lime trees can be grown successfully in some warm areas in the U.S. My garden, apparently, is not one of them.

⇀ SPICE PASTE ↽
4 walnut-size shallots
2 fresh red jalapeño chilies, seeded
4 candlenuts or 8 almonds
2 teaspoons turmeric powder
1/4 cup water

1/4 pound Chinese long beans
1/2 pound cabbage
1 Asian eggplant
1 large carrot
6 okra pods
1 medium tomato
2 tablespoons cooking oil
1 cup diced (1/2-in. cubes) jicama or bamboo shoots
6 kaffir lime leaves (optional)
3/4 cup vegetable broth or water
1/2 cup unsweetened coconut milk
3 tablespoons oyster-flavored sauce
2 green onions, sliced
Soy sauce or salt

Getting Ready
1. Place spice paste ingredients in a blender and process until smooth.

2. Cut vegetables: beans into 2-inch lengths, cabbage into 1- by 2-inch pieces, and eggplant into 1/2-inch cubes. Roll-cut carrot, trim okra stems without piercing pods, and cut tomato into 1/2-inch cubes.

Cooking
1. Heat a 2-quart pan over medium-low heat until hot. Add oil, swirling to coat sides. Add spice paste and cook, stirring, until fragrant, 6 to 8 minutes. Add beans, cabbage, eggplant, carrot, okra, jicama, kaffir lime leaves, broth, coconut milk, and oyster-flavored sauce.

2. Bring to a boil; reduce heat, cover, and simmer for 10 minutes. Add tomato and green onions. Cover and simmer until vegetables are tender, about 5 minutes.

3. Add soy sauce to taste.

Makes 6 servings.

FRIED FISH SAMBAL
(Ikan Goreng Bersambal)

Traditionally, this whole fish with a mildly spicy sweet-sour sauce is deep-fried, but I like to pan-fry it for a lighter presentation. Asian cooks know that when you cook a fish whole, with the head, tail, and bones intact, it comes out wonderfully moist and flavorful. Of course, if you're not comfortable looking your food in the eye, you can also use fish fillets. Just coat them with the cornstarch mixture, then pan-fry, grill, or broil them.

1 or 2 whole fish (1½ lb. total), such as trout or sea bass, cleaned
1 tablespoon cornstarch
½ teaspoon turmeric powder
¼ teaspoon salt

⋟ SPICE PASTE ⋞
1 walnut-size shallot
2 cloves garlic
2 candlenuts or 4 almonds
1 tablespoon chili garlic sauce
1 teaspoon paprika
½ teaspoon dried shrimp paste (blachan)
¼ teaspoon grated lime peel
¼ cup water

Cooking oil
¼ cup tamarind water (see page 71)
2 tablespoons soy sauce or
    ½ teaspoon salt
2 teaspoons sugar
1 tablespoon lime juice
1 piece banana leaf
Sliced fresh chili

Getting Ready
1. Cut 3 diagonal slits, each ½ inch deep, across each side of fish. Combine cornstarch, turmeric, and salt; rub fish inside and out with this mixture.

2. Combine spice paste ingredients in a blender and process until smooth.

Cooking
1. Place a wide frying pan or wok over medium heat. Add oil to a depth of ¼ inch. When oil is hot, add fish and pan-fry, turning once, until fish is golden brown and flesh turns opaque, 3 to 5 minutes per side, depending on size of fish. Remove and drain on paper towels.

2. Remove all but 2 tablespoons oil from pan; turn heat to medium-low. Add spice paste and cook, stirring, until fragrant, 6 to 8 minutes. Add tamarind water, soy sauce, sugar, and lime juice. Simmer until sauce thickens slightly, 1 to 2 minutes.

3. Serve fish on a plate lined with banana leaf. Pour sauce over and garnish with chili.

Makes 4 servings.

Lucky you! You've been invited to visit a traditional Malaysian household. May I share some tips on etiquette? It's polite to bring a simple gift of food— often sweets or fruit. There's even a name for this custom: buah tangan, or "fruit of the hand." Remove your shoes before entering your host's home. Accept drinks and dishes of food with both hands or with your right hand. If you're invited to sit on the floor, tuck your feet under you—showing the soles of the feet is considered rude. Be gentle and respectful, and most important of all, smile! I have witnessed this phenomenon all over the world: People smile back!

This traditional Malay house is more than 100 years old.

BAKED FISH IN BANANA LEAF

(Ikan Bakar Daun Pisang)

If you like to entertain, this makes a dramatic centerpiece for a special-occasion meal. Your family and friends may think you've gone bananas when you bring a whole fish baked in a banana leaf to the table. But when they discover its delicate, succulent texture and marvelous spicy flavor, they'll realize you haven't taken "leave" of your senses after all! By the way you can also cook this fish in its banana leaf wrapper on the grill as people often do in Malaysia.

1 whole fish (1 1/2 to 2 lb.), such as
 sea bass or red snapper,
 cleaned
1/2 teaspoon salt
1/4 teaspoon white pepper

➤ SPICE PASTE ◄
1 stalk lemongrass
6 walnut-size shallots
3 cloves garlic
6 fresh red jalapeño chilies, seeded
1/2 teaspoon dried shrimp paste
 (blachan)
1/2 tablespoon lime juice
1/4 cup water

1 or 2 pieces banana leaf large
 enough to wrap around fish
1 piece foil large enough to enclose
 wrapped fish
Lime slices

Getting Ready
1. Cut 3 diagonal slits, each 1/2 inch deep, across each side of fish. Sprinkle fish inside and out with salt and pepper.

2. Very thinly slice bottom 6 inches of lemongrass. Place in a blender with remaining spice paste ingredients and process until smooth.

3. Dip banana leaf into a pot of boiling water for 3 to 4 seconds to soften; wipe dry. Center leaf, shiny side down, on foil. Fill the cavity and slits of fish with about one-third of the spice paste. Spread another third of the spice paste on banana leaf. Lay fish on paste and top with remaining paste. Fold leaf over fish, then fold foil around fish to enclose. Place wrapped fish on a baking sheet.

Cooking
1. Preheat oven to 425°F. Bake until fish turns opaque, about 30 minutes.

2. Place fish on a serving platter. Open foil and banana leaf, and turn foil back and under fish. Garnish with lime slices.

Makes 4 servings.

SEAFOOD NONYA-STYLE

Nonya cooking is famous for its appealing contrasts of flavors, textures, and colors. Try this simple layered salad of fresh vegetables and shrimp in a sweet and tangy dressing and you'll see (and taste, and crunch) what I mean.

DEEP-FRIED SHALLOTS

Crispy deep-fried shallot flakes are a popular Southeast Asian garnish. Sprinkled over food, they add a delicate crunch and a burst of sweet, oniony flavor. You can find packaged shallot and onion flakes in some Asian markets. To make your own, peel and very thinly slice shallots; separate each slice into rings. Deep-fry slowly at 325°F until golden brown and crisp, 3 to 5 minutes. Drain on paper towels. Store in an airtight container in the refrigerator.

⇒ DRESSING ⇐

3 fresh red jalapeño chilies, seeded
4 cloves garlic
1/3 cup lime juice
1/4 cup plum sauce
2 tablespoons honey
2 tablespoons soy sauce
1 teaspoon sesame oil
2 tablespoons chunky peanut butter

1/2 head romaine or leaf lettuce, shredded
1 small carrot, julienned
1/2 cup julienned jicama
1 small European cucumber, halved lengthwise, seeded, and sliced
1 starfruit, halved lengthwise and sliced (optional)
2 tomatoes, cut into wedges
1/2 pound medium peeled cooked shrimp
1/4 cup roasted peanuts, coarsely chopped
1/4 cup cilantro
Deep-fried shallots (at left)

Getting Ready

1. Place dressing ingredients in a blender and process until smooth.

Assembly

1. Divide lettuce, carrot, jicama, cucumber, starfruit, tomatoes, and shrimp among 6 plates, starting with the lettuce and finishing with the shrimp.

2. Stir peanuts into dressing. Pour dressing over salad; top with cilantro and deep-fried shallots.

Makes 6 servings.

WOK-SEARED SCALLOPS WITH CHILI-WINE SAUCE

My friend Chef Kevin Cape is the brilliantly talented executive chef of the luxurious Eastern and Oriental Express. Now that's what I call a chef on a fast track! As we headed up the Malay Peninsula toward Thailand, he showed me how to prepare this simple, elegant dish in the train's tiny yet remarkably efficient kitchen.

³/₄ pound sea scallops
2 teaspoons cornstarch
¹/₂ teaspoon salt

≽ CHILI-WINE SAUCE ≼
¹/₄ cup tomato sauce
¹/₄ cup dry sherry
2 teaspoons chili garlic sauce
2 teaspoons oyster-flavored sauce
1¹/₂ teaspoons sugar

1 tomato
2 tablespoons cooking oil
1 teaspoon minced garlic
1 teaspoon minced ginger
Cilantro sprigs

Getting Ready

1. Pat scallops dry with paper towels. Place in a small bowl with cornstarch and salt; let stand for 5 minutes.

2. Combine sauce ingredients in a small bowl.

3. Slice tomato and reserve for garnish.

Cooking

1. Heat 1 tablespoon oil in a small pan over high heat. Add garlic and ginger; cook, stirring, until fragrant, about 10 seconds. Add sauce; simmer over medium heat, 2 to 3 minutes. Remove sauce from heat and keep warm.

2. Place a wok over medium heat until hot. Add remaining 1 tablespoon oil, swirling to coat sides. Add scallops; cook until they turn opaque, about 2 minutes on each side.

3. Pour sauce onto a rimmed serving plate; arrange scallops over sauce. Garnish with tomato and cilantro.

Makes 4 servings.

CULINARY "TRAINING"

The Eastern and Oriental Express is Malaysia's version of the famous Orient Express. It was introduced in 1993, but you'd never know it. Every detail has been designed to re-create the look and feel of the golden age of luxury train travel. I'll never forget the two-night journey from Singapore to Bangkok by way of Kuala Lumpur and the Cameron Highlands, through 1,250 miles of lush scenery and greenery. In between feasting my eyes on the show outside the window, I was pampered with fine wines and Asian and European haute cuisine in the lavish dining car, where every meal was truly a moving experience!

Dining aboard the fabulous Eastern and Oriental Express. At 70 miles per hour, this is what I call "fast food!"

MELAKA FISH
(Asam Pedas Ikan)

Since I started work on this book, I've been keeping a jar of Malaysian spice paste in the refrigerator so it's always easy to throw together a quick braised or curried dish. I recommend you do the same!

⇰ SPICE PASTE ⇐
1 stalk lemongrass
2 candlenuts or 4 almonds
2 cloves garlic
2 dried red chilies
1 fresh red jalapeño chili, seeded
2 walnut-size shallots
1 teaspoon dried shrimp paste (blachan)
½ teaspoon turmeric powder
¼ cup water

2 tablespoons cooking oil
¼ pound okra pods
¾ pound firm white fish steaks or fillets such as sea bass
½ cup fish bouillon (from bouillon cube and water)
½ cup tamarind water (see page 71)
1 tomato, cut into quarters
2 tablespoons sugar
2 tablespoons soy sauce

Getting Ready
1. Thinly slice bottom 6 inches of lemongrass. Place in a blender with remaining spice paste ingredients and process until smooth.

2. Place a wide frying pan over medium-low heat until hot. Add oil, swirling to coat sides. Add spice paste and cook, stirring, until fragrant, 6 to 8 minutes.

3. Trim okra without piercing pods.

Cooking
1. To spice paste in frying pan add okra, fish, fish bouillon, and tamarind water. Simmer, covered, until fish is opaque, about 10 minutes.

2. Add tomato, sugar, and soy sauce; cook 2 minutes longer.

Makes 4 servings.

MELAKA
Melaka is often called the most historic city in Malaysia, and its eclectic architecture, a blend of Chinese, Portuguese, Dutch, and British influences, reflects its history of occupation by European colonial powers. It was the most important port and trading outpost in the region as early as the 15th century, when the Portuguese took possession of it. The Dutch took control in 1641, and the British in 1795. Today, it's a charming backwater, with Chinese streets and temples, a massive Dutch town hall, and the ruins of a Portuguese church. Personally, I come here for the food. This is one of the best places to sample Eurasian and Nonya specialties.

SQUID SAMBAL

(Sambal Sotong)

I love to balance the tender, chewy texture and mild flavor of squid with a robust sauce—like this one made with a classic Malaysian spice paste enriched with coconut milk and flavored with tangy tamarind. Keep an eye on the squid as it simmers in the sauce, making sure to cook it just until tender. Avoid overcooking or you will wind up with "Rubber Band Sambal"!

⇒ SPICE PASTE ⇐

8 walnut-size shallots
3 cloves garlic
1 teaspoon dried shrimp paste (blachan)
2 tablespoons chili garlic sauce
¹/₄ cup water

1 pound squid, cleaned
2 tablespoons cooking oil
¹/₂ cup unsweetened coconut milk
¹/₄ cup tamarind water (see page 71)
1 tablespoon sugar
¹/₂ teaspoon paprika
Soy sauce or salt
1 fresh red jalapeño chili, sliced

Getting Ready

1. Combine spice paste ingredients in a blender and process until smooth.

2. Cut squid crosswise into ¹/₄-inch slices to make rings; leave tentacles whole.

Cooking

1. Heat a wok over medium-low heat until hot. Add oil, swirling to coat sides. Add spice paste and cook, stirring, until fragrant, 6 to 8 minutes.

2. Add coconut milk, tamarind water, sugar, and paprika, and soy sauce to taste. Simmer over low heat until sauce thickens slightly, about 4 minutes.

3. Add squid and simmer until tender, 2 to 4 minutes, depending on size.

4. Arrange squid on a plate and garnish with chili.

Makes 4 servings.

Palm reading: Inspecting a cluster of freshly harvested palm kernels at a plantation outside Kuala Lumpur.

BUTTER SHRIMP

Two Eurasian touches—butter and toasted coconut—make these succulent stir-fried prawns irresistibly appealing.

³/₄ pound large raw shrimp
2 teaspoons cornstarch
¹/₂ teaspoon salt
2 tablespoons unsweetened
    desiccated coconut
2 tablespoons cooking oil
1 tablespoon butter
1 tablespoon minced garlic
1 fresh red jalapeño chili, seeded
    and minced
1 fresh green jalapeño chili, seeded
    and minced
2 green onions, minced
1 tablespoon rice wine or dry sherry
1 tablespoon soy sauce
    or ¹/₄ teaspoon salt
¹/₂ teaspoon sugar

Getting Ready

1. Shell and devein shrimp, leaving tails intact, then butterfly them. Place in a medium bowl with cornstarch and salt; stir to coat. Let stand for 10 minutes.

Cooking

1. Toast coconut in a wok over low heat, stirring frequently, until golden brown, 4 to 5 minutes. Remove coconut from wok.

2. Place wok over high heat until hot. Add 1¹/₂ tablespoons oil, swirling to coat sides. Add shrimp; stir-fry for 2 minutes. Remove shrimp.

3. Reduce heat to medium. Add remaining ¹/₂ tablespoon oil and butter to wok, swirling to coat sides. Add garlic and stir-fry for 1 minute. Add chilies and green onions; stir-fry for 2 minutes.

4. Return shrimp to wok and add wine, soy sauce, sugar, and toasted coconut. Cook until heated through.

Makes 4 servings.

SHRIMP
MADE SIMPLE
Deveining and butterflying a fresh shrimp is easier than you might think. To devein: Remove the legs and peel off the shell; run a sharp paring knife along the back of the shrimp to expose the black vein (which is actually the intestine); use the tip of the knife to remove the vein, then rinse the shrimp quickly under cold water. To butterfly: Leave the tail on during peeling. Make a deeper cut along the same groove where the vein was, slicing along the entire length of the shrimp, almost all the way through from the back to the other side. Open the shrimp along this cut and flatten it.

SHRIMP ON LEMONGRASS SKEWERS

STALKING THE WILD LEMONGRASS

If you've ever wondered what that mysteriously floral, delicately lemony aroma and flavor is in so many Southeast Asian dishes, wonder no more. It's lemongrass, an herb that grows in slender green stalks that look a bit like woody leeks. Only the bottom 4 to 6 inches of the stalk is used in cooking (unless, of course, you're using the tops for skewers!). After peeling away any outside layers that look dry and fibrous, you can gently crush the stalk and use it to flavor soups (remove it before serving); or mince, pound, or grind it for use in sauces. You can find lemongrass in Asian markets, and these days I'm seeing it in a lot of supermarkets, too. In a pinch, substitute 1 teaspoon fresh lemon peel for one stalk lemongrass.

My mom comes from the "whole hog" school of cooking—in other words, "use every part, from the feet to the ears." She'd love this recipe, because it makes thrifty use of the otherwise unusable lemongrass stalks as skewers. For me, it's the unusual appearance of the skewers and the subtle flavor they impart to the shrimp that make this cooking method so special.

⇒ SPICE PASTE ⇐
6 small dried red chilies
4 walnut-size shallots
5 cloves garlic
2 candlenuts or 4 almonds
1 teaspoon galangal powder
1 teaspoon turmeric powder
1/2 teaspoon dried shrimp paste (blachan)
1/4 cup water

4 stalks lemongrass
3/4 pound large raw shrimp
2 tablespoons cooking oil
1/2 cup unsweetened coconut milk
1 tablespoon packed brown sugar
1 tablespoon lime juice
1 tablespoon soy sauce

Cooking oil
8 wooden skewers

Getting Ready
1. Soak chilies in warm water to cover for 20 minutes; drain. Place in a blender with remaining spice paste ingredients and process until smooth.

2. Cut off bottom 6 inches of lemongrass and save for another use. Cut the remaining woody stalks in half to make 8 skewers.

3. Shell and devein shrimp, leaving tails intact.

4. Place a wok over medium-low heat until hot. Add 2 tablespoons oil, swirling to coat sides. Add spice paste and cook, stirring, until fragrant, 6 to 8 minutes. Add coconut milk, brown sugar, lime juice, and soy sauce. Cook for 1 minute. Let mixture cool; divide in half.

5. Place shrimp in half of the coconut milk mixture; cover and refrigerate for 30 minutes.

Cooking
1. Remove shrimp from marinade and drain briefly. Thread onto skewers and place on an oiled grill 4 to 6 inches above a solid bed of low-glowing coals. Grill, turning and basting with cooking oil, until shrimp turn pink, 3 to 4 minutes on each side. Serve with remaining half of coconut milk mixture.

Makes 8 skewers, 4 servings.

SATAY
(Sate)

Wherever you go in Malaysia, from big cities to little villages, you'll always find a roadside vendor selling satay—skewers of chicken, beef, or lamb marinated in an intense spice paste and grilled over hot coals—made from his own closely guarded secret recipe. Malaysians claim to have invented satay, though it's probably an adaptation of the much older Middle Eastern kebab. Whatever its origin, it has become one of the country's best-loved snacks—and one of mine, too. Serve it with Peanut Sauce (recipe at right), along with pieces of pressed rice cake (page 72) and wedges of cucumber and red onion.

≽ SPICE PASTE ≼

2 stalks lemongrass
4 walnut-size shallots
3 cloves garlic
1 teaspoon fennel seed
1/4 cup water
2 tablespoons packed brown sugar
1 teaspoon ground cumin
1 teaspoon ground coriander
1 teaspoon turmeric powder
1 teaspoon galangal powder
1 tablespoon soy sauce
    or 1/4 teaspoon salt

1 pound boneless beef sirloin or top round, or boneless, skinless chicken
20 bamboo skewers
Satay Peanut Sauce (see page 133)
Lettuce leaves
Sliced cucumber, onion, and red chili

Getting Ready
1. Thinly slice bottom 6 inches of lemongrass. Place in a blender with shallots, garlic, fennel seed, and water; process until smooth. Pour into a medium bowl. Add brown sugar, cumin, coriander, turmeric, galangal, and soy sauce; mix well.

2. Cut meat across the grain into thin diagonal slices, then cut crosswise into 2-inch pieces. Add meat to spice paste and stir to coat. Cover and refrigerate for 2 hours or as long as overnight.

3. Soak skewers in water for 15 minutes or until ready to use.

Cooking
1. Thread 2 pieces of meat on each skewer. Place skewers on a preheated oiled grill. Cook, turning skewers frequently, until meat is seared, 2 to 3 minutes.

2. Serve with satay sauce for dipping, and garnish with lettuce leaves, cucumber, onion, and chili.

Makes 4 servings.

SATAY PEANUT SAUCE
(Kuah Kacang)

This peanut dipping sauce is the classic accompaniment to satay. To make life a little easier, you can substitute ¾ cup peanut butter for the peanuts, but make sure it's chunky and made only from peanuts with no additives. Before adding the peanut butter to the wok, blend it with about half of the water.

⪢ SPICE PASTE ⪡
1 stalk lemongrass
1 walnut-size shallot
2 cloves garlic
½ teaspoon ground cumin
½ teaspoon ground coriander
½ teaspoon galangal powder
¼ cup water

1 cup roasted peanuts
3 tablespoons cooking oil
1 cup water
¼ cup packed brown sugar
3 tablespoons chili garlic sauce
2 tablespoons soy sauce or
⠀⠀½ teaspoon salt

Getting Ready
1. Thinly slice bottom 6 inches of lemongrass. Place in a blender with remaining spice paste ingredients and process until smooth.

2. In a food processor, chop peanuts very fine.

Cooking
1. Place a wok over medium-low heat until hot. Add oil, swirling to coat sides. Add spice paste and cook, stirring, until fragrant, 6 to 8 minutes.

2. Add water, peanuts, brown sugar, chili garlic sauce, and soy sauce; stir until evenly blended. Bring to a boil. Reduce heat and simmer, stirring frequently, until sauce is slightly thickened, 4 to 5 minutes.

3. Serve with satay for dipping.

Makes about 2 cups.

POSTCARD FROM KUALA KANGSAR
While filming in Kuala Kangsar, the royal residence of the Sultan of Perak, my crew and I caught our first glimpse of the Ubadiah Mosque. It was evening, and as we rounded a corner, the gold-domed minarets suddenly loomed before us, catching the last rays of sunlight. The streets grew silent as a muezzin chanted the Muslim call to worship. And we were silent, too, as we stared in awe at this spectacular symbol of the meaning— and the majesty—of Islam in Malaysia.

The Ubadiah Mosque in Kuala Kangsar.

TANDOORI CHICKEN
(*Ayam Tandoori*)

TANDOORI

In Malaysia and Singapore, it's not unusual to find North Indian restaurants specializing in tandoori cooking, and I am all fired up about this wonderful technique! A tandoor is basically a huge clay vat with a narrow opening on top. Originally, this vat was buried underground for insulation, with just the opening exposed. In restaurants, it's usually surrounded by thick plaster walls. Burning coals are placed at the bottom of the tandoor, which gets so hot it can cook a small chicken in a just a few minutes. Marinated meats are placed on long metal skewers and suspended inside the tandoor above the coals. The intense, dry heat sears and crisps the outside of the food, leaving the inside juicy and tender.

One of the most famous of all Indian dishes throughout the world, tandoori chicken gets its name from the clay oven (tandoor) in which it is cooked. If you don't have time to install a tandoor oven in your backyard (and these days, who does?), here's an easy way to make this succulent, addictively flavorful chicken dish on the barbecue.

1½ pounds chicken thighs

⇒ MARINADE ⇐
⅓ cup unflavored yogurt
3 tablespoons lemon juice
1 tablespoon soy sauce
1 tablespoon minced garlic
1 tablespoon minced ginger
1 tablespoon chopped cilantro
1 tablespoon chopped green onion
2 teaspoons sugar
2 teaspoons chili garlic sauce
½ teaspoon turmeric powder
½ teaspoon ground coriander
¼ teaspoon ground cardamom
¼ teaspoon white pepper

Cooking oil
Lime wedges
Mint sprigs

Getting Ready
1. Place chicken, skin side down, on a cutting board. With a sharp knife, cut slits ½ inch deep along both sides of the bone.

2. Combine marinade ingredients in a large bowl. Add chicken and stir to coat. Cover and refrigerate for 2 hours or up to overnight.

Cooking
1. Lift chicken from marinade and drain briefly. Brush with oil. Arrange chicken, skin side down, on a lightly oiled grill 4 to 6 inches above a solid bed of low-glowing coals. Cook, turning and basting occasionally with oil, until meat is no longer pink when slashed near bone, about 30 minutes.

2. Arrange on a platter and garnish with lime wedges and mint sprigs.

Makes 4 servings.

Fresh turmeric

CAPTAIN'S CURRY
(Kari Kapitan)

This creamy curried chicken is one of my favorite Nonya specialties. It originated in old Melaka and got its name from the Kapitan China, a high-ranking Chinese official who served as the liaison between the Chinese community and the Malay rulers of Melaka.

⇒ SPICE PASTE ⇐
2 stalks lemongrass
4 walnut-size shallots
6 fresh red jalapeño chilies, seeded
2 cloves garlic
8 candlenuts or 16 almonds
1/4 cup water

2 pounds chicken legs or thighs
About 1 teaspoon salt
3 tablespoons cooking oil
1 teaspoon turmeric powder
1 can (13 1/2 oz.) unsweetened
    coconut milk
1/4 cup water
2 to 3 tablespoons lime juice

Getting Ready
1. Thinly slice bottom 6 inches of lemongrass. Place in a blender with remaining spice paste ingredients and process until smooth.

Cooking
1. Season chicken with 1 teaspoon salt. Place a deep frying pan over medium-high heat until hot. Add 2 tablespoons of the oil, swirling to coat sides. Add chicken and cook, turning as needed, until browned on all sides, 2 to 3 minutes per side. Remove chicken from pan.

2. Reduce heat to medium-low. Return pan to heat and add remaining 1 tablespoon oil. Add spice paste and cook, stirring, until fragrant, 6 to 8 minutes. Stir in turmeric, coconut milk, and water. Return chicken to pan. Cover and simmer until chicken is no longer pink near bone, 40 to 45 minutes.

3. Just before serving, stir in lime juice and salt to taste.

Makes 6 servings.

SHEDDING LIGHT ON THE CANDLENUT
Many Malaysian and Indonesian spice pastes, sambals, and curries include candlenut—a small, round nut indigenous to the region—for richness, body, and flavor. Why the nutty name? These waxy nuts have such a high oil content that some tribal people actually pound them up and use them to make candles with palm leaves for wicks. You can buy candlenuts shelled and roasted in Asian markets; or substitute almonds, Brazil nuts, or macadamia nuts.

INDIAN LAMB CURRY
(Korma Kambing)

A korma is a North Indian braised curry, often made with lamb or chicken, that simmers slowly so that the meat absorbs much of the liquid, and becomes tender and deeply infused with flavor.

ALL HANDS ON DISH
Many people will tell you that curries taste better when eaten with the hands, the traditional Indian way. I am one of them. There's something about touching food with your fingertips and feeling its textures that makes the eating experience complete. Besides, it's fun. And you save time washing silverware! Some tips on etiquette if you find yourself eating with your hands anywhere in Asia: Wash your hands first. Use only the right hand, never the left, which is considered unclean (though you can use it to hold your drinking glass). Pick up food with your fingertips, hold it in the curve of the bent fingers, and use your thumb to push it into your mouth. Try not to get food on your palm or below the second knuckle of your fingers. And remember, it's rude to lick or suck your fingers, no matter how great the food tastes!

⇒ SPICE PASTE ⇐
4 walnut-size shallots
4 cloves garlic
3 slices ginger, each the size of a quarter
4 fresh red or green jalapeño chilies, seeded
1/4 cup water

1/2 cup unflavored yogurt
1 tablespoon curry powder
1/2 teaspoon ground cardamom
1 cinnamon stick
1 pound boneless lean lamb
1 medium onion
8 okra pods
2 medium potatoes
2 tablespoons cooking oil
4 cups water
3 tablespoons soy sauce or 3/4 teaspoon salt
2 tablespoons lemon juice
1 tomato, cut into wedges

Getting Ready
1. Combine spice paste ingredients in a blender and process until smooth.

2. Place paste in a medium bowl and add yogurt, curry powder, cardamom, and cinnamon stick; mix well. Cut meat into 1-inch cubes. Add to yogurt mixture and stir to coat. Cover and refrigerate for 1 hour.

3. Cut onion in half lengthwise, then thinly slice crosswise. Trim okra stems without piercing pods. Peel potatoes and cut into 1-inch cubes.

Cooking
1. Place a 3-quart pan over medium-high heat until hot. Add oil, swirling to coat sides. Add onion and cook until soft, 4 to 5 minutes. Add meat and marinade; cook, turning, for 3 minutes. Add water and bring to a boil. Reduce heat, cover, and simmer until meat is tender, about 1 hour.

2. Add okra, potatoes, soy sauce, and lemon juice; cover and simmer until potatoes are tender when pierced, about 20 minutes. Add tomato; cover and simmer until heated through, about 2 minutes. Discard cinnamon stick. Ladle stew into bowls.

Makes 4 servings.

BEEF STEW IN ONION-FLAVORED SAUCE

Here's a hearty beef curry that goes together quickly, leaving you free for other things as it simmers on the stovetop. Serve it with plenty of rice.

1 1/2 pounds boneless beef chuck
2 tablespoons soy sauce
1 tablespoon cornstarch
4 to 6 small dried red chilies
1/4 cup warm water
2 medium onions
2 stalks lemongrass
2 tablespoons cooking oil
4 cups water
2 tablespoons lemon juice
1 cinnamon stick
10 dried curry leaves (optional)
2 tablespoons black bean garlic
    sauce
2 tablespoons oyster-flavored
    sauce
1 tablespoon sugar

Getting Ready

1. Cut meat into 1-inch cubes. Place in a bowl with soy sauce and cornstarch; stir to coat. Let stand for 30 minutes.

2. Crumble dried chilies into a blender; add warm water and let stand for 20 minutes to soften. Process chilies with water until smooth.

3. Cut onions into 1/4-inch cubes. Crush the bottom 6 inches of lemongrass stalks.

Cooking

1. Heat oil in a 3-quart pan over medium-high heat. Add meat and cook, turning, until browned on all sides, 4 to 5 minutes. Remove meat from pan.

2. Reduce heat to medium. Add onions and cook, stirring once or twice, until onions are soft, 4 to 5 minutes. Add puréed chilies and cook for 1 minute.

3. Return meat to pan and add water, lemon juice, cinnamon stick, curry leaves, and lemongrass. Bring to a boil; reduce heat, cover, and simmer until meat is tender, 1 to 1 1/4 hours.

4. Stir in black bean sauce, oyster-flavored sauce, and sugar; simmer, uncovered, until sauce thickens slightly, 10 to 15 minutes.

5. Ladle meat and sauce into a serving bowl.

Makes 6 servings.

JOURNEY TO THE WILD, WILD EAST

I call the state of Sabah, on the eastern side of Borneo, the "wild, wild east" of Malaysia. This is a rugged, mountainous land of lumberjacks and frontier cowboys (or maybe I should say "water buffalo boys!"), where horses and four-wheel-drive vehicles are often the only way to get around. On Sundays in Kota Belud, everybody gets together at the tamu, an open-air market and meeting place, to catch up on gossip and buy and sell everything from herbal remedies to livestock.

Horsing around in a bajau (cowboy) outfit in Sabah. (The tennis shoes are not traditional.)

VENISON ON A SIZZLING HOT PLATE
(Rempah Ratus)

Sarawak, on the island of Borneo, is the largest state in Malaysia, and its lush rain forests are teeming with more than 9,000 types of flowering plants. You can see hundreds of kinds of birds and wildlife here. And for the adventurous, there's even a restaurant that specializes in the exotic wild game of the region, from venison and boar to fruit bats. That's where I learned to make this tasty venison dish, sizzling with chilies, onions, lime, and curry. If venison is not to your liking (or the price is too "dear"), you can substitute a tender cut of beef.

⇒ MARINADE ⇐
1 tablespoon oyster-flavored sauce
2 teaspoons cornstarch

3/4 pound venison steaks, cut 1/2 inch
    thick; or flank steak
1 1/2 tablespoons cooking oil
1 green onion, cut into 1-inch
    lengths
2 fresh red jalapeño chilies, thinly
    sliced
2 cloves garlic, thinly sliced
1 small onion, cut into 1/2-inch cubes
2 teaspoons lime juice
1 teaspoon curry powder
    or 2 tablespoons curry sauce

Getting Ready
1. Combine marinade ingredients in a bowl. Cut meat across the grain into 1/8-inch-thick slices. Add to marinade and stir to coat. Let stand for 10 minutes.

Cooking
1. Place a wok over high heat until hot. Add 1 tablespoon of the oil, swirling to coat sides. Add green onion, chilies, and garlic; stir-fry until fragrant, about 10 seconds. Add meat and stir-fry until barely pink, about 2 minutes. Remove all from wok.

2. Heat remaining 1/2-tablespoon oil in wok. Add onion and stir-fry until tender-crisp, about 2 minutes. Return meat to wok; add lime juice and curry powder. Cook until heated through, 30 seconds.

3. Place on a serving plate. (If you wish to make the dish sizzle, serve on a preheated cast-iron serving plate.)

Makes 4 servings.

LONGHOUSE LIFE
Many of the Iban, Dayak, and Daru tribespeople of Sarawak have moved to cities and towns or gone to work in the timber industry. But in the more than 1,500 longhouse communities of the region, you can still get a glimpse of tribal life the way it used to be. I'll never forget the sight of these simple huts made of bamboo and tin, perched way up in the air on tall stilts to guard against floods and wild animals— or the warm hospitality of the families who live there. Home to many generations all living together, the houses are attached in stair-stepped chains along riverbanks. I was truly moved by the simplicity of life and the spirit of communal cooperation here. These structures may be primitive, but they are an enduring symbol of the power of family and the rich heritage of tribal tradition.

NOODLES IN RICH COCONUT MILK
(Laksa Lemak)

Laksa lemak, which began as a Nonya creation in Melaka, is fun to eat. The taste buds are simultaneously piqued by the spicy chili broth and soothed by the creamy coconut milk. It's often eaten as a midmorning snack. Talk about a wake-up call!

8 ounces fresh Chinese egg noodles
4 ounces dried rice stick noodles
1/2 of a 14 oz. package regular tofu
Cooking oil for deep-frying
1 teaspoon cooking oil
2 eggs, lightly beaten

⇒ SPICE PASTE ⇐
1 stalk lemongrass
3 walnut-size shallots
2 fresh red jalapeño chilies, seeded
3 candlenuts or 6 almonds
1 teaspoon galangal powder
1/2 teaspoon turmeric powder
1/2 teaspoon dried shrimp paste
    (blachan)
1/4 cup water

2 tablespoons cooking oil
1 cup unsweetened coconut milk
4 cups water
1/4 cup soy sauce

⇒ GARNISHES ⇐
1/4 pound bean sprouts, blanched
1/4 pound cooked medium shrimp
1 large chicken breast half,
    poached and shredded
1/2 of an English cucumber, cut into
    matchstick strips
2 fresh red jalapeño chilies, thinly
    sliced
Lemon or lime wedges

Getting Ready

1. Cook egg noodles according to package directions. Drain, rinse, and drain again. Soak rice stick noodles in a warm water, for about 30 minutes; drain.

2. Drain tofu; cut into 1-inch cubes. Place between paper towels and gently press out excess water. In a wok, heat oil for deep-frying to 350°F. Deep-fry tofu, turning once, until golden on all sides, 3 to 4 minutes. Drain on paper towels.

3. Make omelet shred garnish: See Getting Ready, step 3, on page 141.

4. Thinly slice bottom 6 inches of lemongrass. Place in a blender with remaining spice paste ingredients and process until smooth.

Cooking

1. Place a wok over medium-low heat. Add oil, swirling to coat sides. Add spice paste and cook, stirring, until fragrant, 6 to 8 minutes. Add coconut milk and cook for 3 minutes. Add water and soy sauce.

2. To serve, put noodles in a serving bowl. Pour soup over and arrange garnishes decoratively on top.

Makes 4 to 6 servings.

FRIED RICE NOODLES

(Meehoon Goreng)

Here's my version of one of the most popular quick-fried noodle dishes in Malaysia and Singapore.

¼ of a 14-ounce package firm tofu
Cooking oil for deep-frying
1 teaspoon cooking oil
2 eggs, lightly beaten
2 tablespoons dried shrimp
¼ pound medium raw shrimp
6 ounces dried rice stick noodles
3 tablespoons cooking oil
2 cloves garlic, minced
1 fresh red jalapeño chili, thinly
    sliced
1 tablespoon chili garlic sauce
¼ pound bean sprouts
2 ounces garlic chives or 4 green
    onions, thinly sliced
3 tablespoons oyster-flavored
    sauce
¼ teaspoon white pepper
¼ English cucumber, sliced

Getting Ready

1. Drain tofu; cut into ¾-inch cubes. Place between paper towels and gently press out excess water.

2. In a wok, heat oil for deep-frying to 350°F. Add tofu and deep-fry, turning once, until golden on all sides, 3 to 4 minutes. Remove from oil and drain on paper towels.

3. Place a nonstick 8- to 9-inch frying pan over medium heat until hot. Brush with ½ teaspoon cooking oil. Add half of eggs and cook until lightly browned on bottom and set on top, about 1 minute. Turn over and cook for 5 seconds; remove from pan. Repeat with ½ teaspoon oil and remaining egg. Roll omelets into cylinders and cut into ¼-inch-wide strips.

4. Soak dried shrimp in warm water to cover for 20 minutes; drain and finely chop. Shell and devein raw shrimp.

5. Soak rice stick noodles in warm water until soft, about 30 minutes; drain.

Cooking

1. Heat a wok over high heat until hot. Add the 3 tablespoons oil, swirling to coat sides. Add dried shrimp, garlic, and chili; stir-fry until fragrant, about 10 seconds. Add chili garlic sauce and raw shrimp; stir-fry for 2 minutes. Add rice stick noodles, bean sprouts, garlic chives, oyster-flavored sauce, and pepper. Stir-fry until bean sprouts are limp, about 2 minutes. Add tofu and omelet strips; cook, stirring, until heated through, about 1 minute.

2. Garnish with cucumber slices.

Makes 4 servings.

RICE NOODLE NEWS

Dried rice noodles tend to come in two widths, thin (sold as "rice vermicelli") and wide (which are about as wide as fettuccine and are sometimes called "rice sticks.") To use them in a soup or a stir-fry, begin by soaking them in warm water to soften (30 minutes is usually sufficient), then gently untangle them before draining. Thin dried rice noodles are deep-fried (without soaking) to create those fluffy nests and garnishes you sometimes see in Asian restaurants. Separate the noodles inside a bag (so they don't fly all over the place), and deep-fry them a handful at a time in hot oil. They will puff up immediately and dramatically on contact with the oil; it's a thrilling trick, so make sure you have an audience!

FRAGRANT LENTIL RICE
(Nasi Parpu)

Rice is the basic staple of the Malaysian diet—but how it is cooked is anything but basic. The infinitely varied nasi (the word for cooked rice) dishes of Malaysia are perfumed with spices, simmered with coconut milk and nuts, or combined with legumes and vegetables, as in this tasty dish. Serve it as the centerpiece of a meatless meal (lentils and rice make a complete protein), or as a side with "saucy" dishes, such as Captain's Curry (page 135) or Beef Stew in Onion-Flavored Sauce (page 137).

1/3 cup lentils
1 cup long-grain rice
2 tablespoons cooking oil
2 teaspoons minced ginger
1 walnut-size shallot, chopped
1 green onion, sliced
2 1/4 cups water
1/2 carrot, cut into 1/4-inch cubes
8 green beans, cut into 1/4-inch pieces
2 tablespoons soy sauce or 1/2 teaspoon salt

Getting Ready

1. Soak lentils in warm water to cover for 30 minutes; drain. Wash and drain rice.

Cooking

1. Heat oil in a 2-quart pan over medium heat. Add ginger, shallot, and green onion. Cook, stirring, for 2 minutes.

2. Add lentils and rice; mix well. Add water and bring to a boil. Cook, uncovered, until craterlike holes appear on the rice, 8 to 10 minutes.

3. Reduce heat to low. Add carrot and green beans; cover and continue cooking until liquid is absorbed and rice is tender, about 15 minutes.

4. Add soy sauce and mix well.

Makes 4 to 6 servings.

SCENTED RICE
(Nasi Minyak)

A DIFFERENT KIND OF STEAMER TRUNK

I thought I knew all about cooking rice until I visited a remote longhouse village of the Daru tribe, deep in the jungle of Sarawak, where I tasted some of the most tender, moist rice I've ever had. Then I discovered the secret: It had been cooked in bamboo! Cooking alongside the tribespeople, I learned how to wash and soak glutinous rice, then stuff it into thick, green trunks of bamboo, seal the ends with leaves, and prop the trunks up over the smoldering embers of an open fire to slowly steam. The same method is also used for cooking chicken and meat, which might be seasoned with pounded garlic, shallots, and lemongrass, then mixed with chopped cassava leaves and stuffed into lengths of bamboo and slowly steamed to tender perfection.

Baking rice in bamboo in the longhouse village of the Daru tribe in Sarawak.

A rich Malaysian pilaf, cooked with butter and coconut milk and perfumed with aromatic cloves, cinnamon, and cardamom, nasi minyak (literally "oiled rice") is often served at wedding feasts and other celebrations. It's the perfect accompaniment to spicy curries and sambals.

1¼ cups long-grain rice
1 tablespoon butter
2 teaspoons cooking oil
1 teaspoon minced ginger
1 teaspoon minced garlic
1 small red onion, thinly sliced
1 whole star anise
1 cinnamon stick
4 whole cloves
2 cardamom pods, crushed
1¼ cups water
½ cup unsweetened coconut milk
1 tablespoon minced green onion
   or cilantro
2 tablespoons golden raisins
2 tablespoons sliced almonds

Getting Ready

1. Wash and drain rice.

Cooking

1. Melt butter with oil in a 2-quart pan over medium heat. Add ginger, garlic, red onion, star anise, cinnamon stick, cloves, and cardamom. Cook, stirring, for 2 minutes. Add rice and cook, stirring, until lightly toasted, about 2 minutes.

2. Add water and coconut milk. Bring to a boil. Cover, reduce heat, and simmer until rice is tender and liquid is absorbed, 18 to 20 minutes.

3. Place rice in a serving bowl and sprinkle with green onion, raisins, and almonds.

Makes 4 to 6 servings.

JACKFRUIT PUDDING

(Bubur Nangka)

Malaysian desserts are often based on tapioca (from the root of the cassava plant) or sago (a similar starch extracted from palm trees), sweetened with sugar and tropical fruit. My creamy jackfruit and tapioca pudding is equally good warm or chilled. If you can't find canned jackfruit, substitute canned or fresh papaya or fresh mango. A tapioca tip: Once it cooks to the point of translucency and begins to cool, don't stir it. Stirring at this point can alter the structure of the starch chains and quickly transform tapioca from a velvety pudding to a stringy mess!

$^1\!/_2$ cup small ($^1\!/_8$ in.) pearl tapioca
I cup cold water
I can (20 oz.) jackfruit
I can (13$^1\!/_2$ oz.) unsweetened
    coconut milk
I$^3\!/_4$ cups warm water
$^3\!/_4$ cup sugar

Getting Ready

1. Soak tapioca in cold water for 30 minutes (most of water will be absorbed); drain.

2. Drain jackfruit. Finely dice 1 or 2 slices and set aside for garnish; cut the rest into $^1\!/_2$-inch cubes.

Cooking

1. Combine coconut milk, warm water, and sugar in a heavy saucepan. Cook, stirring, over medium heat, until sugar dissolves. Add tapioca and bring to a boil. Reduce heat to medium-low and cook, stirring, until mixture thickens and tapioca becomes translucent, about 15 minutes.

2. Remove from heat and stir in cubed jackfruit.

3. Serve warm in individual bowls garnished with diced jackfruit. Or let cool, cover, and refrigerate until chilled.

Makes 6 servings.

YOU DON'T KNOW JACKFRUIT?

If you've never tried jackfruit, do! Its yellow-orange flesh reminds me of a cross between a banana, a pineapple, and a mango. Jackfruit trees are native to the rain forests of Malaysia and India. In a single year, one tree can bear hundreds of gigantic fruits, each weighing in at up to 100 pounds! The oddly fermented smell of a fresh, ripe jackfruit can be off-putting, to put it mildly, but don't worry, you're not likely to find it fresh. Canned jackfruit, sold in many Asian markets, has a sweet, mild aroma and flavor.

As jackfruits go, this one is on the small side!

145

NONYA PANCAKES
(Kueh Dadar Nonya)

These tender pancakes, rolled around a filling of sweetened coconut and walnuts, make a delicate dessert or brunch dish.

⇝ PANCAKES ⇜
1 large egg
1½ cups water
¼ cup milk
1 cup flour
¼ teaspoon salt
3 or 4 drops green food color

⇝ FILLING ⇜
1 tablespoon butter
2 cups sweetened shredded coconut
¼ cup water
2 tablespoons packed brown sugar
½ teaspoon vanilla extract
¼ cup finely chopped walnuts

1 tablespoon butter

⇝ SAUCE ⇜
1 cup unsweetened coconut milk
½ cup water
⅓ cup sugar
1 tablespoon cornstarch dissolved
    in 2 tablespoons water

¼ cup chopped walnuts (optional)

Getting Ready

1. In a bowl, blend egg, water, and milk with a wire whisk. Add flour and salt; mix until smooth. Add color to tint batter pale green. Pour batter through a strainer into a bowl.

2. To make filling: Melt butter in a wide frying pan over medium heat. Add coconut and cook, stirring, until golden brown, 4 to 5 minutes. Add water, brown sugar, vanilla, and nuts. Continue to cook until water has evaporated and mixture is golden brown, 2 to 3 minutes.

Cooking

1. Heat a nonstick 8-inch frying pan over medium heat. Brush with about ¼ teaspoon butter. Add ¼ cup batter to pan; tilt pan in all directions so batter covers entire surface. Cook until pancake is set and bottom is lightly brown, about 2 minutes; turn over and cook until lightly browned, about 1 minute longer. Remove from pan; repeat to make remaining pancakes.

2. To prepare sauce: In a small pan, combine coconut milk, water, and sugar. Cook, stirring, over medium-low heat until sugar dissolves. Add cornstarch solution and cook, stirring, until sauce bubbles and thickens slightly. Remove sauce from heat.

3. To assemble, place about ¼ cup filling in center of each pancake. Roll to enclose filling; place on a serving plate. Drizzle sauce over pancakes; garnish with chopped nuts, if used.

Makes 8 pancakes.

PANDAN PANACHE

The pale green color of many Malaysian desserts comes from the addition of the pandan leaf (also known as the screwpine or pandanus leaf), a favorite Nonya seasoning that also imparts a delicately grassy flavor. Pandan leaves are long and spiny, and grow on palmlike shrubs. Fresh Hawaiian pandan leaves can sometimes be found in Asian markets. If you can't track them down, I suggest substituting a touch of green food coloring. (Just don't tell any Nonyas you may know.)

STEAMED BANANA-NUT CAKES
(*Lepat Pisang*)

I go bananas for these exotic tropical pudding cakes made with tapioca, bananas, peanuts, and coconut, steamed in banana leaf cups.

THE ENDURING DURIAN

Durian is a mystery to me. It's a brownish yellow fruit covered with pointed spines that's eaten all over Southeast Asia. Once you open a durian, you understand immediately why the outside looks so foreboding. The flesh smells like a combination of cheese, onions, wine, and a few other things I wouldn't want to discuss in a cookbook. This fruit is the ultimate acquired taste, and I must confess, it's a taste I have yet to acquire. But durian has legions of loyal fans, who swear that once you begin eating, you stop noticing the smell and you can appreciate the custardy, sweet flavor.

2 tablespoons small (1/8 in.) pearl tapioca
2 ripe medium bananas
3 tablespoons coarsely chopped peanuts
2 tablespoons sweetened grated coconut
2 1/2 tablespoons sugar
3 tablespoons cornstarch
4 banana leaves, each cut into a 4- by 6-inch rectangle
4 pieces jackfruit, each about 1 by 2 inches

Getting Ready

1. Soak tapioca in warm water to cover for 45 minutes; drain.

2. Peel bananas and mash them in a small bowl. Add peanuts, coconut, sugar, cornstarch, and tapioca; mix well.

3. Dip banana leaves into a pot of boiling water for 3 to 4 seconds to soften; wipe dry, (or if using frozen banana leaves - thaw).

4. Fold each banana leaf into a 3- by 5-inch cup. Secure folds with wooden picks.

5. Divide mixture into 4 portions. To make each cake, spoon 1 portion into a banana leaf cup. Top with 1 piece of jackfruit.

Cooking

1. Prepare a wok for steaming (see page 14). Steam cakes until set and no longer sticky, about 10 minutes. Serve warm or chilled.

Makes 4 servings.

My friend Datin Zabidatul Ali Piah and I in front of the Palace of the Sultan of Perak. We're smiling now, but that's because we haven't cut open the durian.

PINEAPPLE GINGER SODA

It's hot and humid in most of Malaysia most of the time. To help beat the unrelenting heat, street vendors sell refreshing concoctions of fresh fruits and juices, often spiked with lime or ginger and sweetened with sugar syrup. I like my version so much I'm thinking about going into the roadside concession business myself! Serve this in tall glasses over ice, preferably while sitting in the shade of a palm tree. For an extra "punch," you can add rum, tequila, or champagne.

½ fresh pineapple
1 piece ginger (3 oz.), about
    1½ inches across and
    3½ to 4 inches long
1 cup water
1½ cups sugar
2 tablespoons lime juice
1½ cups lemon-lime soda
Ice cubes

Getting Ready

1. Peel and core pineapple; dice flesh to make 2 cups fruit. Peel and thinly slice ginger.

Cooking

1. Combine ginger, water, and sugar in a 2-quart pan; cook over medium heat until syrup simmers and sugar is dissolved. Simmer for 4 minutes longer. Let syrup cool.

2. In a blender, process syrup until ginger is finely chopped. Strain syrup and discard ginger. Return syrup to blender; add pineapple and lime juice. Process until pineapple is puréed.

3. Pour into a large pitcher and chill until ready to serve.

4. Just before serving, stir in lemon-lime soda. Serve over ice.

Makes 6 servings.

A TASTE OF THE HIGH LIFE

The best way to escape the heat in Malaysia is to head for the hills—the Cameron Highlands, that is. A series of hill stations that rise more than a mile above sea level in the center of the Malay Peninsula near Ipoh, the Highlands are a tropical paradise of jungles, waterfalls, exotic plants and flowers, and acres of lush green tea plantations.

In the Camaron Highlands, a tribal hunter gives me some "tips" on the art of the blowgun.

The Philippines The Latin Quarter of Asia

How do you get to the Philippines? Go to Spain, make a right, and keep going, all the way to Southeast Asia.

Geographically speaking, the more than 7,000 islands that make up the Philippine archipelago stretch from just below Taiwan to just above Borneo. But culturally the place feels more like the Latin Quarter of Asia, thanks to the Spanish, who showed up in the late 16th century and stayed for more than 300 years.

Traveling in the Philippines can be delightfully "dis-Orienting." One minute you're watching water buffalo plow emerald green rice paddies, and the next you're in the middle of a fiesta in a town square that could pass for Mexico.

This is the only country in Asia where Roman Catholicism is the dominant religion, and other legacies of the Spanish influence are everywhere: in surnames like Santos and Ramos and city names like Valenzuela and Las Piñas, in Spanish-style buildings with terra-cotta tile roofs, and in the kitchen in foods like the famous *adobo* and *escabeche*.

Luzon

Manila

Philippines

Mindanao

plates. You don't need to be a geologist to know that this makes for some pretty shaky ground. There is earthquake activity somewhere in the islands every other day! Not to mention the notoriously active volcanoes that continue to bring tragedy and devastation.

But plenty of other ingredients have also found their way into the lively stew that is Filipino culture. Malays, Indonesians, and Chinese have each added flavors of their own. The United States governed here from the turn of the century until the late 1940s, and today the Philippines remains the fourth largest English-speaking country in the world.

And then there's the land itself—a land that is more alive and constantly changing than any place I have ever seen. That's because the Philippines lies along the edge of the Pacific "Ring of Fire," at the juncture of two massive undersea

One minute you're watching water buffalo plow emerald green rice paddies, and the next you're in a town square that could pass for Mexico.

Filipinos are no strangers to upheaval, both geological and political. Yet through it all they remain warmly hospitable and delightfully good-humored. Their musical laughter is contagious, and they are so fun-loving they think I am too serious!

Filipino Foods and Flavors

Along with rice, fish—often simply grilled over an open fire—is the main dietary staple of the Philippines. No surprise there: The islands have more miles of coastline than any country on earth—enough to stretch almost completely around the world! Freshwater fish from inland rivers are also plentiful.

Signs of welcome and hospitality are everywhere in the Philippines.

When you leave the coast and head inland, you find more meat on the menu, especially the national favorite, pork (or, in the case of Muslims, goat), as well as chicken and duck. Root vegetables, onions, and garlic show up in many dishes, along with coconut and all kinds of wild and wonderful tropical fruits. From the more than three centuries of Spanish colonial rule come techniques like sautéing foods in oil or lard; ingredients like cheese (made from water buffalo's milk), *chorizo* sausage, garlic, and tomatoes; and dishes like *pochero*, a rich stew of beef, pork, chicken, or a combination of all three (cooking several meats together is very Filipino), simmered with sausage and vegetables.

The Philippines lie along the edge of the Pacific "Ring of Fire." There is earthquake activity in the islands every other day.

Picnicking with newfound local friends in the shadow of the Mayon volcano.

My favorite Spanish culinary legacy is the *merienda*, a morning or midafternoon snack with a Spanish accent. There are sweet cakes and pastries along with savory Spanish-style tidbits and *tapas*—like shrimp or sweet potato fritters, cheese buns, stir-fried noodles, and sandwiches—all washed down with coffee and frothy whipped hot chocolate. Now *that's* a snack!

The famous Filipino sweet tooth may have Spanish "roots" as well. Confections of all kinds—from baked goods and candies to ice cream, fritters, and *flan* custards—are much loved here, and this is one of the few parts of Asia where they're actually served at the end of the meal, as dessert.

My countrymen from China—traders and immigrants who came in search of work and opportunity—have left their mark on the food of the Philippines, too. Thanks to them, stir-frying is an

Helping out with the rice harvest.

important part of the cuisine, along with soy sauce, noodles (*pancit*), dumplings (*siomai*), and the world-renowned Filipino egg roll, *lumpia*.

Meanwhile, this *is* Southeast Asia, and there are plenty of indigenous Malay culinary influences to remind you of that, from fish sauce (*patis*) and shrimp or fish paste (*bagoong*) to the coconut and coconut milk that enrich so many dishes.

On a sour note, palm vinegar, tamarind, and *calamansi* (a small native citrus fruit) lend their tart flavors to *adobo* stews, pickled fish dishes, and *sinigang*, a tangy soup with seafood or chicken.

For the most part, Filipino food is mildly spiced—especially the northern-style cooking of Manila and the rest of the is

land of Luzon, where the Spanish influence is strongest. Though in the more Muslim- and Malay-style cooking of the southern Philippines, chilies are used.

Wherever I traveled in the islands, from Manila to a remote tribal village in the Cordillera Central, I found that food, family, friendship, and hospitality all go hand in hand. Like most things in the Philippines, eating is relaxed and informal, and meals are full of warmth and good humor. This is a true home-style cuisine in the best sense of the word. And once you discover its charms, it's sure to find a place in your home, too.

Hitching a ride on a six kid-power hand cart in Laguna.

FRESH LUMPIA
(*Lumpiang Sariwa*)

Lumpia are among the most famous of all Filipino dishes. These are not the fried, eggroll-like lumpia you may have tried, but a lighter, home-style version, in which delicate egg pancakes are rolled around lettuce and a tasty chicken, shrimp, and vegetable filling. If you have adventurous guests, let everybody make their own lumpia right at the table—it's a great way to get a dinner party rolling!

IT'S A WRAP

If you don't have the time to make pancake wrappers for fresh lumpia, you can also use Vietnamese rice paper wrappers, which are sold in many Asian grocery stores. Look for round wrappers about 8 inches across. They're paper-thin, translucent, and brittle, with a delicate lattice pattern from the woven drying racks on which they're made. To soften them, dip them briefly in a bowl of warm water, shaking off the excess before you put the wrapper on your plate. In a few seconds, the wrapper will be soft enough to roll around the lettuce and the filling.

⇒ WRAPPERS ⇐
2 large eggs
1¼ cups water
½ cup cornstarch
½ cup flour
⅛ teaspoon salt

About 3 tablespoons cooking oil

⇒ FILLING ⇐
½ cup julienned onion
1 teaspoon minced garlic
1 boneless, skinless chicken breast half, thinly sliced
¼ pound medium raw shrimp, shelled, deveined, and halved
1½ cups finely julienned jicama
½ small carrot, finely julienned
2 green onions, finely julienned
2 teaspoons oyster-flavored sauce
1 teaspoon Filipino fish sauce (patis)
¼ teaspoon black pepper

5 tender lettuce leaves

Getting Ready
1. Prepare wrappers: In a bowl, whisk together eggs, water, cornstarch, flour, and salt until smooth. Strain batter.

2. Place a nonstick 8-inch omelet pan over medium heat until hot; brush with ¼ teaspoon oil. Pour ¼ cup batter into pan; tilt pan so batter covers entire surface. Cook until edge of wrapper is lightly browned and surface looks dry, about 45 seconds. Loosen edge with a spatula, turn wrapper, and cook 10 seconds longer. Turn wrapper out of pan onto a plate. Repeat to use all batter.

Cooking
1. Prepare filling: Place a wok over high heat until hot. Add 1 tablespoon oil, swirling to coat sides. Add onion and garlic; stir-fry for 30 seconds. Add chicken and shrimp; stir-fry for 2 minutes. Remove from pan. Heat 1 tablespoon oil. Add jicama and carrot; stir-fry for 1 minute. Add green onions; cook until vegetables are tender-crisp, about 2 minutes. Return chicken mixture to pan; add oyster-flavored sauce, fish sauce, and pepper; cook for 1 minute. Cool.

2. Cut lettuce in half lengthwise. For each lumpia, place a piece of lettuce on wrapper. Spoon about ⅓ cup filling into center of wrapper. Fold bottom third of wrapper over filling, then fold in sides.

3. Serve with garlic dipping sauce (page 156) or a mixture of hoisin sauce and soy sauce.

Makes 10.

MINI LUMPIA
(Lumpiang Shanghai)

These crispy rolls are a bit like Chinese egg rolls, but they're longer, thinner, and open at the ends. In Manila, where they are extremely popular, they're sometimes called lumpia Shanghai, after the region in China known for its fried spring rolls.

PALMS OF PLENTY

You could make a whole salad out of a coconut palm: hearts of palm with a dressing made from coconut oil, coconut vinegar, and coconut nectar! Coconut vinegar, one of the most popular sources of sour flavor in Filipino cuisine, is made from the sap of coconut palms. It has a lower acid content than most vinegars and a cloudy white, appearance. It's sold in many major supermarkets. If you can't find it, use rice vinegar as a substitute.

½ pound ground lean pork, chicken, or turkey
1 green onion, minced
6 water chestnuts, minced
2 tablespoons grated carrot
1 teaspoon sesame oil
½ teaspoon salt
¼ teaspoon black pepper
5 lumpia wrappers
2 tablespoons flour
2 tablespoons water

⇒ GARLIC DIPPING SAUCE ⇐

4 tablespoons palm vinegar or rice vinegar
4 teaspoons soy sauce
2 teaspoons minced garlic
¼ teaspoon sugar

Cooking oil for deep-frying
Sweet and sour sauce

Getting Ready

1. In a bowl, combine meat, green onion, water chestnuts, carrot, sesame oil, salt, and pepper; mix well.

2. Cut lumpia wrappers in half horizontally. Mix flour and water together until smooth.

3. To fill each lumpia: Shape 2 tablespoons filling in a band along one long side of wrapper. Roll bottom edge over filling, then roll up completely to enclose filling. Seal edge with flour-water paste. (Ends of wrapper should remain open.) Place rolls in a shallow pan, cover, and refrigerate until ready to cook.

4. Combine dipping sauce ingredients in a small bowl.

Cooking

1. Cut each roll into 3 equal pieces. In a wok, heat oil for deep-frying to 350°F. Deep-fry lumpia, a few at a time, and cook, turning occasionally, until golden brown, about 3 minutes. Remove and drain on paper towels.

2. Serve hot with sauces for dipping.

Makes 10 lumpia, 30 pieces.

Call me a sap, but I climbed all the way up this giant coconut palm, in a coconut plantation in Liliw, to collect sap for making vinegar.

SAVORY MEAT TURNOVERS

(Empanadas)

In the Philippines, these golden turnovers with a sweet and savory meat filling are often served between meals as part of a merienda. At my house, they're often served as an appetizer, and they're always a huge hit. They're equally good warm or cool, which makes them perfect for a picnic. If you don't have time to make the pastry, just use a packaged mix or frozen pie dough. For an authentic and colorful touch, add ¼ cup sliced pimiento-stuffed olives to the cooled filling.

≥ FILLING ≤

1 tablespoon cooking oil
½ pound ground lean beef or chicken
½ cup chopped onion
1 small potato, peeled and cut into ¼-inch cubes
1 teaspoon minced garlic
1 tablespoon soy sauce or oyster-flavored sauce
2 teaspoons chili garlic sauce
½ teaspoon ground cinnamon
¼ teaspoon black pepper
⅓ cup raisins

Flaky pastry for a 9-inch double-crust deep-dish pie

1 egg yolk mixed with 1 teaspoon water

Getting Ready

1. Prepare filling: Place a wok or wide frying pan over high heat until hot. Add oil, swirling to coat sides. Crumble in meat; cook, stirring, for 1 minute. Add onion, potato, and garlic; cook, stirring occasionally, for 3 minutes. Add soy sauce, chili garlic sauce, cinnamon, and pepper. Cover and cook over medium heat until potato is tender, 6 to 8 minutes. Stir in raisins; let mixture cool.

2. Preheat oven to 375° F. Roll out pastry, one half at a time, on floured board, to a thickness of ⅛-inch; cut into 5-inch rounds. For each turnover, place ¼ cup filling on half of a round, moisten edges of dough with water, then fold other half over to enclose filling. Crimp edges to seal.

Cooking

1. Place turnovers, 1 inch apart, on lightly oiled baking sheets; brush with egg yolk mixture. Bake until golden brown, 25 to 30 minutes. Serve warm.

Makes 10.

PASTRY TIPS

Whether you're baking a pie or making an Asian-style turnover, here are a few tips for making tender, flaky pastry. If your conscience permits, use a little lard in the dough, as Asian bakers often do. Whatever shortening you use, make sure it is chilled, so that when you cut it into the flour, it remains in little bits; when these melt during baking, they form the air pockets that make the pastry flaky and light. Handle the dough as little as possible to avoid toughening it. To make rolling easier, pat the dough into a flat circle, wrap it in plastic wrap, and refrigerate it for 30 minutes. Once it's chilled, pound it lightly with a rolling pin to flatten it further, then roll from the center outward, stopping just before you reach the edge, and turning the dough as you go.

STUFFED EGGPLANT
(Rellenong Talong)

"Relleno" or stuffed dishes are a whole category of their own in Filipino cooking. Crab, fish, squid, even boned whole chickens are stuffed with savory fillings. This stuffed eggplant with its filling of seasoned ground beef or chicken gets dressed up with an extra touch—an omelet wrapper—so the stuffed eggplant itself becomes a stuffing. Maybe I should have called it "Egg Stuffplant"!

1 teaspoon soy sauce
1 teaspoon cornstarch
1/4 pound ground beef or ground chicken
Cooking oil for deep-frying
2 Asian eggplants, each 8 to 9 inches long
2 tablespooons cooking oil
1 teaspoon minced garlic
1/4 cup chopped onion
1/4 cup thinly sliced green onion
1 teaspoon chili garlic sauce

⇒ OMELET ⇐
4 large eggs
1/2 teaspoon salt
1/4 teaspoon white pepper

Getting Ready

1. Combine soy sauce and cornstarch in a bowl. Add meat and stir to coat. Let stand for 10 minutes.

2. In a wok, heat oil for deep-frying to 350°F. Deep-fry eggplants until soft and skin is slightly wilted, 4 to 5 minutes; drain on paper towels. Strip off skin; leave stems on. Flatten eggplants slightly with a fork.

Cooking

1. Place a wok over high heat until hot. Add 2 teaspoons oil, swirling to coat sides. Add garlic, meat, and onion; stir-fry for 2 minutes. Add green onion and chili garlic sauce; cook for 30 seconds.

2. In a bowl, whisk eggs with salt and pepper.

3. Place a nonstick 8-inch omelet pan over medium-low heat until hot. Add 2 teaspoons oil. Pour in half of egg mixture. Lay 1 eggplant across center of pan; spoon half of meat mixture over eggplant. Cook until bottom of omelet sets, 2 to 3 minutes. Fold in sides so omelet partially covers eggplant; cook until center of omelet is cooked, about 1 minute longer.

4. Slide out of pan onto a serving plate. Repeat to cook the other omelet and eggplant.

Makes 2 to 4 servings.

CANDIED YAMS
AND SWEET POTATOES

(Ube Kendi At Minatamis Na Kamote)

Although this is a traditional side dish served with the famous lechon (roast suckling pig), it would also make a perfect accompaniment to a Thanksgiving turkey.

1 pound yams
1 pound sweet potatoes
²/₃ cup sugar
2 tablespoons water
3 tablespoons butter
¹/₂ teaspoon salt
1 teaspoon grated lemon peel
2 tablespoons lemon juice
2 tablespoons unsweetened
    desiccated coconut
2 tablespoons finely chopped
    roasted peanuts

Getting Ready

1. In a 3-quart pan, boil yams and sweet potatoes in water, covered, until tender when pierced, 20 to 30 minutes; drain and let cool. Peel and slice crosswise, ¹/₄-inch thick.

2. Alternating yam and sweet potato, overlap slices slightly in a buttered 1¹/₂-quart baking dish. Start from the outer edge and work toward the center.

3. In a small heavy pan, heat sugar and water over medium heat. Shake pan frequently until sugar melts and turns a light caramel color. Remove from heat and stir in butter, salt, lemon peel, and lemon juice. Pour syrup over the slices.

Cooking

1. Preheat oven to 425°F. Bake, uncovered, until hot and bubbly, 10 to 15 minutes. Sprinkle coconut and peanuts over the top, and serve.

Makes 8 servings.

A LESSON IN LECHON

What turns a Filipino party into a true fiesta? When it comes to food, the answer is lechon, a whole suckling pig. The pig is stuffed with aromatic herbs and tamarind leaves, brushed with crushed garlic and cracked peppercorns, and grilled on a bamboo spit suspended over glowing coals until the skin is red and crispy. The meal begins with the skin, and it's a great honor to be offered the first portion. Then comes the succulent meat, served with a sauce made from pork liver (which is a lot tastier than it sounds!).

Preparing to make a pig of myself at a festival in the countryside.

TAMARIND-FLAVORED SOUP
(Sinigang)

The best-known soup of the Philippines, sinigang is refreshingly tangy. My version is made with seafood, but you'll also find it made with chicken, pork ribs, or beef ribs. The egg noodles are not traditional, but they seem right at home here and turn this into a fantastic one-dish meal.

2 teaspoons cooking oil

1/2 small onion, thinly sliced

1 teaspoon minced garlic

2 1/2 cups seafood bouillon (from bouillon cube and water)

1 cup green beans, cut into 1-inch lengths

1 medium tomato, peeled and diced

1 1/2 tablespoons tamarind powder

2 tablespoons soy sauce or 1 tablespoon oyster-flavored sauce

1 tablespoon Filipino fish sauce (patis)

1/4 teaspoon black pepper

1/4 pound firm white fish fillets, such as sea bass, diced; or bay scallops

1/4 pound medium raw shrimp, shelled and deveined

1 cup packed spinach leaves, coarse stems trimmed

4 ounces fresh Chinese egg noodles (optional)

Cooking

1. Heat oil in a 3-quart pan over high heat. Add onion and garlic; cook, stirring, until fragrant, about 1 minute. Add bouillon, beans, tomato, tamarind powder, soy sauce, fish sauce, and pepper. Bring to a boil; simmer for 2 minutes.

2. Add fish and shrimp; simmer for 3 minutes. Add spinach and cook for 1 minute.

3. If using noodles, in a large pan of boiling water, cook noodles according to package directions. Drain, rinse, and drain again; divide among 4 soup bowls. Ladle soup over noodles.

Makes 4 servings.

LESS WASTE, MORE TASTE

Filipino cooks know that in cooking, saving and savoring go hand in hand—especially when they cook shrimp and rice. They save shrimp heads and shells and pound them in a mortar and pestle, then simmer them in lightly salted water or grind them in a blender to make a shrimp-flavored liquid that is strained and used to season all kinds of soups and stews. Rice water, the water used for the second and third washings of rice before cooking, is saved, too. It gives a special flavor and light viscosity to soup stocks and is often used in sinigang.

Tamarind

161

FILIPINO BRAISED NOODLES
(Pancit)

Pancit, which simply means "noodles," is the generic name for a variety of tasty dishes, mostly made from rice noodles, throughout the Philippines.

ENTRANCED WITH PANCIT

The Chinese brought noodles to the Philippines, where they were reborn as pancit and have become a mainstay of the cuisine. While Chinese noodles are often stir-fried, pancit dishes are usually braised in a small amount of liquid. The noodles soak this liquid up and become wonderfully flavorful. You can find all kinds of pancit in Chinese restaurants in the Philippines (which are sometimes even referred to as panciterias). There's pancit bihon, (rice noodles), pancit sotanghon (bean thread noodles), pancit molo (a garlicky soup with wontons), and more. Filipinos tend to think of pancit as a snack, but it's usually so full of goodies that I like to make it a meal.

6 ounces dried rice stick noodles
¼ pound boneless, skinless chicken
¼ pound medium raw shrimp
½ small carrot
1 stalk celery
½ medium onion
½ small red bell pepper
3 cloves garlic, thinly sliced
2 tablespoons cooking oil
1 cup julienned cabbage
1 cup chicken broth
2 tablespoons soy sauce
2 tablespoons oyster-flavored sauce
½ teaspoon black pepper

Getting Ready

1. In a large pot of boiling water, cook rice stick noodles for 1 minute. Drain, rinse with cold water, and drain again. Cut noodles into about 4-inch lengths.

2. Thinly slice chicken. Shell, devein, and butterfly shrimp. Cut carrot and celery into thin diagonal slices. Cut onion and bell pepper into julienne strips.

Cooking

1. Place a wok over high heat until hot. Add oil, swirling to coat sides. Add garlic and stir-fry until fragrant, about 10 seconds. Add chicken and cook for 1 minute. Add shrimp and cook until pink, about 1 minute.

2. Add carrot, celery, onion, bell pepper, and cabbage; cook for 1 minute. Add noodles, broth, soy sauce, oyster-flavored sauce, and pepper. Simmer, uncovered, stirring frequently, until vegetables and noodles are tender and liquid is absorbed, 3 to 4 minutes.

Makes 4 servings.

SPICY FISH SALAD IN COCONUT CREAM
(Kinilaw)

Another country, another salad of raw fish "poached" in citrus juices. This one traces its lineage directly back to the Spanish seviche, but it gets a distinctly Southeast Asian addition of coconut cream, which helps smooth out the tartness of the lime and the heat of the chili.

1 pound firm white fish steaks or
    fillets, such as halibut, sea bass,
    or red snapper
1/4 cup plus 2 tablespoons lime juice
1/4 cup palm vinegar or rice vinegar
1/2 cup coconut cream
1 teaspoon white sesame seeds
1/2 small red onion, diced
1 large tomato, diced
1 fresh red or green jalapeño chili,
    seeded and minced
2 teaspoons minced ginger
1 teaspoon sesame oil
1 teaspoon salt
1/2 teaspoon black pepper
Butter lettuce leaves

Getting Ready

1. Remove skin and bones from fish; cut fish into 1/2-inch cubes and place in a nonreactive bowl. Add 1/4 cup lime juice and the vinegar; cover and refrigerate until fish turns opaque throughout, about 4 hours.

2. For coconut cream, open a can of unsweetened coconut milk (do not shake it first), and spoon the thick cream off the top.

3. Toast sesame seeds: Place seeds in a small frying pan over medium heat; cook, shaking pan frequently, until lightly browned, 3 to 4 minutes. Immediately remove from pan to cool.

Assembly

1. Drain lime juice-vinegar mixture from fish and discard. To the fish, add remaining 2 tablespoons lime juice, onion, tomato, chili, ginger, coconut cream, sesame oil, salt, and pepper; stir gently to combine.

2. Line a plate or bowl with lettuce leaves; spoon mixture over them and sprinkle with sesame seeds.

Makes 6 servings.

SWEATY PALMS

While filming in the Philippines, I spent two days working in a coconut plantation in Liliw. It's an incredible sight: miles of "bamboo highways" suspended from the trees like scaffolding, some as high as 40 feet in the air. We watched in amazement as the nimble-footed workers climbed effortlessly up the trees and ran along the bamboo bridges like tightrope walkers, harvesting clusters of green-hulled coconuts, which they lower to the ground on long ropes. When my turn came, it took me almost 45 minutes to climb a single tree, and every time I looked down, I almost passed out from fear. By the end of the day, I was a nervous wreck, and I was glad we still had the segment on coconut wine to film!

Up a tree: collecting nectar from the flowers of a coconut palm.

MUSSELS IN BLACK BEAN SAUCE
(Tahong Sa Tawse)

Mussels are everywhere in the Philippines, particularly the beautiful green-lipped kind. This is my version of Filipino-style mussels, steamed in a lively hot-and-sour sauce.

MAKE A MUSSEL

Fresh mussels may look a little intimidating, but don't be put off: Their flavor is sweet and delicate, and they're easy to clean and cook—especially the farmed mussels that are now sold in most fish markets. Mussels must be alive when you buy them, which means that they should be either tightly closed, or they should close quickly when you tap them. Avoid chipped shells or shells that slide back and forth easily. Scrape off the "beard" with a small knife, and rinse each mussel well under cool running water. Keep mussels iced until you cook them, because they're quite perishable. Once cooked, mussels lose their muscle and open up. If they don't open, don't eat them.

2 pounds mussels
1½ tablespoons cooking oil
2 teaspoons minced garlic
2 teaspoons minced ginger
1 fresh red or green jalapeño chili, thinly sliced
½ cup chopped onion
¼ cup seafood bouillon (from bouillon cube and water)
1 tablespoon black bean sauce
2 tablespoons palm vinegar or rice vinegar
1½ teaspoons sugar
1 teaspoon cornstarch dissolved in 2 teaspoons water

Getting Ready

1. Scrub mussels; remove beards and discard any with open shells that don't close when tapped.

Cooking

1. Place a wok over high heat until hot. Add oil, swirling to coat sides. Add garlic, ginger, and chili; cook, stirring, until fragrant, about 10 seconds. Add onion and stir-fry for 1 minute. Add mussels, bouillon, black bean sauce, vinegar, and sugar. Cover and cook over medium heat until mussel shells open, 6 to 8 minutes. Add cornstarch solution and cook until pan juices thicken slightly, 1 to 2 minutes longer.

2. Place mussels in a serving dish. (Discard any mussels whose shells have not opened.)

Makes 4 servings.

SWEET AND SOUR FISH
(Escabeche)

Another Filipino dish with Spanish roots, escabeche is fried or poached fish (usually lapu lapu or mackerel) with a tangy sweet and sour sauce. The sauce is wonderful on pan-fried fillets, too.

A GRATE INVENTION

One of the greatest kitchen inventions of all time is the ginger grater. It's a small, rectangular, ceramic plate covered with little bumps (but no holes). This amazing little invention doesn't look like it should work, but it does. You peel a small knob of fresh ginger and rub it across the bumps, holding the grater over a bowl, and instantly you have grated ginger pulp. Nothing is wasted, and the pulp doesn't get stuck in the holes, like it would with a box grater, because there aren't any holes! These handy little gems are sold in Asian markets and cookware stores, usually for just a few dollars.

1 whole fish (1 1/2 to 2 lb.), such as striped bass or red snapper, cleaned
1/4 teaspoon salt
1/4 teaspoon white pepper
Cornstarch

⇒ SAUCE ⇐
3/4 cup water
6 tablespoons distilled white vinegar
1/4 cup catsup
1/4 cup sugar
1 tablespoon soy sauce
2 teaspoons chili garlic sauce

Cooking oil for deep-frying
2 tablespoons cooking oil
3 tablespoons finely julienned ginger
1/2 small onion, sliced
2 teaspoons minced garlic
1/2 small carrot, finely julienned
1/2 green or red bell pepper, seeded and julienned
2 teaspoons cornstarch dissolved in 1 tablespoon water
1/2 English cucumber, thinly sliced

Getting Ready

1. Cut 3 diagonal slits, each 3/4 inch deep, across each side of fish. Sprinkle fish inside and out with salt and pepper. Dust fish with cornstarch; shake to remove excess.

2. Combine sauce ingredients in a bowl.

Cooking

1. In a wok, heat oil for deep-frying to 375°F. Deep-fry fish, turning once, until golden brown, about 3 minutes on each side. Remove and drain on paper towels.

2. Place a wok over high heat until hot. Add 2 tablespoons oil, swirling to coat sides. Add ginger, onion, and garlic; cook, stirring, for 1 minute. Add carrot and bell pepper; stir-fry for 1 minute. Add sauce; reduce heat and simmer for 3 minutes. Add cornstarch solution and cook, stirring, until sauce thickens.

3. Place fish on a serving platter, garnish with cucumber, and serve with sauce.

Makes 4 to 6 servings.

CRAB IN COCONUT MILK

(Ginataang Alimango)

When crab's in season, try cooking it in a decidedly Filipino sauce of coconut milk, garlic, onion, and tomato.

1 live Dungeness crab or 4 live blue
    crabs
1 tablespoon cooking oil
1 teaspoon minced garlic
1/4 cup minced yellow onion
1 small tomato, peeled and diced
1 teaspoon chili garlic sauce
1 cup unsweetened coconut milk
1/4 teaspoon salt
1 teaspoon soy sauce
1 green onion, thinly sliced

Getting Ready

1. In a pot of boiling water, parboil crab for 2 minutes. Drain, rinse with cold water, and drain again. Remove and discard the gills and spongy parts under the shell. Twist off the claws and legs; crack them with a cleaver or mallet. Cut body into 4 pieces (cut blue crab in half).

Cooking

1. Heat a wok over medium heat until hot. Add oil, swirling to coat sides. Add garlic and onion; cook for 2 minutes. Add tomato and cook until soft, 3 to 4 minutes. Add chili garlic sauce and crab; stir to coat crab with seasonings.

2. Add coconut milk, salt, and soy sauce. Cover and simmer over low heat until crab is cooked, 8 to 10 minutes. Stir in green onion and cook for 1 minute.

3. Arrange crab and sauce on a serving plate.

Makes 4 servings.

A VISIT TO THE IFUGAO
I won't soon forget the time I spent with the people of the Ifugao tribe in the mountains of northern Luzon. Once famous for their ferocity in battle, the Ifugao resisted conquest by the Spanish for more than 300 years (and kept more than a few Spanish heads as trophies!). They have been living in pyramid-shaped huts built on stilts for more than 2,000 years. Ifugao families are close-knit, and deeply spiritual. Life is not easy in these remote villages, where survival is a matter of resourcefulness and hard work. But I felt a sense of uncomplicated tranquillity and happiness here that I try to keep alive in my mind. Whenever the pace of my own life gets going a little too fast, the Ifugao remind me to slow down and enjoy the dance of life.

Yan can dance: Sharing the joy of a tribal celebration with the Ifugao.

CHICKEN ADOBO
(Adobong Manok)

Your attention, please. This is the Filipino national dish. And once you try it, you'll know why! This recipe was inspired by my friend Joyce Lapus, who lives in the Zambales region of southern Luzon. This is one of those dishes that taste even better when you reheat it, so be sure to make extra.

¾ cup palm vinegar or rice vinegar
¼ cup soy sauce
1 tablespoon minced garlic
1 bay leaf
1 teaspoon sugar
½ teaspoon salt
½ teaspoon black pepper
4 each chicken legs and thighs, fat trimmed
¾ cup water
2 tablespoons cooking oil
2 teaspoons cornstarch dissolved in 1 tablespoon water

Getting Ready
1. In a 3-quart pan, combine vinegar, soy sauce, garlic, bay leaf, sugar, salt, and pepper. Add chicken and stir to coat each piece with marinade. Let stand for 30 minutes.

Cooking
1. Add water. Bring to a boil; reduce heat, cover, and simmer until meat near bone is no longer pink when cut, 45 to 50 minutes. Remove chicken with a slotted spoon; pat dry with paper towels. Reserve sauce and discard bay leaf.

2. Place a wok over medium heat until hot. Add oil, swirling to coat sides. Add chicken and cook until browned on all sides, 5 to 6 minutes total.

3. Heat reserved sauce. Add cornstarch solution and cook, stirring, until sauce boils and thickens.

4. Return chicken to sauce; stir until chicken is well glazed.

5. Lift chicken from sauce and arrange on a serving platter. Pass extra sauce at the table.

Makes 4 servings.

Pork Adobo
Follow directions for chicken adobo, but omit chicken and use 1½ pounds pork shoulder, cut into 1½-inch chunks. Simmer pork until tender, 1 to 1¼ hours, before frying.

ADOBO
As my friend Joyce Lapus explained to me, adobo originally referred to a Spanish technique of cooking meat in a vinegar sauce. The technique became popular in the hot, humid climate of the Philippines as a way to preserve meat. Adobo is traditionally made with chicken or pork or both. The secret is in the three-step preparation process. First, the meat is marinated with vinegar, soy sauce, and plenty of garlic and seasonings. Then it's slowly braised in the marinade, and finally, once it's cooked, it's fried in oil until it's browned and slightly crispy on the outside and meltingly tender inside. The whole thing gets topped with a rich sauce made from the reduced braising liquid.

Checking out the chickens at the country home of Joyce Lapus in Zambales.

CHICKEN TINOLA
(Tinolang Manok)

Tinola refers to chicken, meat, or fish cooked with ginger. This is both a soup and a main dish. The chicken and vegetables are served over rice, and the broth is drunk separately.

WILY CHAYOTE

I've used chayote as a stand-in for the traditional green papaya in my Chicken Tinola for two reasons. One: It's easier to find. Two: I like it! A mainstay in many Latin and Asian cuisines, chayote (also known as mirliton or christophine) is a pear-shaped, pale green squash (okay, technically, it's a fruit) with a single seed and a furrowed skin. Its flesh is mildly sweet, and it can be cooked like any summer squash—even though you're more likely to find it in stores during the winter—or peeled, sliced, and eaten raw in salads. An added plus: Eating chayote is a great way to get your potassium.

1 tablespoon cooking oil
8 slices ginger, each the size of a quarter
2 cloves garlic, thinly sliced
1 frying chicken (about 3 lb.), cut up, fat trimmed
5 cups water
2 tablespoons Filipino fish sauce (patis)
1 chayote or 1/2 small green papaya
2 cups packed spinach leaves, coarse stems removed

Cooking

1. Heat oil in a 5-quart pan over medium-high heat. Add ginger and garlic; cook, stirring, until fragrant, about 30 seconds. Add chicken and cook, turning, until browned on all sides, 5 to 6 minutes total. Add water and fish sauce. Bring to a boil; reduce heat, cover, and simmer until meat near bone is no longer pink when cut, 40 to 45 minutes.

2. Wash chayote; do not peel unless skin is tough or spiny. Cut into 3/4-inch cubes (no need to discard seed). (If using papaya, peel, discard seeds, and cut into cubes.) Add chayote to chicken; cover and simmer until tender, 6 to 8 minutes. Add spinach; cook for 1 minute.

3. To serve, ladle chicken, vegetables, and broth into a tureen.

Makes 4 to 6 servings.

Market economy: buying fresh vegetables for dinner at a farmers' market on the road to Banaue

BEEF AND SAUSAGE STEW
(Pochero)

The French have cassoulet. The Irish have boiled dinner. In the Philippines, it's Spanish-style pochero, a slow-cooked stew of meat, sausage, and vegetables that's often served as the centerpiece of a big Sunday lunch. At my house, we sometimes "Yan-itize" this dish, by throwing in a few tasty Chinese sausages (lop cheong).

2 pounds beef shanks, sliced about 1 inch thick
4 cups water
1 teaspoon salt
3 green onions
2 chorizo de Bilbao or 5 ounces linguisa
2 teaspoons sesame oil
2 tablespoons cooking oil
1 medium onion, cut in half lengthwise, thinly sliced crosswise
2 teaspoons minced garlic
1 can (8¾ oz.) garbanzo beans, drained
2 small thin-skinned potatoes, peeled and cut into chunks
¼ pound green beans, cut into 2-inch lengths
½ head cabbage, cut into wedges 1½ inches wide
½ cup canned tomato sauce

⤞ CONDIMENTS ⤝
Chopped dill pickle
Sliced pimiento-stuffed olives
Capers
Chopped parsley
Hard-cooked egg, white and yolk chopped separately

Cooking
1. In a 2-quart pan, boil shank slices in water to cover for 3 minutes; drain. Add water, salt, and green onions. Bring to a boil; reduce heat, cover, and simmer for 1 hour. Add sausages and simmer until shanks are tender, about 1 hour longer.

2. Remove meats from broth with a slotted spoon; pat shanks dry with paper towels. Discard green onions. Measure broth; add water if necessary to make 3 cups. Stir in sesame oil.

3. Heat cooking oil in a 5-quart pan over medium heat. Add onion and garlic; cook for 3 minutes. Place shanks in pan and brown lightly on all sides, 5 to 6 minutes.

4. Cut sausages into ½-inch slices and scatter over meat. Place garbanzo beans, potatoes, and green beans over meat. Lay cabbage wedges on top. Pour in reserved broth and the tomato sauce. Bring to a boil; reduce heat, cover, and simmer until vegetables are tender, about 20 minutes.

5. Place shanks in a wide, shallow serving bowl. Surround with sausages and vegetables. Serve broth separately. Serve condiments in small bowls.

Makes 6 to 8 servings.

CHORIZO MADE EASY
Chorizo de Bilbao gets its name from the Spanish city Bilbao, though you're more likely to find this air-dried sausage, flavored with garlic and paprika, in Filipino markets than in Spain. Not to be confused with fresh Mexican chorizo, these sausages are usually around 6 inches long by 1 inch in diameter, and are always cooked before eating. They're usually cut into chunks or slices and added to other foods as a flavor enhancer. Substitutes include Italian pepperoni and Portuguese linguisa.

MEAT AND VEGETABLE STEW
(Pinakbet)

After a bumpy ride in a tiny airplane, and an even bumpier one in a jeep, I found myself 4,000 feet up in the mountains of northern Luzon, standing in front of a sign that reads: "Welcome to the gateway of the eighth wonder of the world: the Banaue Rice Terraces." This is no tourist hype. The terraces are a moving and mind-boggling sight: a hundred square miles of steeply tiered rice paddies carved into the sides of the mountains with nothing but simple stone retaining walls to hold them up. The locals call them the "Giant Steps to the Sky." The terraces seem to go on forever, and I was told that if they were lined up, they'd stretch halfway around the world. It's a staggering feat of engineering, especially when you realize that these terraces were carved out by hand as long ago as 1000 B.C.

In the Philippines, vegetables are often cooked with a small amount of meat, used more as a flavor accent than as a main ingredient. Pinakbet is a tasty example. It's a rich ratatouille-style stew of bitter melon, eggplant, squash, and tomato, braised with just a bit of shrimp and pork (or chicken).

1/4 pound medium raw shrimp
1/4 pound boneless pork or chicken
1 bitter melon
1 Asian eggplant
1/4 pound winter squash, such as butternut or kabocha
6 okra pods
2 tablespoons cooking oil
2 teaspoons minced garlic
1 small onion, thinly sliced
1/2 cup chicken broth
2 tablespoons oyster-flavored sauce
1 teaspoon Filipino shrimp paste (bagoong)
1/2 teaspoon salt
1/8 teaspoon black pepper
1/4 teaspoon sugar
1 medium tomato, cut into wedges

Getting Ready

1. Shell and devein shrimp. Thinly slice meat. Halve bitter melon lengthwise and discard seeds. Slice melon and eggplant 1/4 inch thick. Peel squash; cut into pieces similar in size to those of melon. Trim okra stems without piercing pods.

Cooking

1. Place a wok over high heat until hot. Add oil, swirling to coat sides. Add garlic and meat; stir-fry for 1 minute. Add shrimp and cook for 1 minute.

2. Add bitter melon, eggplant, squash, okra, onion, broth, oyster-flavored sauce, shrimp paste, salt, pepper, and sugar. Cover and simmer over medium heat for 10 minutes.

3. Add tomato and cook until all vegetables are tender, about 5 minutes.

Makes 4 to 6 servings.

BRAISED OXTAIL WITH FRAGRANT PEANUT SAUCE

(Kare Kare)

Kare kare is a hearty stew of oxtails and tripe (don't worry: I've spared you the tripe), flavored with peanuts and tinted orange-yellow with annatto seeds. The oxtails give the sauce lots of meaty flavor and a thick, rich consistency. Serve kare kare with rice and its traditional accompaniment: achara (recipe opposite).

3 tablespoons rice
2 pounds oxtail, cut into segments
4 cups water
2 tablespoons soy sauce
2 tablespoons cooking oil
2 tablespoons annatto seeds or
    1 teaspoon annatto powder
1 medium onion, cut in half length-
    wise, thinly sliced crosswise
2 cloves garlic, thinly sliced
3 tablespoons creamy peanut butter
1/2 pound Asian eggplants, quartered
    lengthwise and cut into 2-inch
    lengths
1/4 pound Chinese long beans or
    green beans, cut into 2-inch
    lengths
1/4 teaspoon black pepper
Salt

Getting Ready

1. Place rice in a small frying pan and cook over medium heat, shaking pan frequently, until golden, 3 to 5 minutes. Transfer to a spice grinder or blender; whirl until rice is a fine powder; set aside.

2. In a 2-to 3-quart pan, parboil oxtail in water to cover for 3 minutes; drain.

Add 4 cups water and soy sauce. Bring to a boil; reduce heat, cover, and simmer until oxtail is tender, 2 to 2½ hours. Remove oxtail from broth with a slotted spoon and pat dry. Reserve and measure broth; add water if necessary to make 3 cups.

Cooking

1. Place oil and annatto seeds in a 5-quart pan; cook over low heat until oil is brick red, 3 to 4 minutes. Pour oil and seeds into a sieve placed over a bowl. Discard seeds; return oil to pan. (If using powder, dissolve powder in oil.) Add onion and garlic; cook, stirring, over medium heat for 3 minutes. Place oxtail in pan and brown lightly on all sides, 5 to 6 minutes.

2. In a bowl, whisk peanut butter with ½ cup of the reserved broth until smooth; stir in remaining 2½ cups broth and rice powder. Pour over oxtails. Bring to a boil; reduce heat, cover, and simmer for 15 minutes. Add eggplants and beans. Cook until vegetables are tender, about 10 minutes. Add pepper and salt to taste.

Makes 4 servings.

SPANISH-STYLE PICKLES

(Achara)

These punchy, crunchy pickled vegetables are great with kare kare (at left) or roast pork. They're a fun alternative to kosher dills at a picnic, too!

1 chayote
1/2 small jicama
1/2 red bell pepper
1/2 green bell pepper
1-inch piece ginger
1 medium carrot
8 walnut-size shallots
1 fresh red jalapeño chili
1 fresh green jalapeño chili
2 teaspoons salt

⇒ PICKLING SOLUTION ⇐
1 cup palm vinegar or rice vinegar
3/4 cup sugar
1 teaspoon salt

Getting Ready

1. Wash chayote; do not peel unless the skin is tough or spiny. Quarter lengthwise, discard seed, then cut each piece crosswise into 1/4-inch-thick slices. Cut jicama and bell peppers into matchstick pieces 1/4-inch-thick, carrot into matchstick pieces 1/8-inch-thick, and ginger into very thin matchstick strips. Thinly slice shallots; halve and seed jalapeños.

2. Place vegetables in a large bowl; rub salt into them with your hands. Cover vegetables with a plate, weight it with a heavy can, and let stand at room temperature for 1 hour.

3. In a small pan, heat ingredients for pickling solution until sugar dissolves, 2 to 3 minutes; let stand until cool.

Assembly

1. Pour vegetable mixture into a colander and rinse well to remove salty juices. Place in a self-sealing plastic bag or a bowl. Pour pickling solution over vegetables. Seal bag or cover bowl.

2. Refrigerate for at least 2 days or up to 1 week.

Makes 10 servings.

CROSS-CULTURAL TRANSPORT

What do you get when you cross a jeep and a jitney? A jeepney, of course! Converted from U.S. Army transport vehicles, some of which date back to the Second World War, jeepneys are a favorite mode of transportation in the Philippines. Each one is an outlandish work of art on wheels, lovingly decorated by its owner with all kinds of colorful sculptures and signs.

Renting a jeepney in Manila is easy. Negotiating the traffic is another thing altogether!

MERIENDA TARTLETS
(Kakanin)

MANAGING A MANGO

Preparing a mango can be tricky. Try this "chef's secret." Stand an unpeeled mango (not too ripe) on its end, with a narrow side facing you. Using a sharp knife, cut straight downward about ¹/₂ inch from the center of the mango so you clear the pit. Turn the mango around and make the same cut on the other side. Lay the cut slices face up and make diagonal cuts about ¹/₂ inch apart in a crosshatch pattern with the tip of the knife, being careful not to cut through the peel. Turn the slice inside out and your crosshatch pattern will open up into a beautiful "flower." You can use this flower as a garnish, or you can trim away the peel, and the flesh will fall away in perfect chunks. Repeat this with the other slice, then use your knife to cut away the flesh that's left around the pit.

Sweets are an everyday indulgence in the Philippines, and there's no better time to indulge than at merienda time, the wonderful break between meals that's almost a meal itself. Here are two of my favorite merienda snacks: miniature tarts filled either with a crunchy peanut and cashew filling or with macapuno—sweet coconut preserves, sold in Filipino markets.

CASHEW-PEANUT FILLING
1 large egg
¹/₂ cup light corn syrup
2 tablespoons sugar
¹/₂ teaspoon vanilla extract
1 tablespoon butter, melted and cooled
3 tablespoons coarsely chopped cashews
3 tablespoons coarsely chopped peanuts

MACAPUNO FILLING
2 large eggs
1 cup macapuno preserves
¹/₂ teaspoon grated lemon peel
2 tablespoons all-purpose flour
2 tablespoons finely chopped peanuts

Flaky pastry for a 9-inch double-crust deep-dish pie

Getting Ready
1. Prepare cashew-peanut filling: In a bowl, lightly beat egg with corn syrup, sugar, vanilla, and butter. Stir in nuts.

2. Prepare macapuno filling: In a bowl, lightly beat eggs. Stir in undrained macapuno preserves, lemon peel, and flour; reserve nuts.

Cooking
1. Preheat oven to 350°F. Roll out pastry, one half at a time, on a floured board, to a thickness of ¹/₈ inch; cut into 3¹/₂-inch rounds. Line 18 oiled 2-inch (measured across the top) muffin cups or fluted tart pans with dough.

2. In half of muffin cups, spoon 2 tablespoons of nut filling. In the other half, spoon 2 tablespoons of macapuno filling; sprinkle peanuts on top.

3. Bake tartlets until golden brown: about 25 minutes for nut tartlets, 30 to 35 minutes for macapuno. Before serving, let cool to room temperature on a rack.

Makes 18 tartlets.

BANANA ROLLS

(Turrones)

Imagine an egg roll with a surprise filling: a banana stuffed with fruit, brown sugar, and cinnamon. These wrapped-up fritters are a popular snack sold by Filipino street vendors. At home, I like to serve them with vanilla ice cream or frozen yogurt for a wonderful hot-and-cold contrast. If canned jackfruit is unavailable, use strips of dried fruit (such as apricots, peaches, or pears) soaked in wine or water to soften them slightly.

4 medium firm-ripe bananas
1/2 cup packed brown sugar
1 tablespoon white sesame seeds
1 teaspoon ground cinnamon
1/2 cup canned jackfruit
8 lumpia wrappers or egg roll
    wrappers
Cooking oil for deep-frying

Getting Ready

1. Peel bananas; halve each lengthwise and crosswise. With a teaspoon, scoop out a channel on the cut side of each banana piece.

2. In a small bowl, combine brown sugar, sesame seeds, and cinnamon. Drain jackfruit and cut into 8 strips to fit along channels in banana pieces.

3. To make each roll, spoon 1 tablespoon brown sugar mixture in channel of 1 banana piece, top with a thin strip of jackfruit, then cover with a second piece of banana placed cut side down.

4. Place a wrapper on work surface with one corner facing you. Place filled banana across wrapper, slightly above the corner. Fold corner over banana, then roll over once. Fold in left and right sides. Brush edges with water and roll up completely to enclose filling.

Cooking

1. In a wok, heat oil for deep-frying to 350°F. Deep-fry banana rolls a few at a time, turning occasionally, until golden brown, about 3 minutes. Remove and drain on paper towels.

2. Let cool for 10 minutes before serving.

Makes 8 rolls.

BANANA BANTER

Bananas are among the most available and frequently eaten fruits in the Philippines, where they're enjoyed as snacks and in cooking. Maybe I'm part Filipino: I go bananas for bananas! The average banana has just 88 calories, almost no fat or sodium, and plenty of potassium and fiber. As bananas ripen, their starches turn to sugar, making them a great source of energy. They can help heal ulcers and lower blood cholesterol, and they're even beneficial to the nervous system. And did you know that they contain tryptophan, which can help you sleep? Plus, they taste good. (Although I must admit, they taste even better sugared and deep-fried!)

Japan *The Art that Conceals Art*

On the face of it, Japan is a country that just shouldn't work.

It's a long, thin island nation, a little smaller than the state of California. Nearly 75 percent of its terrain is so rugged and mountainous as to be uninhabitable, and another 15 percent is devoted to agriculture, leaving only about 10 percent for people to live in. How many people? Oh, about 124 million, or nearly half the population of the entire United States!

Add to this picture a history of devastating earthquakes, tidal waves, volcanic eruptions, typhoons, and fires, and a legacy of isolation from the rest of the world. Now, consider that in spite of all these obstacles—maybe even because of them— this country has not only survived but has become one of the world's greatest industrial and economic powers.

Impossible? Welcome to Japan, where contrasts and paradoxes are an everyday fact of life. The place is crowded and chaotic, yet somehow orderly and safe. It's tied to ancient tradition, yet always on the lookout for the latest technological innovations. Its people revere nature, yet they have created some of the most built-up urban centers on earth. Take

Japan
Hokkaido
Honshu
Tokyo
Shikoku
Kyushu

alpine mountain peaks, fertile river valleys, dairy farms, and coastal sand dunes. I sometimes think of Japan as a *tansu*—a beautiful Japanese chest of drawers with a stately, substantial, and serene exterior and dozens of sliding panels and secret compartments, each concealing a hidden treasure.

my advice: Don't try to resolve all of these contrasts. Just think of them as pieces of the puzzle, and eventually you'll see the whole picture come together.

The Long and the Short of It

Japan is amazingly long and skinny—just 200 miles at its widest point and nearly 1,800 miles from north to south. This translates to an unbelievable range of weather conditions (think of the differences between Maine and Miami, with some wild Pacific and Siberian air currents thrown in), from deep snow-bound winters in the north to humid, subtropical summers in the south.

There are four main islands—Hokkaido, Honshu, Shikoku, and Kyushu—plus nearly 4,000 smaller ones. Hills, mountains, rivers, and inland seas break the country up into thousands of mini-regions and micro-climates, making the landscape infinitely varied and full of surprises: volcanoes,

With so much going on in such a little space, people seem to have a natural sense of compactness and compartmentalization. You see it in the respect for personal privacy and the inward focus of the family and the household. You see it in the love of miniatures, from bonsai trees to micro-chips. And, of course, you see it in the food.

It's there in the small but perfectly pre-pared portions and the neatly divided lacquer trays and dishes. It's the magic in a delectable morsel of sushi, the bite of the crunchy pickled vegetable, the tender tofu and delicate sprouts floating in a simple, clear broth—each a world of flavor and texture to be discovered and savored in all its miniature splendor.

Sure, Japan is a land of contrasts, but it is also a land of well-ordered boundaries and divisions that keep everything in its place and keep things humming right along. In food and in life, the attitude seems to be: Focus on the perfection of the parts—the

treasures in each drawer of the tansu—and the whole will take care of itself.

Japanese Cooking "Zen and Now"

For me, eating Japanese food is a little like paying a visit to a distant cousin, because so many of its essential elements—rice, soy sauce, tofu, tea, and even chopsticks—originally came from my native China, starting as long ago as the fourth century B.C.

But what we think of as Japanese food really began in the sixth century, with the arrival in Japan of Zen Buddhism (another Chinese import). The meatless Zen diet was a perfect fit for Japan with its scarce farming and grazing land and abundant seas on all sides. And ever since, Japanese cooking has revolved around rice, vegetables (particularly root vegetables, which require minimal growing space), seafood, soybean products, and fruit.

The Nikko Toshogu Shrine Festival parade.

Afternoon tea in a country house. (Can you tell, I'm nearly fainting from knee strain?)

Under Zen influence, what had been an austere, poor man's diet was transformed into an organized philosophy of cooking— *shojin ryori*—based on purity, minimalism, harmony with nature, and respect for the fleeting seasonality of foods.

What amazes me is that all of this is very much in evidence in Japan today. The changing of the seasons is still marked with eager anticipation by the arrival of the first seasonal foods—trout and fresh strawberries in spring, eel in summer, and wild matsutake mushrooms in fall, to name just a few.

A typical meal still centers around rice, soup, and pickled vegetables as it has for centuries, and dishes are still classified, as they were in the early days of *shojin ryori*, not by their main ingredient but by how they are prepared.

Foods are either served raw or are cooked by one of four principal methods. Grilling (*yakimono*) in a broiler or brazier is the most common way to cook fish. Simmering (*nimono*), is the method used to make dishes like *shabu-shabu*, in which foods are quickly cooked in a bowl of steaming broth. Steaming (*mushimono*) is used to quickly cook fish and *chawan mushi*, a savory egg custard. And frying (*agemono*) produces light, crispy *tempura*.

The idea is to ensure variety by avoiding the repetition of any one technique in a single meal. But this doesn't apply to the repetition of ingredients. You might find yourself being served an entire meal based on a single ingredient prepared in a variety of ways—a challenge that particularly appeals to the imagination and resourcefulness of Japanese cooks.

Less is More

A Japanese meal is a lot like a haiku. Its form is simple and structured, yet within that ordered framework the food is carefully balanced and full of reverence for the beauty of the natural world.

Don't expect a slab of steak or half a roast chicken. Rather than a single entrée, many small portions are served, each presented on a separate plate or bowl to highlight its distinctive flavors. Typically, food is cut up into bite-size pieces so that it can be artfully arranged on the plate and easily eaten with chopsticks. Portions may be small, but you'll never end a meal feeling hungry, because the overall effect is abundantly varied and satisfying.

Many Asian cuisines are known for their

assertive sauces, but Japanese marinades, sauces, and condiments are more likely to be mild and simple. You'll often find them served not on the food but alongside it as a dipping sauce, so that the food's true flavors and colors can be appreciated. Japanese cooks can create an astonishingly varied and subtle range of tastes from a surprisingly small array of ingredients and seasonings, of which the most common are soy sauce, *mirin* (sweet rice wine), miso, seaweed, sesame seeds, ginger, rice vinegar, and *wasabi* (Japanese horseradish).

Edible Art

Walk into an average restaurant in Japan, and you'll be greeted by a colorful display of dishes and trays filled with food. You can look, but don't eat, because it's all fake—a stunningly realistic visual re-creation of the entire menu, so you can savor everything with your eyes before you order. Talk about an obsession with "see food"!

In Japan, the appearance of food is every bit as important as the food itself, and

A snack and a drink are a typical ending to a grueling work day.

Japanese cooks have elevated food presentation and garnishing to the level of a highly refined culinary art. They treat the plate as a picture frame and balance carefully placed ingredients with "negative space" to create pleasing compositions of shape and exquisite harmonies of color. The whole idea is to begin enjoying the food even before you bite into it.

Round dishes are used to offset square foods and straight-sided ones to frame round foods. Restaurants and some home cooks even use different kinds of dishes for every season—light, clear glassware in summer, heavy earthenware in fall—designed to evoke that season's symbols and complement the colors of its foods.

It's all about creating a delicate interplay between the natural and the artificial, the studied arrangement of ingredients calculated to create an effect of spontaneity—the art that conceals art. And you see it in everything from the humblest one-pot meal to the most elaborate kaiseki banquet (see page 22). The whole may be a feast of special foods, but the individual parts remain pure and artfully simple.

Maki-zushi (clockwise):
Tekka Maki (tuna), Kappa Maki
(cucumber), Takuan Maki
(pickled daikon), Futo Maki
(egg and pickled vegetable),
Maguro Hand Roll (tuna).

I'm happy to see that in the last few decades, culinary inspiration from Japan has begun to show up all over the world, from nouvelle cuisine in France to California cuisine in my neck of the woods.

The thing I love most about Japanese food (aside from eating it!) is that it gently invites you to think about healthful eating, balance, freshness, flavor, seasonality, and presentation in a way that can make anything you prepare look and taste better. Its quiet wisdom translates beautifully to any language. And that's the mark of a truly great cuisine.

Sushi

The Freshest Fast Food in the World

A ball of vinegared rice topped with fish. Only in Japan could such a simple idea become a great social institution, a revered culinary art and a source of infinite pleasure.

Enter a sushi bar in Japan (or an authentic one anywhere in the world), and you'll be greeted by cries of *"Irasshai,"* or "Welcome" from the sushi master and his assistants as they look up to acknowledge you without missing a beat.

If you can swing it, take a front row seat at the counter, as near as possible to the sleek refrigerator case filled with fresh fish and seafood. You'll be welcomed with a cup of tea, a small dish for soy sauce, and a rolled, moist towel to wash your hands. Once you've settled in, the sushi master will raise an inquiring eyebrow and await your first order.

A great sushi master is many things. He is an expert shopper, who selects the freshest seafood early each morning at the local fish market. He is a performer whose dexterity and showman's flair are worthy of a professional magician. He is an unflappable host, who can engage in lively conversation with "regulars" and strangers alike. He is a human computer, who can keep the bills of five or six guests at a time in his head and provide a running total without ever picking up a pencil. And, of course, he is a highly skilled chef who spends years apprenticing and learning his craft.

Now, I'm pretty handy with a Chinese chef's knife, but nothing can compare to the precision and speed of a sushi master as he fillets and slices perfectly uniform rectangles of fish and seafood.

Precision is the name of the game in assembling sushi, too. It's said that as he picks up two fingers-full of sushi rice, a great master can judge the quantity with his hands right down to the number of grains, and that if he is truly skilled, the grains will all line up in the same direction!

In Tokyo and most of Japan (and in sushi bars the world over), sushi is generally prepared in one of three ways: *nigiri-zushi* is seafood and rice pressed together; *maki-zushi* is fish, seafood, or vegetables, and rice rolled in toasted seaweed; and *inari-zushi* is rice stuffed into a pouch of deep-fried tofu.

Sushi Eating Made Simple

Okay, it's time to order. Where do we start? How about a taste of *sashimi*—tender, freshly sliced raw fish—washed down with a cold beer or a bit of warm saké, before we proceed to the main event?

After that, do as the Japanese do: Begin with one of the milder nigiri offerings, like *maguro* (tuna) and gradually work your way up to the more complex and highly flavored sushi. It never hurts to ask the sushi master which fish is freshest or most highly recommended that day.

Nigiri-zushi (clockwise): Tamago (omelet), Maguro (tuna), Ikura (salmon roe), Ebi (shrimp), Toro (tuna belly), Unagi (eel).

As the chef prepares your order, pour a little soy sauce into your dish. You can mix in a bit of wasabi, but many sushi chefs pride themselves on adding the perfect amount to the sushi itself, so you should try the sushi first before adding more.

Fingers or chopsticks? There's no right answer, but sushi aficionados will usually tell you that it's best to pick the sushi up with your fingers, turn it upside down, dip the tip of the fish side in soy sauce (if you dip the rice side, it falls apart), and then place the sushi on your tongue, fish side down, so that your first sensation is tasting the fish. It's polite to eat a whole piece of sushi in one or two bites. If you prefer to use chopsticks, pick nigiri-zushi up on its side, so that the chopsticks hold the rice and fish together.

In any event, go easy on the dipping. The soy sauce is meant to be a light condiment and flavor enhancer.

The thin slices of pink pickled ginger (*gari*) served on the side are intended to be eaten a little at a time between orders of sushi to cleanse the palate. Sips of hot green tea have a similar, refreshing effect.

Inari-zushi

The most difficult part of eating sushi is stopping. When you're feeling content but not overly full, it's time to call it a day. That's the point at which I always enjoy one final order of *tamago*, a rectangle of sweetened omelet attached to a finger of rice with a band of seaweed.

I always leave a sushi bar feeling relaxed and happy. With so much fast food in the world these days, isn't nice to know that the fastest food of all is also the freshest?

Rolling Your Own

Sushi making is a near-sacred art in Japan, and most people would never attempt to make it themselves at home. But don't let that stop you! With a few good recipes and some basic techniques, you can make delicious sushi any time you feel the urge.

Sushi Essentials

These days, most of the ingredients for sushi making can be found in the Asian foods section of major supermarkets. In addition to very fresh fish or seafood, you'll need medium-grain rice, Japanese rice vinegar, *mirin*

(Japanese sweet cooking rice wine) and *wasabi* (Japanese horseradish). A traditional wooden paddle (*shamoji*) is just the right shape for tossing the vinegar into the rice, and it sticks less than a metal spoon. A hand-held fan (a homemade one made from folded paper works fine) is helpful for cooling the rice. For maki rolls, you'll also need square sheets of seaweed (*nori*) and a sushi-rolling mat (*sudare*).

Sushi Rice Tips

Sushi rice (page 186) should be cooked so that it's a bit firmer than ordinary rice. You'll need about 2 tablespoons of cooked rice for each piece of nigiri, or 1 cup for a single maki roll. I use a ratio of 1 part water to 1 part rice. To judge quantities, figure that the amount of cooked rice will be equal to the amount of raw rice plus the amount of water.

While the rice cooks, you can make the vinegar mixture known as *su*, a combination of rice vinegar, sugar, and salt. I also add a little mirin to make the rice extra-shiny. Be sure to use a nonaluminum pot to heat the vinegar (aluminum will react with the acid in the vinegar and result in a metallic taste). You can also skip this step and simply use a premixed seasoned rice vinegar.

The trick to making great sushi rice is tossing and cooling it with the vinegar. Before you transfer the cooked rice to a plastic or wooden tub, rinse the tub with water to keep the rice from sticking. Pour the vinegar over the rice, tossing gently and trying not to mash the rice or cut it up too much (think of folding egg whites). At the same time, fan the rice to cool it and give it a lustrous sheen. You may want to enlist a helper to fan while you do the tossing.

Sushi rice will keep for a few hours, covered with a damp cloth. Don't store it in the refrigerator, where it will quickly become hard and dry. (In general, sushi doesn't keep well in the refrigerator either. You're just going to have to eat it!)

Learning to make sushi is fun, and it will make you very popular with your friends and family. With a little practice, you'll be "on a roll" in no time and ready to add the most important ingredient of all: your imagination. Don't be afraid to experiment with whatever ingredients tickle your fancy. Who knows? You might just invent the world's next sushi sensation!

Sushi Basics

⇒ SUSHI RICE ⇐

2 cups medium-grain rice
2 cups cold water
1/4 cup rice vinegar

2 1/2 tablespoons sugar
1 tablespoon sweet cooking rice wine (mirin)
3/4 teaspoon salt

Getting Ready

1. Place rice in a bowl; add enough cold water to cover, and wash rice well by rubbing it between your hands; drain. Repeat twice more. Pour rice into a strainer, drain, and let stand for 15 minutes.

Cooking

1. Place rice and 2 cups cold water in a 2- to 3-quart pan. Bring to a boil; cover, reduce heat, and simmer for 20 minutes. Turn off heat and let rice stand for 10 minutes.

2. In a small pan, heat vinegar, sugar, mirin, and salt over medium heat until sugar dissolves.

3. Turn cooked rice into a large wooden or plastic bowl; pour vinegar mixture over rice. Fold liquid in with a wooden rice paddle. At the same time, fan the rice to bring out the luster of the grains. Continue folding and fanning until rice absorbs all liquid. Cover with a damp cloth and let stand until ready to use.

Makes 4 cups.

⇒ NIGIRI-ZUSHI ⇐

1/2 pound boneless, skinless fish such as
     tuna or sea bass; or 12 sea scallops;
     or 12 large raw shrimp
1 1/2 cups sushi rice (see above)

Wasabi paste
Soy sauce
Thinly sliced Japanese pickled ginger
     (beni-shoga)

Getting Ready

1. Cut fish into thin slices about 1 by 1 1/2 inches. (If using scallops, parboil until opaque, then butterfly. If using shrimp, parboil until pink, 3 to 4 minutes; shell and devein, then butterfly.)

Assembly

1. Shape about 2 tablespoons sushi rice into a 1- by 2-inch finger. Top with a dab of wasabi paste. Drape a piece of the fish of your choice over the top of the rice.

2. Serve with wasabi paste, soy sauce, and ginger.

Makes 12 pieces.

⇒ KAPPA MAKI ⇐

2 thin strips (each 7 in. long) peeled cucumber	Wasabi paste
Salt	Soy sauce
1 sheet nori	Thinly sliced Japanese pickled ginger
1¹/₃ cups sushi rice (see opposite)	(beni-shoga)

Getting Ready

1. Sprinkle cucumber strips lightly with salt; let stand for 15 minutes. Rinse cucumber with cold water and pat dry. Cut nori in half.

Assembly

1. Place a half-sheet nori, shiny side down, on a bamboo mat (sudare). Spread ²/₃ cup rice evenly on nori.

2. Spread a thin film of wasabi down center of rice, top with a strip of cucumber, and roll sushi into a cylinder. Press mat around rolled sushi to seal the edges. Repeat to make a second roll.

3. Place sushi on a cutting board; slice each roll into 6 pieces. Serve with wasabi paste, soy sauce, and ginger.

Makes 12 pieces.

Variations

Tuna Sushi (Tekka Maki). Follow instructions for cucumber kappa maki, but also use 2 ounces boneless raw tuna, cut into thin strips 7 inches long. Spread a thin film of wasabi down center of rice, top with a strip of fish, and roll.

Makes 12 pieces.

Pickled Daikon Sushi (Takuan Maki). Follow instructions for cucumber kappa maki, but instead of cucumber, cut pickled daikon into 2 thin strips each 7 inches long. Place 1 teaspoon sesame seeds in a small frying pan over medium heat; cook, shaking pan frequently, until lightly browned, 3 to 4 minutes. Immediately remove from pan to cool. Sprinkle seeds down center of rice, top with a strip of daikon, and roll.

Makes 12 pieces.

YAN CAN ROLL

Yan can wok, and Yan can roll. And with a little practice, so can you! Here's my contribution to the world of sushi. The filling is made from raw tuna dressed with soy sauce, sesame oil, chili garlic sauce, and a bit of creamy mayonnaise (which, by the way, has become quite a popular ingredient in sushi in Japan.)

1 tablespoon mayonnaise
1 teaspoon chili garlic sauce
1/2 teaspoon soy sauce
1/2 teaspoon sesame oil
1/3 cup coarsely chopped raw tuna
2 tablespoons finely shredded lettuce
2 teaspoons minced green onion
1 sheet Japanese seaweed (nori)
1 teaspoon sesame seeds
2 cups sushi rice (see page 186)
2 thin strips (each 7 in. long) carrot, blanched
2 thin strips (each 7 in. long) peeled cucumber
Wasabi paste
Soy sauce
Thinly sliced Japanese pickled ginger (beni-shoga)

Getting Ready

1. In a small bowl, combine mayonnaise, chili garlic sauce, soy sauce, sesame oil, and tuna. In another small bowl, combine lettuce and green onion. Cut nori in half.

2. Place sesame seeds in a small frying pan over medium heat; cook, shaking pan frequently, until lightly browned, 3 to 4 minutes. Immediately remove from pan to cool.

Assembly

1. Place a piece of nori, shiny side down, on a bamboo mat (sudare). Spread nori evenly with 1 cup rice. Sprinkle 1/2 teaspoon sesame seeds over rice.

2. Place a piece of plastic wrap on top of rice. Turn nori-rice over so plastic wrap forms a layer between rice and mat.

3. Spread half of tuna mixture lengthwise down center of nori. Sprinkle half of lettuce mixture over tuna. Place 1 strip of carrot along one side of tuna mixture and 1 strip of cucumber along the other side.

4. Tuck edge of plastic wrap out of the way; using mat to help you, roll sushi into a cylinder. Press mat around rolled sushi to seal the edges. Repeat to make a second roll.

5. Place sushi on a cutting board; slice each roll into 6 pieces. Serve with wasabi paste, soy sauce, and ginger.

Makes 12 pieces.

SCATTERED SUSHI
(Chirashi-zushi)

This traditional dish is sushi made simple. A bowl of sushi rice is scattered (artfully, to be sure) with seafood and other typical sushi toppings. In Japan, it's often served in a lacquered box.

1 Japanese cucumber or ½ English
  cucumber
½ teaspoon salt
6 fresh shiitake mushrooms, stems
  discarded
1 teaspoon cooking oil
3 cups sushi rice (see page 186)
1 package (3 oz.) lox or other
  cold-smoked salmon, cut into
  ¼-inch-wide strips

Getting Ready
1. Cut cucumber into paper-thin slices. (If using English cucumber, cut in half lengthwise before slicing.) Reserve 6 slices for garnish. Place remaining cucumber in a colander and rub in salt; let stand for 30 minutes. Rinse with cold water, then squeeze or press out liquid.

Cooking
1. Place a grill pan or wide frying pan over medium heat. When pan is hot, add oil, swirling to coat surface. Add mushrooms and cook until lightly browned and tender, 2 to 3 minutes per side. Cut caps into thin slices.

2. In a bowl, toss sushi rice with cucumber, mushrooms, and salmon. Place in a serving bowl and garnish with unsalted cucumber slices.

Makes 6 servings.

A FISH STORY
You have to get up pretty early in the morning to catch the show at Tokyo's Tsukiji wholesale fish market, the sprawling 56-acre, thousand-stall labyrinth that's the largest of its kind in the world. We arrived just as the fish did, at around 4 A.M. On a typical day, 5 million pounds of seafood move through here in just a few hours! The fish come in by boat and truck from all over the country and all over the world. By 5:20, the tuna auction was underway, with some enormous fish weighing up to 800 pounds and fetching more than $10,000. Soon, the wholesalers began carting their prizes to their stalls, where retailers and sushi chefs were already waiting to buy the catch of the day. For breakfast, we checked out the food stalls, where I had the freshest sushi I've ever tasted.

Tunas anyone? Fresh fish on display at the Tsukiji Market.

189

SAVORY STEAMED CUSTARD

(Chawan Mushi)

Comfort food, Japanese style. This delicate custard made with dashi stock, chicken, shrimp, and vegetables has just enough egg to make it hold its shape. In Japan, it's steamed and served in special lidded cups, but you can use any heatproof custard cup.

6 small dried shiitake mushrooms or black mushrooms
1 boneless, skinless chicken breast half
2 teaspoons Japanese rice wine (sake)
1 teaspoon cornstarch
1/2 teaspoon salt
6 small raw shrimp
6 ginkgo nuts
6 slices Japanese fish cake (kamaboko)
4 spinach leaves, shredded

⇒ CUSTARD ⇐

3 large eggs
2 cups Japanese soup stock (dashi)
2 teaspoons sweet cooking rice wine (mirin)
1 teaspoon soy sauce
1 teaspoon salt

1 1/2 teaspoons soy sauce

Getting Ready

1. Soak mushrooms in warm water to cover until softened, about 20 minutes. Discard stems.

2. Cut chicken into 1/4-inch cubes. Add 1 teaspoon sake, cornstarch, and salt; stir to coat evenly. Let stand for 10 minutes. Shell and devein shrimp and place in a separate bowl; sprinkle with the remaining 1 teaspoon sake.

3. In each of 6 chawan mushi or custard cups (2/3-cup size), place equal amounts of chicken, shrimp, ginkgo nuts, fish cake, and spinach.

4. In a bowl, lightly beat eggs. Add remaining custard ingredients; stir just to blend (custard should not be foamy). Pour custard equally into cups. Place a mushroom on top of each.

Cooking

1. Prepare a wok for steaming (see page 14). Place cups in steamer; drape waxed paper loosely over the cups. Steam over medium heat for 15 minutes. Turn off heat and let stand, covered, 5 minutes longer. Sprinkle each custard with 1/4 teaspoon soy sauce, and serve.

Makes 6 servings.

JAPANESE POTSTICKERS
(Gyoza)

Japanese potstickers are lighter and thinner-skinned than their Chinese counterparts, with a zesty, garlicky filling. I like to make extras and freeze them (I spread them on a baking sheet, cover with plastic, then transfer them to a plastic bag once they're frozen). To cook frozen gyoza, take them directly from the freezer into the pan, and increase the cooking time by about 2 minutes.

⇲ FILLING ⇱
1½ cups finely chopped cabbage
½ teaspoon salt
⅔ pound ground chicken or pork
¼ cup chopped water chestnuts
2 green onions, minced
3 tablespoons Japanese rice wine
    (saké)
1 tablespoon oyster-flavored sauce
1 tablespoon minced ginger
1 teaspoon minced garlic
1 teaspoon cornstarch
¼ teaspoon black pepper

⇲ DIPPING SAUCE ⇱
¼ cup seasoned rice vinegar
¼ cup soy sauce
2 teaspoons chili garlic sauce
2 teaspoons sesame oil
1 green onion, minced
2 teaspoons minced ginger

30 potsticker wrappers (gyoza)
3 tablespoons cooking oil
1 cup chicken broth

Getting Ready
1. In a bowl, toss cabbage with salt; let stand for 10 minutes. Drain, rinse, and drain again. Press cabbage to extract excess moisture. Add remaining filling ingredients to cabbage; mix well.

2. In another bowl, combine dipping sauce ingredients.

3. To shape each potsticker, place a rounded teaspoon of filling in center of one wrapper. Brush edges with water; fold wrapper over filling to form a half-moon. Press and pleat edges to seal. On a tray dusted with cornstarch, set filled potsticker down firmly, seam side up, so that it will sit flat. Cover while you shape remaining potstickers.

Cooking
1. Place a wide nonstick frying pan over medium heat until hot. Add 1 tablespoon oil, swirling to coat sides. Add one-third of potstickers, seam side up, and cook until bottoms are golden brown, 3 to 4 minutes. Add ⅓ cup broth; reduce heat to low, cover, and cook until dumplings are tender and liquid has evaporated, 6 to 8 minutes.

2. With a wide spatula, remove potstickers from pan and place them browned side up on a serving platter. Repeat to cook remaining potstickers. Serve hot with dipping sauce.

Makes 30 potstickers.

BENTO: BANQUET IN A BOX
The lunch box is a thing of the past for many Americans, but for millions of Japanese people, lunch still comes this way. Whether prepared at home or purchased, the neatly packed compartments of the bento box contain a complete meal of rice and all kinds of tasty tidbits—seafood, pickles, egg, meat, fresh fruit, and a pickled plum. You can buy bento lunches all over Japan, and they're a regular feature at most train stations (eki)—where they're called ekiben—a great way to sample the specialties of each city and region as you travel the country by rail. Bento is one of my favorite Japanese traditions. It's like opening a present for lunch!

DASHI

Dashi is one of the essential keys to Japanese cooking. It's what gives many Japanese soups and sauces their distinctive taste. If you can track down the ingredients at a Japanese market, dashi is quite easy to make. Granulated dashi concentrate (hon dashi or dashi-no-moto), is even easier—just add boiling water—and quite tasty.

KELP YOURSELF
Japanese cuisine relies on the sea for more than just seafood. All kinds of seaweed are harvested, processed, and dried for use in cooking, adding flavor and important minerals to a variety of dishes. Konbu (giant sea kelp) looks like a dusty strip of speckled olive-brown leather and is used to make dashi stock. Before cooking, don't rinse it, but wipe it gently with a damp cloth to preserve its flavor. Nori is a black seaweed that's dried in paper-thin sheets that are used for sushi and cut into strips for garnishing. And wakame is a leafy seaweed that's sold fresh or dry (to be softened in water before using). It adds a nice chewy texture and oceany flavor to salads and soups.

2 pieces ($\frac{1}{2}$ oz. total) dried kelp (konbu), each about 4 by 6 inches
4 cups cold water
$\frac{3}{4}$ cup ($\frac{1}{3}$ oz.) loosely packed flaked dried bonito (katsuo-bushi)

Cooking

1. Wipe kelp with a damp cloth. Place in a 2- to 3-quart pan with water; bring slowly to a boil over medium heat, 6 to 8 minutes. Remove kelp and discard.

2. Add bonito, remove from heat, and let stand until shavings settle to bottom of pan. Strain broth and discard flakes.

Makes 4 cups.

WINTER MISO SOUP

From breakfast to dinner, miso soups are the most popular soups in Japan. The secret to perfect miso soup is to blend the miso paste and broth well and avoid boiling or overcooking once the miso is added.

4 dried black mushrooms
1 large carrot
$\frac{1}{2}$ pound sweet potatoes or yams
$\frac{1}{2}$ of a 14-ounce package regular-firm tofu
$\frac{1}{4}$ cup diced bamboo shoots
4 cups Japanese soup stock (dashi)
2 tablespoons sweet cooking rice wine (mirin)
4 slices ginger, each the size of a quarter
$\frac{1}{3}$ cup fermented soybean paste (white miso)
2 green onions, cut into $\frac{1}{2}$-inch lengths

Getting Ready

1. Soak mushrooms in warm water to cover until softened, about 20 minutes; drain. Discard stems; cut caps into $\frac{1}{2}$-inch squares. Cut carrot and sweet potatoes into $\frac{1}{2}$-inch cubes. Drain tofu and cut into $\frac{1}{2}$-inch cubes.

Cooking

1. Place mushrooms, carrot, sweet potato, bamboo shoots, dashi, mirin, and ginger in a 2-quart pan. Bring to a boil; reduce heat, cover, and simmer until vegetables are tender, 6 to 8 minutes. Remove ginger.

2. Stir in miso; blend until smooth. Add tofu and green onions. Simmer until tofu is heated through, 2 to 3 minutes. Ladle into individual soup bowls.

Makes 4 to 6 servings.

SOUP FOR ALL SEASONS

(Suimono)

Start with a lightly seasoned dashi stock and add a few simple garnishes, chosen from whatever is at the peak of freshness. What could be more quintessentially Japanese—or more perfectly satisfying?

⇒ GARNISHES ⇐

(choose three)

Small cooked clams in the shell

Small cooked shrimp

Poached bay scallops

Slices of Japanese fish cake
(kamaboko)

Tiny cubes of poached chicken
breast

Hard-cooked quail eggs

Cubes of tofu

Finely shredded raw zucchini

Thin slivers of snow peas or
mushrooms, cooked 1 minute

Diced carrot, potato, bamboo
shoots, or daikon, cooked until
tender

Dried shiitake mushrooms, soaked,
drained, and cooked until tender

1-inch bundle of cooked spinach

Blanched watercress sprigs

Strands of cooked thin Japanese
noodles (somen)

Thinly sliced green onion

Thin strips of lemon or lime peel

Tiny shiso leaves

⇒ BROTH ⇐

6 cups Japanese soup stock (dashi)

1 teaspoon soy sauce

1 teaspoon Japanese rice wine
(saké)

Getting Ready

1. Prepare garnishes of your choice.

Cooking

1. In a 2- to 3-quart saucepan, heat dashi over medium heat to simmering. Add soy sauce and saké.

2. Divide garnishes among 6 individual soup bowls. Just before serving, ladle hot broth into bowls.

Makes 6 servings.

SEASON TO TASTE

The Japanese word kisetsukan means "sense of season," and it's almost like a sixth sense in Japan. You see it in the way people dress and in the way they decorate their homes. And you see it in the foods they eat, from chilled soba noodles in the summertime to mushrooms in fall and fresh bamboo shoots in spring. Even the garnishing of foods has seasonal meaning. In winter, a dish may be served with a scattering of pine needles (evergreens symbolize longevity) or plum blossoms (representing tenacity, because they bloom in the midst of the January snows). In spring, cherry blossoms, or even foods carved to resemble them, are reminders of the fleeting beauty of life.

NEW YEAR'S SOUP
(Ozoni)

THE MEANING OF MOCHI

The ushering in of the new year (Oshogatsu) is Japan's most important holiday. And the eating is pretty incredible, too! People begin cooking weeks in advance, and the rice cakes called mochi are always at the top of the list. Friends and family get together for all-day mochitsuki (rice-pounding) parties, where steaming-hot sweet glutinous rice is ladled into big tubs and pounded rhythmically with wooden mallets amid cries of "yoi-sho!" until it is mashed into a smooth paste, which is formed into little cakes. Symbolic of longevity and prosperity (the word motsu means "to have"), sweet, chewy mochi cakes are eaten throughout the new year holiday, and many people freeze them to be enjoyed all year long.

This soup with its sweet rice cakes (mochi) is the first food to be savored after the traditional saké toast on New Year's morning. You can buy fresh mochi cakes around the end of the year in Japanese markets, and they're sold frozen year-round. I love to eat them as a snack, toasted in a skillet and dipped in sweetened soy sauce.

6 dried black mushrooms
1/2 pound boneless, skinless chicken
1 tablespoon Japanese rice wine (saké)
1/8 teaspoon salt
8 glutinous rice cakes (mochi)
4 cups Japanese soup stock (dashi)
2 teaspoons soy sauce
1 large carrot, thinly sliced
2-inch length Japanese fish cake (kamaboko), thinly sliced
1/4 cup sliced bamboo shoot
1 cup (packed) spinach leaves, or 2 ounces garland chrysanthemum (shungiku)

Getting Ready

1. Soak mushrooms in warm water to cover until softened, about 20 minutes; drain. Discard stems and cut caps in half.

2. Thinly slice chicken. Place in a bowl with saké and salt; mix well. Let stand for 10 minutes.

Cooking

1. Heat rice cakes in a frying pan over medium heat until softened and browned, 2 to 3 minutes on each side.

2. In a 3-quart pan, heat dashi and soy sauce to simmering. Add mushrooms, chicken, carrot, fish cake, and bamboo shoot; simmer until vegetables are tender, about 5 minutes. Add spinach and simmer for 1 minute.

3. Divide rice cakes and soup solids among 4 soup bowls, then ladle broth into each bowl.

Makes 4 servings.

CRAB AND CUCUMBER SUNOMONO

Sunomono refers to a vegetable salad dressed with rice vinegar. With their crisp, cool slices of cucumber, these two versions are delicate and refreshing, perfect for starting off a summer meal of grilled fish. The dressing for the crab salad is entirely fat-free.

SHICHIMI
Like five-spice powder in China, Japanese shichimi, or "seven-spice," isn't always made from the same seven spices—or even from seven spices at all! A lively mixture of ground seasonings and herbs, it might include ground chilies, sansho (prickly ash pods), black hemp seeds, flakes of nori (dried seaweed), dried mandarin orange peel, white poppy seeds and white sesame seeds. Shichimi is sprinkled over bowls of udon noodles and used to season salads and other foods. In Japan, you can have it mixed to your liking by spice vendors. In the West, you'll find it in Japanese grocery stores in small shaker-top jars or bags. Use it sparingly at first: It's tasty, but often quite hot.

½ English cucumber
½ teaspoon salt
½ pound cooked crabmeat, flaked

⇒ DRESSING ⇐
3 tablespoons rice vinegar
1 tablespoon Japanese soup stock (dashi)
1 tablespoon sugar
2 teaspoons soy sauce

2 teaspoons flying fish roe (tobiko), or 1 hard-cooked egg yolk, mashed

Getting Ready
1. Cut cucumber in half lengthwise, trim end, and thinly slice crosswise. Place in a medium bowl. Mix cucumber with salt; let stand for 15 minutes. Turn into a colander, rinse with cold water, and press to squeeze out liquid. Return cucumber to bowl. Add crabmeat. Cover and chill until ready to serve.

2. In a small pan, heat dressing ingredients over medium heat just until sugar dissolves; let cool.

Assembly
1. Pour dressing over salad and mix well; garnish with roe.

Makes 4 servings.

SHRIMP AND CUCUMBER SUNOMONO

½ English cucumber
½ teaspoon salt
½ pound shelled small cooked shrimp
2 tablespoons grated daikon

⇒ DRESSING ⇐
2 tablespoons seasoned rice vinegar
1 teaspoon sugar
2 teaspoons lemon juice
1 teaspoon soy sauce
½ teaspoon sesame oil
⅛ teaspoon red pepper mix (shichimi togarashi)

Getting Ready
1. Follow steps 1 and 2 for Crab and Cucumber Sunomono (above), using shrimp instead of crab and adding daikon.

Assembly
1. Pour dressing over salad and mix well. Mound salad on a serving plate.

Makes 4 servings.

GREEN BEANS WITH SESAME DRESSING
(Sayaingen Goma-ae)

Toasted black and white sesame seeds add a nutty flavor to this simple salad of crisp-tender green beans.

1 teaspoon black sesame seeds
1/4 cup white sesame seeds

⟫ DRESSING ⟪
2 tablespoons oyster-flavored
    sauce
2 tablespoons sweet rice cooking
    wine (mirin)
2 teaspoons rice vinegar
1 tablespoon sugar

1/2 teaspoon salt
3/4 pound green beans, cut in half

Getting Ready
1. Place black sesame seeds in a small frying pan over medium heat; cook, shaking pan frequently, until seeds smell toasted, 3 to 4 minutes. Repeat with white sesame seeds but cook until lightly browned, 3 to 4 minutes. Immediately remove from pan to cool. Grind white seeds in a spice grinder; leave black seeds whole.

2. In a small pan, heat oyster sauce, mirin, vinegar, and sugar over medium heat just until sugar dissolves. Remove from heat and wisk in ground seeds until dressing is smoothly blended. Let cool.

Cooking
1. In a saucepan, heat 2 inches of water with salt to boiling. Add beans and cook until tender-crisp, 4 to 5 minutes. Drain, rinse with cold water until cold, and drain again.

2. Place beans in a bowl, add dressing, and toss lightly to mix.

3. Place on a serving plate and sprinkle with black sesame seeds.

Makes 4 servings.

ONE NATION, TWO FAITHS

Two religions, Shinto and Zen Buddhism, coexist side by side in Japan, and many Japanese adhere to both. It's not uncommon to be married in a Shinto ceremony and buried in a Buddhist ceremony. Shinto is native to Japan and is based on the worship of nature and the ancestors, while Zen Buddhism, which came to Japan in the sixth century by way of China, teaches meditation and a simple lifestyle as ways to achieve enlightenment. Shinto shrines are recognizable by their torii arches (two straight pillars with one or two curved crossbeams), while Buddhist temples often have an entrance gate with heavy doors, and sometimes a pagoda.

Wishes on the wind: At the Toshogu Shinto shrine in Nikko, visitors write their wishes on wooden plaques.

GRILLED MUSHROOMS WITH PONZU SAUCE

Grilled mushrooms served with a classic citrus-soy ponzu dipping sauce and a woodsy garnish of green pine needles are a Japanese autumn tradition.

THE FACTS OF KNIFE

My trusty cleaver is an all-purpose chef's knife that does almost every job in the kitchen. But in Japan, there's no such thing as "one knife fits all." Chefs and home cooks alike have a knife for every purpose, whether it's boning a fish, cutting noodle dough, or paring vegetables. Chefs are judged first and foremost on the basis of their knife skills—from wielding a cleaver to slicing a paper-thin sheet from a carrot. In fact, the Japanese word for chef means "in front of the cutting board." Knife making is something of a sacred art in Japan, too. It takes more than 200 steps to make a knife, and the Japanese believe that at each step, the knife maker must pour his soul into the steel so that his spirit becomes one with it.

At the Sakai Cutlery workshop, just outside Osaka, carbon steel is hand-pounded to make some of the finest and most expensive knives in the world.

⇒ PONZU SAUCE ⇐

1/4 cup sweet cooking rice wine (mirin)
1/4 cup lemon juice
3 tablespoons soy sauce
4 teaspoons sugar
1 tablespoon minced green onion

8 fresh shiitake mushrooms
8 large button mushrooms
1 1/2 tablespoons sesame oil
Pine needles

Getting Ready

1. Combine ponzu sauce ingredients in a bowl; divide among 4 small dipping sauce bowls.

2. Discard shiitake stems. Cut button mushrooms through cap and stem into 1/4-inch-thick slices. Brush mushrooms with sesame oil.

Cooking

1. Heat a grill pan or wide frying pan over medium heat until hot. Add mushrooms and cook until lightly browned and tender, about 3 minutes per side.

2. Arrange mushrooms in a serving bowl. Garnish with pine needles and serve with dipping sauce.

Makes 4 servings.

MRS. NANAO'S STUFFED SHIITAKE MUSHROOMS

If you're a fan of stuffed mushrooms, wait till you taste this version: shiitakes filled with shrimp and chicken and braised in a sweet dashi sauce. It's the invention of one of the most esteemed Japanese cooks I know, Mrs. Akiko Nanao, wife of San Francisco's Japanese consul general.

5 large raw shrimp
2 ounces ground chicken
2 teaspoons Japanese rice wine (saké)
2 teaspoons soy sauce
1/2 teaspoon grated ginger
1/2 teaspoon sesame oil
6 large fresh or dried shiitake mushrooms or button mushrooms, each 2 1/2 inches in diameter

⋟ BRAISING SAUCE ⋞
2/3 cup Japanese soup stock (dashi)
3 tablespoons soy sauce
3 tablespoons sweet cooking rice wine (mirin)
1 tablespoon sugar

Pine needles

Getting Ready

1. Shell, devein, and finely chop shrimp.

2. Place shrimp in a bowl with chicken, saké, soy sauce, ginger, and sesame oil; mix well.

3. If using fresh shiitake mushrooms, discard stems. If using dried mushrooms, soak in warm water to cover until softened, about 20 minutes; drain. Discard stems.

4. Spread 1 tablespoon of filling inside each mushroom cap.

Cooking

1. Combine braising sauce ingredients in an 8-inch frying pan. Place mushrooms, filled side up, in sauce.

2. Bring to a boil; reduce heat, cover, and simmer until mushrooms are tender and filling is cooked, about 25 minutes. Remove cover and simmer until sauce is slightly syrupy, about 5 minutes.

3. Lift mushrooms from sauce and place on a serving plate; drizzle remaining sauce over each mushroom. Garnish with pine needles.

Makes 6.

GARDENS OF THE MIND

In Japan, a garden is more than a place of rest and recreation. It is a meticulously arranged miniature landscape designed to present nature at its most perfect state within a small space. And it is a place of contemplation and meditation. Some gardens include miniature ponds, streams, and waterfalls. Others, like the famous Ryoanji temple garden in Kyoto, use stones and raked sand or pebbles to create the effect of rippling water. In my own home, every room looks out on the garden, and it is my favorite "room"— the place I go to slow down and think things over. Seeing the first buds appear on the lemon tree, watching the fish swim lazily in the little pond, or marveling at the hummingbirds as they flutter around the fuchsias—these are some of the quietest and deepest pleasures I know.

A moment of contemplation in the garden of the Ryoanji temple in Kyoto.

GRILLED VEGETABLES WITH MISO GLAZE

You don't have to be serving a Japanese meal to enjoy these tasty grilled vegetables: slices of eggplant, zucchini, onion, and shiitake mushrooms, cooked on a griddle and finished with a miso glaze.

1/4 cup Japanese soup stock (dashi)
3 tablespoons sweet cooking rice
    wine (mirin)
2 tablespoons sugar
1 tablespoon soy sauce
2 tablespoons fermented soybean
    paste (red miso)
1 tablespoon cooking oil
1 tablespoon sesame oil
2 Asian eggplants, each about
    5 inches long
2 zucchini, each about 5 inches long
1 medium onion
8 fresh shiitake mushrooms
1 teaspoon white sesame seeds

Getting Ready

1. In a small pan, heat dashi, mirin, sugar, and soy sauce over medium heat just until sugar dissolves. Remove from heat and whisk in miso until sauce is smoothly blended.

2. Combine cooking oil and sesame oil in a small bowl.

3. Cut eggplants and zucchini diagonally to make ovals about 1/4 inch thick and 3 inches long. Cut onion in half length- wise, then cut crosswise into 1/4-inch-thick slices. With a wooden pick, skewer each slice to keep rings together. Discard mushroom stems.

4. Place sesame seeds in a small frying pan over medium heat; cook, shaking pan frequently, until lightly browned, 3 to 4 minutes. Immediately remove from pan to cool.

Cooking

1. Heat a Japanese iron griddle (teppan) or wide frying pan over medium heat. Brush hot griddle with some of the oil. Place vegetables on griddle and brush with oil. Cook, turning once and brushing again with oil, until vegetables are tender, about 3 minutes on each side.

2. Reduce heat to low. Brush half of miso glaze on vegetables and cook for 30 seconds. Turn vegetables, brush with remaining glaze, and cook 30 seconds longer. Place on a serving plate and sprinkle with sesame seeds.

Makes 4 servings.

MIGHTY MISO

Miso—fermented soybean paste—is one of the most important staples in Japanese cooking, used in everything from soups to sauces and glazes. It's rich in protein and makes a great "secret" flavor enhancer for all kinds of cooking. Miso is made by mixing crushed boiled soybeans with rice, barley, or wheat; inoculating this mash with a yeast culture; and allowing the whole thing to ferment for several months. White miso (miso shiru), made with rice, has a sweet, delicate flavor, while red miso (aka miso), made with barley, is saltier and more robust. Both are sold in plastic tubs in many supermarkets and most natural food stores. In our house, there's always some miso in the fridge, so we can make a quick, nutritious soup by combining it with dashi (page 192), tofu, and whatever vegetables are on hand.

VEGETABLE AND TOFU STEW

(Oden)

*This is my version of a traditional vegetarian stew that's a home-style winter favorite.
Unlike most stews, which take time to make, this one comes together in a matter of
minutes. Devil's tongue jelly is a grayish starchy product made from the devil's
tongue root (konnyaku). It doesn't add much flavor, but soaks up other flavors nicely
and has an appealingly smooth texture on the tongue.*

1 large carrot
1/2 pound daikon
1/3 pound yams
1/4 pound potatoes
1/4 pound napa cabbage
8 ounces devil's tongue jelly
(konnyaku)
1 package (14 oz.) regular-firm or
extra-firm tofu
2 tablespoons dry mustard powder
2 tablespoons water
5 cups Japanese soup stock (dashi)
1/4 cup soy sauce
1/4 cup sweet cooking rice wine (mirin)
6 hard-cooked quail eggs

Getting Ready
1. Peel carrot, daikon, yams, and
potatoes. Roll-cut carrot; cut other
vegetables into 1-inch pieces.

2. Cut cabbage into 1½-inch pieces. Cut
jelly into 1-inch cubes. Drain tofu and
cut into bite-size triangles.

3. Mix mustard with water; place in a
small serving dish.

Cooking
1. Place carrot, daikon, yams, potatoes,
dashi, soy sauce, and mirin in a 3-quart
pan. Bring to a boil; reduce heat, cover,
and simmer until vegetables are barely
tender, 10 to 12 minutes.

2. Add cabbage; cook until all vegetables
are tender, 4 to 6 minutes. Add jelly,
tofu, and quail eggs. Cook until heated
through.

3. Ladle into individual bowls. Serve
with mustard.

Makes 4 to 6 servings.

SPINACH AND TOFU WITH WASABI DRESSING

Here's a novel appetizer or vegetable side dish: golden squares of pan-fried tofu, topped with sesame-flavored spinach in a lively soy-wasabi dressing.

1 tablespoon white sesame seeds
1 teaspoon sesame oil
¹/₄ teaspoon salt
¹/₄ teaspoon sugar

⋟ DRESSING ⋞
1 teaspoon wasabi paste
2 teaspoons water
2 teaspoons soy sauce
1 ¹/₂ teaspoons sugar

³/₄ pound spinach
¹/₂ of a 14-ounce package regular-
   firm or extra-firm tofu
1 tablespoon cooking oil

Getting Ready

1. Place sesame seeds in a small frying pan over medium heat; cook, shaking pan frequently, until lightly browned, 3 to 4 minutes. Immediately remove from pan to cool. When seeds are cool, grind 2 teaspoons of it in a spice grinder; reserve remainder.

2. In a medium bowl, combine ground seed, sesame oil, salt, and sugar.

3. In a small bowl, blend dressing ingredients until smooth.

4. Wash spinach and remove coarse stems.

Cooking

1. Place spinach in a large pot with 1 inch of water. Parboil for 30 seconds; drain, then rinse with cold water. Gently squeeze to remove all water. Coarsely chop spinach and add to ground sesame seed mixture; toss lightly to mix.

2. Drain tofu and cut into pieces about ¹/₂ inch thick and 2¹/₂ inches square.

3. Heat oil in a wide nonstick frying pan over medium heat. Add tofu and cook until lightly browned, 2 to 3 minutes on each side. Remove from pan and drain on paper towels.

4. Place tofu on a serving platter. Using a teaspoon, shape 2 teaspoons of spinach mixture at a time into ovals. Place 1 oval on each square of tofu. Drizzle dressing over spinach and garnish with the reserved whole sesame seeds.

Makes 12 pieces.

TOFU

Tofu, or bean curd, originated in China more than 2,000 years ago, but Japan has made it its own. It is rich in protein, inexpensive to make, and takes to just about any method of preparation. To make it, soybeans are soaked in water, then ground, boiled, and strained to extract soy milk. From here, the process is just like cheese-making. A coagulant is added to the soy milk, separating it into curds and whey, and the curds are poured into molds, where they set up in blocks. I'm crazy about the texture and mild flavor of tofu, and I've been known to design entire menus around it, from creamy dressings and soups to grilled "steaks" and even homemade tofu ice cream for dessert!

RICE WITH CHICKEN AND EGG
(Oyako Donburi)

AN ODE TO RICE

Rice is more than just a staple in Japan. It is a symbol of prosperity, health, and well-being. Its name, gohan, also means "meal," because it is the true central core of any meal—and sometimes it is the meal itself. Onigiri, rice balls—either plain or with seaweed or pickled plums—are sold as snacks and light meals, and often eaten as picnic foods. Rice is a part of the landscape as well, lush green in summer and golden in fall. In many parts of the country, it is still planted by hand. I've always loved rice, but after spending several days helping plant rice on a farm in the countryside near Mashiko, I learned to appreciate it in a whole new way.

Every cuisine has its unique one-dish meal, and in Japan, it's donburi: a healthy helping of steamed white rice with a variety of toppings. The original Japanese fast food, it is served in small mom-and-pop restaurants all over the country. Donburi may be topped with pork cutlet and egg (katsudon), tempura (tendon), or my favorite, chicken and egg, whose name, oyako donburi, literally means "parent and child."

1 dried shiitake mushroom
3/4 cup donburi sauce (recipe follows)
1 green onion, cut diagonally into
    1/2-inch lengths
3 ounces boneless, skinless chicken
    breast, thinly sliced
1 egg, lightly beaten
1/2 cup coarsely chopped spinach or
    thinly sliced napa cabbage
1 1/2 cups hot cooked medium-grain
    rice
Japanese seaweed (nori), cut into
    thin strips

Getting Ready

1. Soak mushroom in warm water to cover until softened, about 20 minutes; drain. Discard stem and slice cap.

Cooking

1. Heat donburi sauce in a small frying pan or 1-quart pan over medium heat. Add mushroom, green onion, and chicken. Simmer until chicken is no longer pink, 3 to 4 minutes.

2. Pour egg over chicken; sprinkle spinach over egg. Reduce heat to low, cover, and cook until egg is softly set, 2 to 3 minutes.

3. Place rice in a donburi bowl or deep soup bowl. Spoon topping and broth over rice. Garnish with nori.

Makes 1 serving.

⇒ DONBURI SAUCE ⇐

1 cup Japanese soup stock (dashi)
1/4 cup sweet cooking rice wine (mirin)
1/4 cup soy sauce
2 tablespoons sugar

Cooking

1. Combine dashi, mirin, soy sauce, and sugar in a saucepan. Cook, stirring, over medium heat until sugar dissolves. Use, or refrigerate up to 1 week.

Makes 1 1/2 cups.

Planting rice by hand near Mashiko

TOFU WITH MISO GLAZE
(Dengaku)

At Japanese temples, dengaku is a popular festival treat. Domino-shaped pieces of tofu are skewered on flat, pronged wooden skewers, then grilled over charcoal and coated with a sweet miso glaze as they finish cooking. Dengaku is popular among home cooks in Japan, too. When I make it at home, I skip the skewers and brown the tofu in a nonstick frying pan.

SHIRA-AE DRESSING

Shira-ae is a traditional Japanese dressing for vegetables made from puréed tofu. It's used to dress blanched vegetables, such as watercress, spinach, or carrot. I've also tried it with great success on asparagus, broccoli, cauliflower, and green beans. To make shira-ae, finely grind 1/4 cup sesame seeds in an electric spice grinder or mortar and pestle. Drain 1/2 of a 16-ounce package of soft tofu; place it in a food processor with the ground sesame seeds, 1/4 cup fermented soybean paste (white miso), and 1/4 cup sugar. Process to a smooth paste. Makes about 1 1/4 cups.

1/4 cup Japanese rice wine (saké)
1 tablespoon sugar
3 tablespoons fermented soybean paste (white miso)
1 package (14 oz.) regular-firm tofu or 1 package (16 oz.) soft tofu
1 tablespoon cooking oil

Getting Ready

1. In a small pan, heat saké and sugar over medium heat just until sugar dissolves. Remove from heat and whisk in miso until sauce is smoothly blended.

2. Drain tofu and cut in half horizontally. Cut each half into sixths to make a total of 12 rectangles.

Cooking

1. Heat oil in a wide nonstick frying pan over low heat. Place tofu in pan and cook until lightly colored, about 3 minutes on each side. Drain oil.

2. Add miso glaze and simmer for 2 minutes. Turn tofu and simmer for 2 minutes longer.

Makes 4 servings.

TEMPURA

Tempura—crispy deep-fried seafood and vegetables—is one of Japan's most famous dishes. But did you know it was brought there in the 1500s by Spanish and Portuguese missionaries?

⮞ DIPPING SAUCE ⮜

1 cup Japanese soup stock (dashi)
1/4 cup sweet cooking rice wine (mirin)
1/4 cup soy sauce
2 tablespoons sugar

⮞ BATTER ⮜

1 cup flour
1/4 cup cornstarch
1/8 teaspoon baking soda
1 egg yolk
1 1/3 cups ice water

8 large raw shrimp
1 zucchini
1 medium onion
1 green bell pepper
1 carrot
2 Asian eggplants
1 sweet potato
8 white button mushroom caps
1/4 pound green beans, trimmed
1/4 pound broccoli florets, trimmed
2 sheets Japanese seaweed (nori),
   cut into 2-inch squares
Cooking oil for deep-frying

⮞ CONDIMENTS ⮜

Grated daikon, grated ginger, and
   lemon slices

Getting Ready

1. Combine dipping sauce ingredients in a saucepan. Cook until sugar dissolves; cool. In a bowl, mix dry ingredients for batter. Refrigerate.

2. Shell and devein shrimp, leaving tails intact. Make several cuts across back of shrimp, then butterfly; set aside.

3. Prepare vegetables: Cut zucchini into 2½-inch pieces, then lengthwise into ¼-inch-thick slices. Cut onion in half lengthwise, then crosswise about ¼ inch thick; run a wooden pick through all layers to hold rings together. Cut bell pepper into lengthwise strips about ¼ inch wide and 2 inches long. Cut carrot, eggplants, and sweet potato diagonally into ⅛-inch-thick slices. Halve mushroom caps if large. Dry all vegetables. Coat with cornstarch, shaking off excess.

Cooking

1. Finish batter: Mix egg yolk and ice water; stir quickly into dry ingredients (batter will be lumpy). Do not overmix.

2. In a wok or 2-quart saucepan, heat oil for deep-frying to 350°F. Dip shrimp, vegetables, and nori, a few pieces at a time, into batter, shaking off excess, then put immediately into hot oil. Deep-fry until batter is golden brown and shrimp and vegetables are cooked, about 1½ minutes. Remove with a slotted spoon and drain on paper towels.

3. Serve with dipping sauce and condiments.

Makes 4 servings.

TEMPURA TIPS

Psst! Here are my seven secrets for light, crispy tempura: Keep the oil at a constant 350°F (an electric wok or fryer is helpful). Always use ice water in the batter (it reacts more "explosively" with the hot oil and gives you lacier tempura). Make the batter just before frying so it's light and cold. Avoid overbeating, and leave the batter lumpy. Before dipping ingredients in the batter, dry them, then dredge them in flour or cornstarch to help the batter adhere. Cook only a few pieces at a time. And most important of all: Enjoy immediately!

FISH IN SOBA BUNDLES

These tender fish fillets steamed in bundles of buckwheat noodles make a great main course for a dinner party. The noodles add a delicate flavor to the fish as it steams. If you prefer, you can use fresh spinach noodles in place of soba.

1/4 cup finely shredded daikon
2 teaspoons chili garlic sauce
2 green onions
3/4 pound firm white fish fillets, such as sea bass, each 1/2 inch thick
1 tablespoon Japanese rice wine (saké)
1 teaspoon cornstarch
1/4 teaspoon salt
1/4 teaspoon white pepper
1/2 pound dried buckwheat noodles (soba)

⇒ SAUCE ⇐
1 1/2 cups Japanese soup stock (dashi)
1/4 cup sweet cooking rice wine (mirin)
3 tablespoons soy sauce
2 tablespoons Japanese rice wine (saké)
1 tablespoon oyster-flavored sauce
1/2 teaspoon chili garlic sauce

Black and white sesame seeds, toasted

Getting Ready

1. In a bowl, cover daikon with ice water and let stand for 30 minutes; drain and toss with chili garlic sauce. Place in a small serving bowl and chill until serving time. Cut green onions into 1 1/2-inch lengths, then into thin shreds.

2. Cut fish into 4 pieces, each about 1 1/2 by 3 inches; place in a bowl with saké, cornstarch, salt, and pepper. Stir to coat fish; let stand for 10 minutes.

3. Divide noodles into 4 equal portions; lay each portion parallel in a bundle. Tie one end of each bundle with string. Slide noodles into a large pot of boiling water; cook until tender but firm, 6 to 7 minutes. Carefully drain noodles, rinse with cold water, and drain again. Cut off and discard string and tied end of noodles; keep bundles straight and separate.

4. Lay one piece of fish across center of each bundle; wrap noodles around fish. Place bundles in a single layer in a heat-proof dish.

Cooking

1. Prepare a wok for steaming (see page 14). Cover and steam fish over high heat until it turns opaque, 7 to 8 minutes.

2. Combine sauce ingredients in a small pan and bring to a boil over medium heat; simmer for 3 minutes.

3. To serve, place fish bundles in 4 individual bowls. Pour sauce over each serving; sprinkle with green onions and sesame seeds. Serve with seasoned daikon.

Makes 4 servings.

THE GREAT WHITE RADISH

Daikon, or "great root," is a white radish that is one of the biggest ingredients in Japanese cooking. Literally. Some kinds weigh up to 30 pounds! Daikon tastes like a cross between a radish and a turnip. In Japan, you'll find it pickled, stewed, and shredded into fine, vermicelli-like strands and for use in salads or as a garnish. Speaking of roots, when I was growing up in China, we always ate daikon cooked. Years later, I discovered the Japanese custom of eating it raw, and now my favorite way to enjoy it in the summertime is simply to peel it, grate it using the fine holes of a box grater, squeeze out a bit of its moisture, and sprinkle it with a little soy sauce. After shredding daikon, soak it in ice water to make it crisp and reduce its turnip-y odor.

HAWAIIAN FISH SALAD
(Aku Poke)

Birds of a feather: Cormorant
trainer Sugiyama-san and one
of his "children" display the
catch of the day.

Traditional sashimi has just one ingredient: raw fish. This Japanese-Hawaiian version with a sweet-savory dressing and chunks of tropical fruit was inspired by my friend Sam Choy, chef-owner of Sam Choy's Restaurant in Honolulu.

⇒ DRESSING ⇐

2 tablespoons oyster-flavored sauce
1 tablespoon plum sauce
1 teaspoon soy sauce
1 1/2 teaspoons sesame oil
1 fresh red jalapeño chili, seeded
   and minced

1/2 pound tuna or salmon fillet
1 medium tomato, diced
1/2 medium onion, diced
1/2 cup diced pineapple
1/2 cup diced papaya
1 green onion, thinly sliced
1 teaspoon sesame seeds
1/2 sheet Japanese seaweed (nori)

Getting Ready

1. In a bowl, combine dressing ingredients.

2. Remove skin and any bones from fish, then cut fish into 1/2-inch cubes. Place in bowl with dressing. Add tomato, onion, pineapple, papaya, and green onion; toss to mix.

3. Place sesame seeds in a small frying pan over medium heat; cook, shaking pan frequently, until lightly browned, 3 to 4 minutes. Immediately remove from pan to cool.

Assembly

1. Place fish mixture in a serving bowl.

2. Fold nori into layers, such as quarters, then cut into fine strips with scissors. Sprinkle nori and sesame seeds on top for garnish.

Makes 4 servings.

SEA SCALLOPS WITH KARAMI SAUCE

These sea scallops, lightly pan-seared and served with a spicy dipping sauce, make a simple first course or light entrée that takes just a few minutes.

⇒ DIPPING SAUCE ⇐

¹/₃ cup Japanese soup stock (dashi)
2 tablespoons sweet cooking rice wine (mirin)
2 tablespoons soy sauce
2 tablespoons lemon juice
2 tablespoons flaked dried bonito (katsuo-bushi)
¹/₂ teaspoon red pepper mix (shichimi togarashi), or 1 teaspoon chili garlic sauce
¹/₄ teaspoon sesame oil

1 cup shredded daikon

⇒ MARINADE ⇐

¹/₄ cup Japanese rice wine (saké)
2 tablespoons soy sauce

1 pound sea scallops
Cornstarch
2 tablespoons cooking oil
1 green onion, thinly sliced

Getting Ready

1. In a small pan, heat dashi, mirin, soy sauce, and lemon juice to simmering. Add flaked bonito; remove from heat and let stand until flakes settle to bottom of pan. Strain broth and discard flakes. Add red pepper mix and sesame oil.

2. In a bowl, cover daikon with ice water and let stand for 30 minutes.

3. Combine marinade ingredients in a bowl. Add scallops and stir to coat; let stand for 10 minutes.

Cooking

1. Lift scallops from marinade and pat dry with paper towels. Coat scallops evenly with cornstarch; shake off excess.

2. Place a wide frying pan over medium heat until hot. Add oil, swirling to coat sides. Add scallops and cook, turning once, until scallops are opaque, about 2 minutes on each side.

3. Pour sauce into individual dipping bowls. Float a few green onion slices in each bowl. Arrange scallops on a serving plate and garnish with daikon.

Makes 4 servings.

FUGU: FISH TO DIE FOR?

Call me crazy, but during one of my visits to Japan, I took my life in my hands and dined at a restaurant specializing in fugu, or blowfish, known for its remarkable flavor—and its potential for being deadly poisonous if wrongly prepared. Its liver and ovaries contain a toxin that's lethal to humans, and they must be removed whole, with what amounts to surgical skill, so only highly trained fugu chefs are licensed to serve it in Japan. In other words, don't try this at home! First, we were served the fins, which had been toasted and steeped in saké. Next came the raw meat of the fugu sliced paper thin and arranged to look like a beautiful flower. Finally, a stew of fugu and vegetables was cooked right at the table. The flavor was so unusual and tasty, I'm dying to try it again!

Dried blowfish are sold as ornamental lanterns throughout Japan.

TOFU CRAB CAKES

KAISEKI

The kaiseki banquet is renowned in Japan as the peak of culinary artistry. More than any other kind of Japanese cooking, kaiseki ryori is based on the idea of shun, the time of year when different ingredients are at their peak of freshness. This is definitely an all-afternoon or evening affair—a parade of small dishes starting with an appetizer, soup, and an uncooked dish; followed by steamed, fried, broiled, simmered, and vinegared foods; and concluding with soup, rice, and pickles. Everything is prepared with meticulous skill and beautifully presented to reflect the symbols and colors of the season. Unlike banquets in many cultures, kaiseki is based not on lavish conspicuous consumption but on an appreciation of simple perfection.

If you like crab cakes, try this Japanese-inspired version: golden croquettes made with crab and tofu, served with a delicate, sweet-savory sauce.

4 dried black mushrooms
1 package (14 oz.) extra-firm tofu
1/2 pound cooked crabmeat, flaked
1/2 cup small cooked shrimp, coarsely chopped
2 green onions, minced
2 eggs
1 tablespoon minced ginger
1 teaspoon sugar
3/4 teaspoon salt
1/4 teaspoon white pepper

⇒ SAUCE ⇐
3/4 cup Japanese soup stock (dashi)
1/3 cup sweet cooking rice wine (mirin)
3 tablespoons soy sauce
1 tablespoon sugar
1 tablespoon minced ginger
1 tablespoon cornstarch dissolved in 2 tablespoons water

1 tablespoon water
Cornstarch or flour
1/2 cup Japanese-style bread crumbs (panko)
Cooking oil
Sliced green onion
Toasted white sesame seeds (see opposite page)

Getting Ready
1. Soak mushrooms in warm water to cover until softened, about 20 minutes; drain. Discard stems; trim and finely dice caps, and place in a large bowl.

2. Drain tofu. Place in a colander and crumble with your hands; let drain for 15 minutes. Place tofu in a clean dish towel; twist towel around tofu to extract all moisture. Add tofu to mushrooms.

3. Add crabmeat, shrimp, minced green onions, white of 1 egg, ginger, sugar, salt, and white pepper. Mix well. Using about 1/4 cup for each, shape mixture into ten 1/2-inch-thick cakes.

Cooking
1. In a small pan, combine dashi, mirin, soy sauce, sugar, and ginger; simmer for 3 minutes. Add cornstarch solution to sauce and cook, stirring, until sauce boils and thickens. Keep sauce warm.

2. Lightly beat remaining egg yolk and egg with water. Dip crab cakes into cornstarch; shake off excess. Dip into egg, drain briefly, then coat with bread crumbs.

3. Place a wide frying pan over medium heat. Add oil to a depth of 1/4 inch. When oil is hot, add crab cakes and pan-fry, uncovered, turning once, until golden brown, 5 to 6 minutes per side. Lift out and drain on paper towels.

4. Arrange cakes on a serving platter. Pour sauce over; garnish with green onion and sesame seeds.

Makes 10 crab cakes.

CHICKEN TERIYAKI

Probably the most famous Japanese dish the world over, chicken teriyaki is one of my favorite backyard barbecue foods. If you live in a high-rise or don't want to fire up the grill, you can also cook it in the broiler. Just remember to watch it closely and to baste and turn it often.

1/3 cup soy sauce
1/3 cup Japanese rice wine (saké)
1/3 cup sweet cooking rice wine (mirin)
1 tablespoon sugar
1 teaspoon minced garlic
1 teaspoon minced ginger
1 1/2 pounds boneless chicken thighs
2 teaspoons white sesame seeds
1 teaspoon cornstarch mixed with
    2 teaspoons water
Sliced green onion

Getting Ready

1. Place soy sauce, saké, mirin, and sugar in a small pan. Bring slowly to a simmer over low heat; simmer for 5 minutes. Remove from heat; stir in garlic and ginger and let mixture cool.

2. Place chicken in a shallow bowl. Pour half of sauce over chicken; reserve remaining sauce. Cover and refrigerate chicken for 2 hours, turning occasionally.

3. Place sesame seeds in a small frying pan over medium heat; cook, shaking pan frequently, until lightly browned, 3 to 4 minutes. Immediately remove from pan to cool.

Cooking

1. Lift chicken from marinade. Arrange chicken, skin side down, on a lightly oiled grill 4 to 6 inches above a solid bed of low-glowing coals. Cook, basting with marinade and turning frequently, until meat is no longer pink, 25 to 30 minutes.

2. In a small pan, heat reserved sauce to simmering. Add cornstarch solution and cook, stirring, until sauce boils and thickens slightly.

3. Place chicken on a platter and pour sauce over. Sprinkle with sesame seeds and green onion.

Makes 4 to 6 servings.

SAKÉ

Saké, the clear alcoholic beverage made from fermented glutinous rice, is the national brew of Japan—an indispensable part of every special occasion and an important ingredient in cooking. It's known as "the drink of the gods," and the gods must love variety, since more than 2,000 brands are produced in Japan! There's no such thing as a vintage saké, since it doesn't improve with age. In fact, it should be consumed within a year of production, and once a bottle is opened, it should be finished relatively quickly. Saké is served warm in little ceramic cups or chilled in square wooden ones. To warm it, pour a small amount into a porcelain serving bottle (tokkuri) and place the bottle in a pan of water over low heat. Kampai!

A thousand pounds of steaming rice in a small room make for some pretty sticky working conditions—like 95 percent humidity and 104°F!

CHANKO NABE

The Japanese are big on sports, and nothing (or maybe I should say "no one") is bigger than sumo. To an outsider, sumo may look like a simple wrestling match. True, the object is to push your opponent outside the ring or make him touch the ground with any part of his body other than his feet. But sumo is more than that. It's a 1,500-year-old martial art that began in the seventh century as a way to pray for a good harvest, and it's still deeply tied to Shinto ritual. You see it in the way the wrestlers purify the ring by sprinkling salt over it before each bout, and in the way they behave with dignity both in and out of the ring. Becoming a sumo wrestler means years of training and body building, but the spiritual responsibility is just as heavy!

Nabemono refers to dishes cooked in a single pot. Sukiyaki and shabu-shabu are probably the most famous examples of this style of cooking, in which everyone simmers bits of meat or vegetables in a communal pot of steaming broth. Chanko means "everything," and chankonabe has just about everything in it, from chicken, beef, and shrimp to tofu and vegetables. No wonder it's the daily mainstay of sumo wrestlers in training. (Don't worry, it's everything else they eat that helps them put on all that weight.) This recipe serves two. Or one very young sumo wrestler!

1 leek (1-in. diameter), white part only
1 large carrot
1 medium piece jicama
6 fresh shiitake mushrooms
1 choy sum or baby bok choy
1/4 pound spinach
1/4 pound boneless, skinless chicken breast, thinly sliced
1/4 pound boneless tender beef, thinly sliced
6 large raw shrimp, shelled and deveined
1/2 of a 14-ounce package firm tofu, drained and cut into 1-inch squares

⇒ COOKING SAUCE ⇐
2 cups Japanese soup stock (dashi)
1 cup water
1/3 cup soy sauce
1/3 cup sweet cooking rice wine (mirin)

Lemon wedges
Hot cooked rice

Getting Ready
1. Prepare vegetables: Cut leek diagonally into 1 1/2-inch lengths. Roll-cut carrot. Slice jicama 1/8 inch thick, then cut into 1- by 2-inch pieces to make 1 cup.

Discard mushroom stems; cut caps in half. Split choy sum lengthwise. Remove coarse stems from spinach; rinse leaves.

2. Arrange vegetables, chicken, beef, shrimp, tofu, and vegetables attractively on a platter; cover and chill until ready to cook.

3. In a small pan, combine cooking sauce ingredients and heat to simmering.

Cooking
1. Place chicken, beef, tofu, shrimp, and all vegetables except spinach in a deep frying pan; keep each ingredient separate. Pour cooking sauce over. Bring to a boil; reduce heat and simmer, uncovered, until vegetables are tender, 4 to 5 minutes. Turn vegetables as needed during cooking, but keep each in its own place. Tuck spinach into edge of pan and continue to cook for 2 minutes.

2. To serve, ladle chicken, beef, shrimp, tofu, vegetables, and broth into 2 deep soup bowls. Pass lemon wedges to squeeze over individual servings; accompany with rice.

Makes 2 servings.

CHIKUZEN CHICKEN

A specialty of the former Chikuzen province on the island of Kyushu, this is one of the few stir-fried dishes in Japanese cooking.

⇒ COOKING SAUCE ⇐
1/4 cup Japanese soup stock (dashi)
3 tablespoons soy sauce
1 1/2 tablespoons sugar
1/2 teaspoon red pepper mix
    (shichimi togarashi) or
    1 teaspoon chili garlic sauce

1/2 pound boneless chicken thighs
1 medium carrot
6 ounces bamboo shoots
6 fresh shiitake mushrooms
1/4 pound fresh lotus root or jicama
2 ounces snow peas
2 tablespoons cooking oil
2 teaspoons sesame oil

Getting Ready

1. Combine cooking sauce ingredients in a small bowl.

2. Thinly slice chicken. Roll-cut carrot and bamboo shoots. Discard mushroom stems; thickly slice caps. Peel lotus root, cut in half lengthwise, then cut crosswise into 1/8-inch-thick slices. Trim snow peas and cut in half diagonally.

Cooking

1. Place a wok over high heat until hot. Add cooking oil, swirling to coat sides. Add chicken; stir-fry for 1 1/2 minutes. Add carrot, bamboo shoots, mushrooms, and lotus root; cook for 1 minute.

2. Add cooking sauce; cover and simmer or until vegetables are tender, about 3 minutes. Add snow peas and cook for 30 seconds.

3. Stir in sesame oil, then serve.

Makes 4 servings.

SKEWERED BARBECUED CHICKEN
(Yakitori)

Skewered grilled chicken in a sweet soy sauce is a specialty of yakitori-ya, the small bars that serve drinks and grilled snacks throughout Japan. You can often spot them by the red lantern hanging outside the door. Traditionally, yakitori skewers are grilled over coals, and this recipe works well on the stove, in the broiler, or on the barbecue.

⟫ GLAZE ⟪

2/3 cup soy sauce
1/3 cup Japanese rice wine (saké)
1/4 cup Japanese sweet cooking rice wine (mirin)
2 tablespoons sugar

12 bamboo skewers, each 8 inches long

1 pound boneless chicken, cut into 1-inch pieces
3 green onions, cut into 1-inch lengths
1/2 red bell pepper, seeded and cut into 3/4-inch squares
1/2 green bell pepper, seeded and cut into 3/4-inch squares
Garlic salt
Cooking oil

Getting Ready
1. Combine glaze ingredients in a small pan. Bring slowly to a simmer over low heat, then simmer, uncovered, until slightly syrupy, about 2 minutes. Remove from heat.

2. Soak skewers in water for 15 minutes or until ready to use.

3. Alternately thread chicken, green onions, and bell peppers on skewers. Sprinkle with garlic salt.

Cooking
1. Lightly oil a grill or wide frying pan; place over medium-high heat until hot. Place skewers on grill and cook until chicken is no longer pink, 2 minutes on each side for breasts, 3 minutes for thighs. Brush glaze on all sides of skewered food and continue to cook for 30 seconds on each side.

Makes 12 skewers.

SALT-GRILLING
Salt-grilling, or shio-yaki, is a perfect example of the "less is more" philosophy of Japanese cooking. It produces succulent, beautifully browned fish and requires just two ingredients: fish and salt. First, thread the fish (or fillet) from head to tail with two or three metal skewers in a wavelike pattern; avoid piercing one side of the fish, which will be the "public" side, to be served facing up. The skewers help hold the fish together and make it easy to handle during grilling. Next, salt the fish with a generous amount of sea salt and let it stand for 10 minutes. This draws out moisture, reduces fishy odors, and aids in browning. Heavily salt the fins and tail to keep them from scorching, then grill or broil the fish, starting with the "public" side to the flame. Remove the skewers and serve the fish with a lemon wedge.

Salt-grilled fish and teriyaki chicken skewers on display at a roadside food stand.

TOKIE'S SESAME CHICKEN
(Kara Age)

Kara age, or dry-frying, refers to foods that are lightly dusted with cornstarch or flour before frying, which seals the moisture into the food and creates a delicate, crispy coating. This recipe is based on one of my favorite dishes served at Tokie's Restaurant in Foster City, California, by my longtime friend, Tokie Onizuka.

⇛ SAUCE ⇚
1/2 cup soy sauce
1/2 cup Japanese rice wine (saké)
1/2 cup Japanese soup stock (dashi)
1/3 cup sugar
2 teaspoons minced garlic
1/2 teaspoon minced ginger
2 teaspoons cornstarch dissolved in
   1 tablespoon water

1 teaspoon white sesame seeds
1/2 pound spinach, stems removed,
   rinsed and coarsely chopped
3/4 pound boneless chicken thighs,
   cut into 2- by 2-inch pieces
Cornstarch
Cooking oil
4 cups hot cooked rice

Getting Ready
1. Combine soy sauce, saké, dashi, sugar, garlic, and ginger in a 2-quart pan. Cook over medium heat, stirring once or twice, until sugar is dissolved. Reduce heat and simmer, uncovered, for 10 minutes. Add cornstarch solution and cook, stirring, until sauce boils and thickens. Keep sauce warm.

2. Place sesame seeds in a small frying pan over medium heat; cook, shaking pan frequently, until seeds are lightly browned, 3 to 4 minutes. Immediately remove from pan to cool.

3. Cook spinach in boiling water for 1 minutes; drain well and keep warm.

Cooking
1. Dredge chicken in cornstarch; shake off excess. Place a wide frying pan over medium heat. Add oil to a depth of 1/4 inch. When oil is hot, add chicken and pan-fry, uncovered, until no longer pink in center, about 4 minutes on each side. Lift out and drain on paper towels.

2. Place rice in 4 individual bowls; top each serving with 1/4 of the spinach. Cut chicken into 1/2-inch-wide strips, dip in sauce, then arrange over spinach. Drizzle 1 to 2 tablespoons additional sauce over each serving, then sprinkle with sesame seeds.

Makes 4 servings.

TAKE A BOW
Bowing is the "handshake" of greeting in Japan, and you can tell a lot from the way it's done. The deeper the bow, the longer it is held, and the more times it is repeated, the more respect is being shown. Bowing is supposed to be done from the waist with the hands at the sides and the back straight. But don't worry, if you're a foreigner you're not really expected to know this, and any kind of bow or nod will be appreciated. Although Japan may seem to have more mysterious rules of etiquette than some countries, I have found that the basic ones are the same as they are anywhere else in the world: Be nice, be humble, and take your cue from the people around you.

GRILLED BEEF AND VEGETABLES
(Teppan-yaki)

HEAD 'EM UP, RUB 'EM DOWN

You've probably heard of Japan's famous—and famously expensive—Kobe beef. But on my last trip to Japan, I visited the Wadakin Ranch, where the even pricier (up to $150 per pound) Matsuzaka beef is raised. As cattle go, these animals have it pretty good. During their last year, they're fed a diet of corn, barley, wheat, and other grains, all washed down with beer! To ensure that their meat is tender and well marbled, they're exercised one at a time, and every other day they're even given a full massage, which includes getting sprayed with mouthfuls of saké by the rancher. I tried this technique, but kept swallowing the saké. I couldn't tell who was getting more relaxed, the cow or me!

Matsuzaka cattle get a bath of saké as part of their regular massage treatment.

Teppan-yaki restaurants feature large flattop griddles with seats all around them. The chef grills the food to order, while you sit back and watch the show. If you enjoy performing, you can take the same approach with an electric griddle, plugged in right at the table. If you're cooking in the kitchen, grill the steaks first and keep them warm while you cook the vegetables. For variety, you can also grill Asian eggplant, sweet potato rounds, green onions, snow peas, or Chinese cabbage.

4 small boneless beef steaks, such as New York, each about ½ inch thick
Salt and pepper
1 medium onion
1 each red and yellow bell peppers
1 each zucchini and crookneck squash
¼ pound bean sprouts, rinsed and drained
8 fresh shiitake mushrooms, stems discarded

⇒ MUSTARD SAUCE ⇐
1½ tablespoons dry mustard powder
¼ cup soy sauce
2 tablespoons Japanese sweet cooking rice wine (mirin)
½ teaspoon sesame oil

1 tablespoon cooking oil
2 tablespoons butter, cut into small cubes

Getting Ready

1. Trim fat from steaks; sprinkle meat lightly with salt and pepper. Cut onion in half lengthwise, then crosswise into half-moons about ¼ inch thick; run a wooden pick through all layers of onion to hold rings together. Cut peppers into ¼-inch-thick slices; remove seeds and veins. Cut squash into ¼-inch-thick slices. Cover and chill all vegetables until ready to cook.

2. In a bowl, combine mustard sauce ingredients until evenly blended; pour into 4 small bowls.

Cooking

1. Heat a Japanese iron griddle (teppan) or electric frying pan to medium-high. Brush griddle with half the oil. Place half of meat and vegetables on griddle. Place half of the butter on top of the vegetables. Cook, turning once, until meat is done to your liking, about 2 minutes per side for rare, and vegetables are tender-crisp. Repeat with remaining meat, vegetables, and butter.

2. Before serving, cut meat into thin strips. Serve with mustard sauce for dipping.

Makes 4 servings.

BEEF SUKIYAKI

Although it's one of the most popular Japanese dishes worldwide, sukiyaki is a relative newcomer to Japanese cuisine, having appeared on the scene in the late 19th century. This recipe is based on the traditional Osaka-Kyoto method, in which slices of beef are first browned at the table in an iron pot, then simmered with vegetables and noodles in a sweet soy-based stock. The meat must be very thin, so it's best to have your butcher slice it for you; if you slice it yourself, partially freeze it first.

1 pound boneless tender beef, sliced paper-thin
4 fresh shiitake mushrooms
4 white button mushrooms
1 medium onion
6 green onions
1 medium carrot
¼ pound napa cabbage
1 package (14 oz.) regular-firm tofu, drained and cut into 1-inch squares
½ cup sliced bamboo shoots, drained
1 package (14 oz.) yam noodles (shirataki), drained
2 small pieces beef suet or 2 teaspoons cooking oil

⇒ COOKING SAUCE ⇐

3 cups Japanese soup stock (dashi)
1 cup soy sauce
1 cup Japanese sweet cooking rice wine (mirin)
¼ cup sugar
6 slices ginger, each the size of a quarter

Getting Ready

1. Cut beef slices into 2-inch squares.

2. Prepare vegetables: Discard stems from shiitake and button mushrooms; slice caps. Slice onion ¼ inch thick. Cut green onions into 1½-inch lengths. Cut carrot diagonally into thin slices. Cut napa cabbage into 1½-inch pieces.

3. Arrange ingredients attractively on a large platter. Cover and chill until ready to cook.

4. In a small pan, heat cooking sauce ingredients over medium heat just until sugar dissolves. Pour sauce into a small pitcher.

Cooking

1. Heat a heavy frying pan over medium heat on a tabletop cooking unit; rub hot surface with suet. Place one-third of meat in pan, and cook just until it loses pinkness, 1 to 2 minutes; push meat to corner of pan.

2. Add one-third of vegetables and noodles, and enough cooking sauce to barely cover pan bottom. Cook until vegetables are tender-crisp, 3 to 5 minutes, turning as needed. Serve as cooked.

3. Repeat with remaining ingredients, adding enough sauce to cover pan bottom for each batch.

Makes 4 servings.

BAMBOO BABIES

Takenoko, the Japanese name for bamboo shoots, literally means "child of bamboo." When spring arrives in Japan, people love to eat fresh bamboo shoots, especially in bamboo rice, cooked with slices of the tender shoots, soy sauce, and mirin. In the West, fresh shoots are not available, but canned ones can be quite tasty. You can find them in supermarkets, though Asian markets offer a wider selection, including whole tips and sliced or diced shoots. If you find that they have a slightly tinny taste, rinse them or blanch them quickly in boiling water.

GRILLED SESAME BEEF

Tender steak with a tangy soy-sesame sauce makes a great entrée. I like to garnish this dish with a lemon wedge and a mound of thinly sliced cucumbers or finely grated daikon.

OPEN SESAME

Black and white sesame seeds are among the most common flavorings and condiments in Japanese cooking. Before using them, toast them briefly by tossing them in a dry pan over medium heat to bring out their flavor and fragrance. If a recipe calls for ground seeds, crush them gently in a mortar and pestle, or pulse briefly in a spice grinder. Don't mash them so hard that they become a paste. Once they're ground, use them right away. Sesame seeds are much cheaper when bought in bulk in Asian markets. They keep longer when stored in a tightly sealed container in the refrigerator.

⇒ MARINADE ⇐

2 tablespoons sesame seeds, finely crushed
1/4 cup soy sauce
1/4 cup Japanese rice wine (saké)
I tablespoon lemon juice
I tablespoon sesame oil
I tablespoon sugar
2 green onions, minced
2 teaspoons minced garlic
2 teaspoons minced ginger

I pound boneless tender beef steaks, such as rib eye or New York, cut into long strips 2 to 3-inches-square
I teaspoon cornstarch dissolved in 2 teaspoons water

⇒ GARNISH ⇐

Sesame seeds, toasted
Thinly sliced green onion

Getting Ready

1. Place sesame seeds in a small frying pan over medium heat; cook, shaking pan frequently, until lightly browned, 3 to 4 minutes. Immediately remove from pan to cool.

2. Combine marinade ingredients in a bowl. Add beef to marinade; turn to coat. Cover and refrigerate for 4 hours or overnight.

Cooking

1. Heat a Japanese iron griddle (teppan) or electric frying pan to medium-high. Lift meat from marinade and drain briefly; reserve marinade in a small pan. Place meat on griddle and cook, turning once, until done to your liking, about 2 minutes per side for rare.

2. While meat is cooking, simmer marinade for 3 minutes. Add cornstarch solution and cook, stirring, until sauce bubbles and thickens slightly.

3. To serve, pour sauce onto a serving plate. Cut meat into crosswise slices, then reassemble in its original shape on sauce.

Makes 4 servings.

PORK CUTLETS
(Tonkatsu)

The word katsu is the Japanese version of "cutlet," and tonkatsu—fried breaded pork cutlet—has been popular in Japan since the 1930s, when the dish was first made at a Tokyo restaurant. Today, tonkatsu shops all over the country specialize in the dish, each with its own secret recipe for the sweet-savory dipping sauce.

IN PRAISE OF PANKO

If you've ever used store-bought bread crumbs to coat fried foods and gotten crummy results, give Japanese panko crumbs a try. You'll never look back! You can find panko in the Asian section of most supermarkets. These crumbs, which give tonkatsu its wonderfully crisp texture, are lighter, coarser and flakier than Western-style bread crumbs. When fried, they create a crunchy golden coating that doesn't taste greasy and stays crisp longer than regular bread crumbs.

⊳ DIPPING SAUCE ⊲
1/2 teaspoon dry mustard powder
2 tablespoons Japanese rice wine (saké)
1/4 cup catsup
1 tablespoon soy sauce
1 tablespoon hoisin sauce or char siu sauce
2 teaspoons sugar
2 teaspoons Worcestershire sauce

1 pound boneless pork loin chops, cut 1/2 inch thick
Salt and black pepper
1/2 cup flour
1 egg, lightly beaten
1 cup Japanese-style bread crumbs (panko)
Cooking oil

⊳ GARNISHES ⊲
Shredded red and green cabbage
Lemon wedges

Getting Ready

1. Combine mustard and saké in a bowl; whisk until smooth. Add remaining dipping sauce ingredients; mix well.

2. Lightly pound pork; sprinkle with salt and pepper. Dredge pork in flour; shake off excess. Dip into egg, drain briefly, then coat with bread crumbs.

Cooking

1. Place a wide frying pan over medium heat. Add oil to a depth of 1/4 inch. When oil is hot, add pork and pan-fry, covered, for 2 minutes on each side. Uncover and cook until pork is no longer pink in center, about 2 minutes longer on each side. Lift out and drain on paper towels.

2. To serve, cut pork into crosswise slices, then reassemble in the original shape on a serving plate. Garnish with cabbage and lemon wedges. Serve with dipping sauce.

Makes 4 servings.

PORK ROAST WITH MISO
(Butaniku No Misozuke)

The famous Nagasaki-style stewed pork dish known as buta kaku-ni takes almost two days to cook. My version is considerably quicker. It braises in just 2 hours and comes out meltingly tender. I serve it with a tangy pineapple sauce made with the braising liquid.

3 pounds boneless pork butt or shoulder

2½ cups water

½ cup soy sauce

1¼ cups fermented soybean paste (white miso)

¼ cup sugar

2 tablespoons hoisin sauce

6 slices ginger, each the size of a quarter

1 cup diced pineapple

1½ teaspoons cornstarch dissolved in 1 tablespoon water

2 green onions, thinly sliced

Cooking

1. Place pork in a close-fitting 2- to 3-quart pan; add enough cold water to cover pork. Heat to boiling; boil for 2 minutes, then drain.

2. In a bowl, whisk together the 2½ cups water, soy sauce, miso, sugar, and hoisin sauce until smooth. Pour over meat in pan; add ginger. Bring to a boil; reduce heat, cover, and simmer 1½ hours. Turn meat several times during cooking. Add pineapple and simmer until meat is very tender when pierced, about 30 minutes longer.

3. Lift out meat and place on a cutting board. Slice meat ⅛ inch thick. Arrange in overlapping rows on a serving platter; cover and keep warm.

4. Place pineapple and 1 cup of cooking liquid in a small pan. Add cornstarch solution to pan and cook, stirring, until mixture boils and thickens. Pour sauce over meat, and sprinkle with green onions.

Makes 8 servings.

THE JOY OF SOY

By far the most commonly used seasoning in Japan is soy sauce. But this magic stuff is anything but common! It's made from steamed soybeans and wheat, which are inoculated with a yeast culture, mixed with salt water, and fermented in tanks for up to half a year. The amino acids in soy sauce have the amazing ability to enhance the flavors of other foods. The Japanese believe that in addition to the four basic tastes— sweet, salty, bitter, and sour—there's a fifth one, umami or "savory." Soy sauce is one of the key ingredients used to achieve this elusive flavor.

Kikkoman's Goyogura soy sauce plant in Noda is a living museum where soy sauce is brewed for the Imperial Household using traditional techniques and equipment, like these beautiful wooden fermentation vats.

FOX NOODLES
(Kitsune Udon)

Some say that these noodles get their name from golden tan color of the fried tofu puffs that top them off.

⇒ SHRIMP PASTE ⇐
1/4 cup water chestnuts
1/2 pound medium raw shrimp, shelled and deveined
1 tablespoon minced green onion
1 teaspoon cornstarch
1/8 teaspoon white pepper

1 package (14 oz.) fresh Japanese-style noodles (udon)
2 packages (1 1/2 oz. each) tofu puffs

⇒ SEASONING ⇐
1 1/2 cups water
2 tablespoons soy sauce
2 tablespoons sweet cooking rice wine (mirin)
1 tablespoon sugar

⇒ BROTH ⇐
5 cups Japanese soup stock (dashi)
1/2 cup sweet cooking rice wine (mirin)
1/4 cup soy sauce
2 teaspoons oyster-flavored sauce

⇒ GARNISHES ⇐
6 small cooked shrimp
1 green onion, thinly sliced
1/2 small carrot, thinly sliced
4 button mushrooms, thinly sliced
Chili garlic sauce

Getting Ready

1. In a food processor, finely chop water chestnuts. Add raw shrimp, green onion, cornstarch, and pepper; process to make a chunky paste.

2. Bring a large pot of water to a boil. Add noodles and cook according to package directions. Drain, rinse with cold water, and drain again; set aside.

3. In a bowl, cover tofu puffs with hot water and let stand for 1 minute; drain and squeeze out water. Cut each puff in half crosswise; gently pull open the center of each to make a little bag. Stuff equal amounts of shrimp paste into each bag.

Cooking

1. Combine seasoning ingredients in a 2-quart pan; cook, stirring once or twice, until sugar dissolves. Add filled tofu puffs and simmer, uncovered, for 5 minutes or until shrimp filling turns pink.

2. Combine broth ingredients in a 2- to 3-quart pan. Bring to a boil; reduce heat and simmer for 5 minutes. Add noodles and cook until heated through, 2 to 3 minutes.

3. Divide noodles and broth among 6 individual soup bowls. With a slotted spoon, lift out tofu puffs and place two pieces in each bowl. Top serving with shrimp, green onion, carrot, and mushrooms. Add chili garlic sauce to taste.

Makes 6 servings.

JAPANESE STIR-FRIED NOODLES
(Yakisoba)

Buckwheat noodles (soba) stir-fried in a tangy brown sauce are a popular favorite at festivals in Japan, even though they're really Chinese in origin. I like to make this dish with Chinese egg noodles. My version is vegetarian, but you can also add beef or chicken.

⇒ SAUCE ⇐
2 tablespoons vegetarian oyster-
    flavored sauce
2 tablespoons Worcestershire sauce
1 tablespoon seasoned rice vinegar
1 teaspoon sugar
2 teaspoons Japanese rice wine
    (saké)

6 dried black mushrooms
1/2 of a 12-ounce package fresh
    Chinese egg noodles
2 tablespoons cooking oil
1/2 onion, sliced
3 slices ginger, each the size of
    a quarter, shredded
1 carrot, thinly sliced
1 cup shredded cabbage
2 tablespoons chicken broth
1/4 pound snow peas, trimmed and
    cut in half diagonally
2 green onions, cut diagonally into
    1 1/2-inch lengths

Getting Ready
1. Combine sauce ingredients in a small bowl; set aside.

2. Soak mushrooms in warm water to cover until softened, about 20 minutes; drain. Discard stems and slice caps.

3. Bring a large pot of water to a boil. Add noodles and cook according to package directions. Drain, rinse with cold water, and drain again; set aside.

Cooking
1. Place a wok over high heat until hot. Add oil, swirling to coat sides. Add onion and ginger; stir-fry for 1 minute. Add mushrooms, carrot, cabbage, and broth; stir-fry until vegetables are tender-crisp, about 1 minute. Add snow peas and green onions; cook for 1 minute.

2. Reduce heat and add reserved sauce; add noodles and toss to coat. Cook until noodles are heated through, 2 minutes.

Makes 3 servings.

OODLES OF NOODLES
Noodle shops are everywhere in Japan. You can duck in for a quick, cheap bowlful of noodles in steaming broth and leave moments later feeling warm and content. Japanese noodles come in two main types: buckwheat flour or wheat flour. Light gray, speckled buckwheat soba and pale green cha-soba, made with green tea, are most popular in Tokyo and the colder northern regions. Flour-and-water noodles—soft, thick udon, fine somen, and broad, flat kishimen—are the favorites in Osaka and the warmer south. Ramen, Chinese egg noodles, are also popular. Look for soba, udon, and egg noodles either dried or fresh in the refrigerator case at Asian markets and many supermarkets. You can substitute one for another in most Japanese noodle soup recipes.

At a country house near Nagoya, I learned the secrets of making tender fresh udon noodles by hand.

CHILLED SUMMER NOODLES
(Somen)

Here's my interpretation of a much-loved summertime dish, zaru soba, in which soba noodles are cooked, chilled, and served over ice with a sweet soy sauce for dipping on the side. I like to make it with delicate somen and sprinkle the sauce on as a dressing.

SLURP!

What you've heard about slurping in Japan is true . . . and then some! When eating noodles, slurping is not only accepted, it's expected. You use your chopsticks to pluck up a few strands from the piping hot broth, then quickly suck them in along with plenty of air to cool them off. This cannot and should not be done quietly. A few months ago, I was eating in a noodle shop in Tokyo, and the place was nearly empty. As I ate, I kept thinking, "What a loud cash register they have in here." As I got up, I noticed it wasn't the cash register. It was an old man slurping a big bowl of soba!

16 medium cooked shrimp
1/3 English cucumber
2 green onions
4 bundles (about 8 oz. total) dried thin Japanese wheat noodles (somen)

⇒ DRESSING ⇐
1 cup Japanese soup stock (dashi)
1/3 cup soy sauce
1/4 cup sweet cooking rice wine (mirin)
2 tablespoons sugar

⇒ OMELET ⇐
2 eggs
1 teaspoon cornstarch
1 teaspoon sugar
1 teaspoon water
Salt
1 teaspoon cooking oil

Getting Ready
1. Shell and devein shrimp, leaving tails on for decoration. Cut cucumber lengthwise, then thinly slice crosswise. Thinly slice green onions.

Cooking
1. Bring a large pot of water to a boil. Add noodles and cook according to package directions. Drain, rinse with cold water, and drain again. Place in a bowl with several ice cubes and chill until ready to serve.

2. In a small pan, heat dressing ingredients over medium heat just until sugar dissolves; let cool. Pour into a small pitcher and chill until ready to serve.

3. In a bowl, beat eggs with cornstarch, sugar, water, and salt to taste. Place a nonstick 8- to 9-inch frying pan over medium heat until hot. Brush with 1/2 teaspoon cooking oil. Add half of the eggs and cook until lightly browned on bottom and set on top, about 1 minute. Turn over and cook for 5 seconds longer; remove from pan. Repeat with 1/2 teaspoon oil and remaining egg. Roll omelets into cylinders and cut crosswise into 1/8-inch shreds.

4. Discard ice cubes and drain noodles. Place noodles in a serving bowl. Toss with 1/2 cup dressing. Garnish with shrimp, cucumber, green onions, and omelet shreds. Pass remaining dressing at the table.

Makes 4 servings.

PLUM WINE SNOW

1 envelope unflavored gelatin
1/4 cup cold water
1/2 cup boiling water
1/2 cup sugar
1/3 cup plum wine
2 tablespoons lemon juice
2 large egg whites

▷ FRUIT-WINE SAUCE ◁
1 cup plum wine
2 tablespoons sugar
1 cup sliced strawberries

Mint sprigs

Cooking

1. In a small saucepan, sprinkle gelatin over cold water; let stand 1 minute to soften. Add boiling water and stir over low heat until gelatin is dissolved. Add sugar and stir until it is dissolved. Add wine and lemon juice. Refrigerate until mixture mounds slightly when dropped from a spoon.

2. In large bowl of an electric mixer, beat egg whites until stiff. Add gelatin mixture and beat until light and fluffy. Pour into 6 dessert dishes; chill until firm, 3 to 4 hours.

3. To prepare sauce, combine ingredients in a small pan. Simmer over medium heat for 3 minutes. Let sauce cool, then chill.

4. Before serving, top each dessert with sauce and a mint sprig.

Makes 6 servings.

MANDARIN ORANGE MOUSSE

1 envelope unflavored gelatin
1/4 cup cold water
3/4 cup sugar
1/2 cup boiling water
1 can (6 oz.) frozen orange juice concentrate
1/2 of a 16-ounce package soft tofu, drained
1 1/2 cups (4 oz.) frozen whipped topping, thawed
1 can (11 oz.) mandarin oranges, drained
Mint sprigs

Cooking

1. Dissolve gelatin in cold water as in step 1 above.

2. In a blender, process sugar, boiling water, softened gelatin, juice concentrate, and tofu until smooth.

3. Pour into a large bowl. Refrigerate until mixture mounds slightly when dropped from a spoon. Fold in whipped topping. Pour into 6 dishes; chill until firm, 3 to 4 hours.

4. Serving, topped with oranges and a mint sprig.

Makes 6 servings.

A SWEET NOTE

The Japanese are sweet on sweets, but they don't usually eat them for dessert. Instead, fruit is served at meals, and sweets are eaten with tea as a between-meal snack. You can find all kinds of Western-style cakes in Japanese bakeries, but traditional Japanese sweets, called wagashi, are something else altogether. They may look like cakes, but they're not made with flour, butter, or yeast. In fact they're not even baked; they're either steamed or uncooked. Wagashi are often made from glutinous rice flour, agar-agar gelatin and filled with pastes of red adzuki beans, sweet potatoes, or chestnuts. These beautifully colored creations are served as part of the tea ceremony—their intense sweetness counteracts the slight bitterness of the tea—and sold in special confectionery shops throughout the country for gift-giving and enjoying at home.

SWEET RED BEAN PANCAKES
(Dora Yaki)

Dora is the Japanese word for "gong," which is just what these delicate pancakes, sandwiched in pairs with a sweet adzuki bean filling, look like. They're a favorite snack sold by street vendors throughout Japan. In place of the red bean paste, you can also use apricot, raspberry, or blackberry preserves sprinkled with a bit of sesame oil.

¼ cup white sesame seeds
1½ cups flour
1 teaspoon baking powder
3 large eggs
⅔ cup sugar
1 tablespoon honey
⅔ cup water
Cooking oil
1½ cups sweetened red bean paste

Getting Ready

1. Place sesame seeds in a small frying pan over medium heat; cook, shaking pan frequently, until lightly browned, 3 to 4 minutes. Immediately remove from pan to cool.

2. Sift flour and baking powder into a large bowl.

3. In a medium bowl, beat eggs lightly. Add sugar and honey; whisk until well blended. Add water and mix well. Pour egg mixture into dry ingredients; whisk until smooth.

Cooking

1. Place a griddle or large skillet over medium heat until hot; wipe griddle with a lightly oiled paper towel. For each pancake, spoon 2 tablespoons batter onto griddle to make a 3-inch circle. Cook until tiny bubbles form on top of pancake, 2 to 3 minutes; turn and cook the other side until golden brown, about 1 minute longer. Repeat until all pancakes are cooked.

2. To assemble, spread 2 tablespoons of bean paste on one pancake; sprinkle with 1 teaspoon sesame seeds. Top with a second pancake and gently press together. Assemble so the more attractive side of each pancake is on the outside. Serve warm or at room temperature.

Makes 2 dozen pancakes, 1 dozen filled pancakes.

Tea for 2 million: visiting a tea plantation in Toba.

GLOSSARY

From Japan to Malaysia and Singapore via Hong Kong and the Philippines is a broad culinary leap, and even if you're somewhat familiar with these cuisines, many of the ingredients won't be on your pantry shelf. While this list isn't all-inclusive, it does include ethnic ingredients used in the recipes in this book. As Asian dishes become more and more a part of home cooking, many of these ingredients can be found in supermarkets. Otherwise, Asian markets (especially ones that cater to a specific country or area) carry good selections including a variety of prepared sauces and fresh ingredients.

In many of the recipes, spice pastes and sauces are made from scratch, but if you're a cook in a hurry, don't worry: a lot of them are available ready-made. Also, many sauces are interchangeable. For example, each country has its own version of fish sauce, so if you find one you like, stick with it. Better one bottle on the shelf than five! The same goes for shrimp paste.

Sauces with a greater proportion of whole ingredients are generally thicker and are referred to as pastes. Sauces and pastes of the same name are used interchangeably depending on the desired appearance of the final product. Both are found in various-sized bottles and jars. Once opened, they should be refrigerated. Most will keep for several months to a year.

Store dry seasonings in a tightly sealed container in a cool, dry place. Most will keep for several months. Before using canned vegetables such as bamboo shoots and straw mushrooms, drain and rinse them to remove any trace of the salty canning liquid. If the vegetables have a metallic taste, blanch them in boiling water with a pinch of salt before cooking further.

Achara: see Pickles, Spanish-style.

Annatto: Seeds of the annatto tree and a powder made from them are used to color Filipino dishes and other foods. Seeds look like fragments of chipped brick. Two tablespoons seeds equal 1 teaspoon powder. For more details, see page 174.

Asian eggplant: see Eggplant.

Asian greens: For some of Martin Yan's favorites, see page 119; see also bok choy, Chinese broccoli, Chinese long beans, choy sum, garlic chives, napa cabbage, peas.

Bagoong: see Filipino shrimp paste.

Bamboo shoots: These are available as whole tips, young tips, sliced, or diced. All are tender-crisp with a sweet taste, but their texture varies. Young winter bamboo tips are the most tender, and sliced shoots are the most fibrous.

Banana leaf : Leaves are used in Southeast Asia as well as in the Americas to wrap foods for steaming or grilling. For more details, see page 122.

Bean curd: see Tofu.

Bean paste, sweetened red: A paste made from cooked, mashed, and sweet-ened adzuki beans is used to fill a variety of savory and sweet dishes, including Japanese pancakes (dora-yaki, page 230).

Bean sprouts: Soybean sprouts have larger heads and are crunchier than mung bean sprouts, but both can be used interchangeably. It is best to use them the day they are purchased, but they will last a couple of days if refrigerated.

Beans, Chinese long: see Chinese long beans.

Blachan: see Shrimp paste, Malay dried.

Black beans, salted: Also called

preserved or fermented black beans, these lend a distinctly pungent, smoky flavor to foods. They come in plastic packages and should feel soft and not look dried out.

Black bean sauce: see Sauce.

Bok choy: This loose-leaved cabbage has thick white stalks and dark green leaves. Stalks have a mildly tangy taste and a crunchy texture; leaves are peppery and soft. Baby bok choy and Shanghai baby bok choy are are sweeter and less fibrous than regular bok choy.

Bonito, flaked dried (katsuo-bushi): Flakes of boiled, smoked, and sun-dried bonito, a kind of tuna, are the main flavoring in Japanese soup stock (dashi); it is also used as a garnish and to flavor dipping sauces for sashimi.

Bouillon, seafood: As a short-cut to making your own fish broth, use 1 fish bouillon cube and 2 cups water, or dilute as directed in recipe.

Candlenut: This mainstay of Malaysian and Indonesian spice pastes is hard in texture and high in fat. For details and for substitutes, see page 135.

Cardamom: This pungent, sweetly aromatic spice, a relative of ginger, is a mainstay of Indian curries and stews, as well as of the spice mix garam masala. Each berry-size pod contains about 20

seeds. Use the whole pod, or whole or freshly ground seeds.

Char siu sauce: see Sauce.

Chayote: For a description of this pear-shaped tropical squash, see page 170.

Chilies, dried: Small dried chilies are fiery hot. Use them whole or broken into smaller pieces. Crushed dried red chilies are simply chopped whole ones. Remember to wash your hands after handling dried and fresh chilies, because their oils can burn or irritate your skin and eyes.

Chilies, fresh: Most of this book's recipes call for red or green jalapeño chilies, which are hot but not too hot, and are widely available. If you prefer, substitute hotter or milder ones. Generally, the smaller the chili, the hotter it is. From hottest to mildest, they include the fiery Thai bird, slightly milder serrano, jalapeño, and mild Anaheim.

Chili garlic sauce: see Sauce.

Chinese barbecued pork (char siu): The honey, soybeans, garlic, and spices in char siu sauce (see Sauce) give Chinese pork and spareribs their pleasantly sweet, rich taste.

Chinese broccoli: It has thin, dusty green stems, deep green leaves, and tiny white flowers. When cooked, the tender stems and leaves have a slight bitter-sweet taste. Choose young, slender stems and unblemished leaves.

Chinese chives: see Garlic chives.

Chinese dried seaweed: see Seaweed.

Chinese five-spice: This cocoa-colored powder is made from combinations of cinnamon, star anise, fennel, cloves, ginger, licorice, Sichuan peppercorns, and dried tangerine peel. It lends a distinct anise and cinnamon flavor to braised meats, roasts, and barbecues.

Chinese long beans: These pencil-thin pale to dark green beans are also called yard-long beans; for details, see page 77.

Chinese parsley: see Cilantro.

Chinese rice wine: see Rice wine.

Chinese sausage (lop cheong): These savory-sweet links, from 4 to 6 inches long, are deep red to brown with a slightly bumpy texture. Most are made from pork, pork fat, duck, or beef. Look for them in Chinese delis, fresh or in vacuum packages.

Chorizo de Bilbao: This Spanish-style sausage flavors Filipino dishes; for more details, see page 171.

Choy sum: This Asian green, also called bok choy sum, looks like a smaller bok choy but with yellow flowers. Cook choy sum as you would bok choy (the flowers are edible, too).

Chrysanthemum, garland (shungiku): It is often referred to as chop suey greens in the markets and on seed packets. Cooked leaves taste very much like the smell of chrysanthemum flowers and foliage (uncooked, they're too overwhelming in flavor for most tastes).

Cilantro: Also known as Chinese parsley or fresh coriander, Cilantro has wide, flat leaves and a distinct, refreshing flavor. Don't confuse it with similar-looking Italian parsley.

Coconut: Coconut milk and cream are commonly used throughout Southeast Asia in curries, stews, and desserts; see instructions on page 140. Coconut water, the liquid in the center of a fresh coconut, is not used in cooking but makes a refreshing drink. Desiccated coconut is sold shredded or flaked, sweetened or unsweetened, in cans or plastic bags; unless a recipe calls for sweetened coconut, use unsweetened.

Coconut chips: see page 70 for how to make your own.

Cooking oil: In Chinese and other Asian cooking, the clear golden oil extracted from peanuts is highly prized for cooking. Its fragrant aroma and distinct nutty flavor make it the ideal oil for stir-frying and deep-frying. Other choices include palm oil (see page 128), canola, and corn oil.

Coriander: The lightly fragrant seeds (more correctly, the dried ripe fruits) of cilantro or Chinese parsley have a sweet flavor of caraway, lemon, and sage that's not at all like the flavor of the fresh herb, (see Cilantro).

Crab: For details on shopping and cooking both Dungeness and blue crabs, see page 83.

Cucumber, English: This hothouse-raised cucumber can reach more than a foot long. It is almost seedless, with a thin, bright green skin. Japanese cucumbers are similar but are only about 1 inch in diameter and 8 inches long.

Cumin: This tiny aromatic seed, which looks like caraway seed, adds pungent, spicy flavor to Asian foods such as curries and satay, though many diners first encounter it in Latin American dishes such as chili con carne. Cumin is available whole or powdered.

Curry: The term generally defines a highly seasoned mixture of various ingredients; it's described on page 107.

Curry leaf: No relation to curry seasoning (see above), these lemon-like leaves do have a decided curry fragrance that goes with many Southeast Asian dishes. For details, see page 92.

Daikon: This Japanese radish, 8 to 14 inches long and 2 to 3 inches in diameter, has crisp white flesh and a sweet, peppery taste; see page 209. Pickled daikon (takuan) is used in some sushi.

Dashi: see Japanese soup stock.

Devil's tongue jelly (konnyaku): Starch from a yamlike tuber called

devil's tongue is made into an almost tasteless dense, gelatinous, and translucent cake that readily absorbs other flavors. Yam noodle (shirataki) is the tuber's filament form, used in sukiyaki. Japanese markets sell both kinds.

Eel, Japanese (unagi): This seasoned and cooked product is ready to eat. Look for it in the refrigerated section of Japanese markets. Use it to top sushi as well as in donburi (see page 204).

Eggplant, Asian: Both Chinese and Japanese kinds range from short and pudgy 3 inches long to thin and slender 9 inches long. Chinese are white to lavender, Japanese light purple to purple-black. Use intechangeably in most recipes; one eggplant equals about 1/4 pound.

Egg roll wrappers: see Wrappers.

Fermented soybean paste: see Miso.

Filipino shrimp paste (bagoong): see Shrimp paste.

Fish sauce: see Sauce.

Flying fish roe (tobiko): Japanese markets sell the salted roe. Just a few of the tiny eggs makes a flavorful and decorative garnish for salads and sushi. Store the roe in the freezer and use as needed. As a substitute, use other types of caviar or the mashed yolk of a hard-cooked egg.

Galangal: This rhizome with translucent pale yellow skin adds a mellow ginger-peppery flavor to stews and

Malaysian spice pastes. For details, see page 82.

Garbanzo beans: These round, beige legumes, also called chickpeas, have a firm, starchy texture and mild flavor. Filipino Beef and Sausage Stew (see page 171) shows Spanish influence. They are sometimes available fresh but more often dried or canned.

Garland chrysanthemum (shungiku): see Chrysanthemum.

Garlic: All of the cuisines in this book make liberal use of garlic this member of the onion family. As a rough equivalent, 1 clove garlic equals 1 teaspoon minced. Fried garlic, often used as a garnish, can be purchased in Asian markets and some supermarkets.

Garlic chives: Chinese cooking uses several kinds of garlic chives. For details, see page 39.

Ginger: Fresh ginger has a smooth golden skin, a fibrous yellow-green interior, and a spicy bite and tantalizing aroma. Young ginger, available seasonally, has a smoother, more delicate flavor and less fibrous texture. Choose ginger that is hard, heavy, and free of wrinkles and mold. A ginger slice the size of a quarter equals 1 teaspoon minced. Japanese pickled ginger (beni-shoga), used as a condiment with sushi, is made from whole fresh ginger preserved in salt and vinegar, then very thinly sliced. It often is dyed pale pink. Pickled ginger, used in Chinese cooking, is cured in brine, then soaked in a sugar-vinegar solution; red pickled

ginger is somewhat sweeter. Preserved ginger is packed in a heavy sugar syrup that becomes infused with a mild ginger taste. Candied ginger is tender young ginger, cooked and sugar-coated.

Ginkgo nuts: Buff-colored seeds of the ginkgo tree have a delicately sweet taste and are popular in Japanese cooking. Asian markets sell fresh nuts in fall and winter; the hard shell must be removed before eating. Or look for dried or canned nuts.

Gyoza: see Wrappers.

Hoisin sauce: see Sauce.

Jackfruit: This spiny oval or oblong tropical fruit has white or yellowish fruit with a bland, sweet flavor. For details, see page 145.

Japanese fish cake (kamaboko): This ready-to-eat fish cake looks something like a long, bright pink sponge on a thin strip of wood. It is made from puréed whitefish and potato starch, which is molded, colored, and steamed. The Japanese eat it as a snack with soy sauce or with wheat noodles in dishes like hot udon soup or cold somen salad. Look for kamaboko in the refrigerated section of Asian markets.

Japanese pepper (sansho): This reddish brown powdered spice is not pepper but the pod of prickly ash; its flavor is tangy rather than hot. Look for

it in Japanese markets.

Japanese pickled ginger: see Ginger.

Japanese rice wine: see Rice wine.

Japanese seaweed (nori): see Seaweed.

Japanese soup stock (dashi): It's easy to make this basic ingredient for many traditional Japanese soups, marinades, and sauces from dried giant sea kelp (konbu), flaked dried bonito (katsuo-bushi), and water; see recipe on page 192. Although homemade dashi has the best flavor, many home cooks find it easier to use instant dashi (dashi-no-moto) granules, powder, or concentrate.

Japanese-style bread crumbs (panko): These dried, toasted flakes, which are larger and coarser than Western-style bread crumbs, give a crunchy coating to deep-fried foods such as pork cutlets (tonkatsu, page 224). Use as you would bread crumbs. Unlike some batter- or crumb-coated foods, panko does not taste greasy after frying, and it retains its crisp texture even after standing.

Japanese wheat noodles (soba, somen, udon): see Noodles.

Jicama: Under its brown, leathery skin is crunchy, slightly fibrous, and sweet white flesh. Although a bit more fibrous and less sweet than fresh water chestnuts, jicama makes a good substitute. Choose small, firm, well-rounded roots that are free of blemishes and mold.

Kaffir lime:  This small Southeast Asian citrus fruit has bright yellow-green skin whose aromatic rind is used in cooking; its glossy, dark green leaves are used for their strong lemon-floral fragrance. Both rind and leaves are available dried, and sometimes fresh in Asian markets.

Kamaboko: see Japanese fish cake.

Katsuo-bushi: see Bonito, flaked dried.

Kecap manis: see Soy sauce, thick.

Kelp: see Seaweed.

Ketupat: See Rice cakes.

Konbu: see Seaweed.

Konnyaku: see Devil's tongue jelly.

Kung pao sauce: see Sauce.

Lemongrass: This herb imparts a delicate lemony flavor and aroma to Southeast Asian foods. To prepare, see page 130.

Longan: Oval fruit, about the size of a small plum, has red, pink, or yellow skin over sweet translucent flesh somewhat similar to that of lychee. Longans are available canned, crystallized, and sometimes fresh.

Longtong: see Rice cakes.

Lop cheong: see Chinese sausage.

Lotus root: This rhizome adds a fibrous crunch to soups and braised dishes. For details, see page 216.

Lumpia: see Wrappers.

Lychee: Fresh fruit looks like a crimson pink berry 1 to 2 inches across. When the bumpy, leathery peel is slipped off, the semitranslucent, juicy flesh is revealed. For details, see page 59.

Macapuno preserves: Shredded meat from a kind of coconut with very soft meat is s cooked with sweetener and water, then used as a filling for Filipino Merienda Tartlets (page 176).

Malay dried shrimp paste (blachan): see Shrimp paste.

Mee: see Noodles

Mirin: see Rice wine

Miso: This protein-rich mainstay of the Japanese diet is appealing because of its taste and aroma. For details on the several types of miso and recipes, see page 201.

Mochi: see Rice cakes, glutinous.

Mushrooms, fresh: The delicate shell-shaped oyster mushroom and long-stemmed, tiny-capped enoki both have a mild flavor. Firm, golden brown shiitake mushrooms have a rich, meaty flavor. All are smooth and velvety in texture.

Mushrooms, dried and canned: Chinese black mushrooms and Japanese shiitake mushrooms share some characteristics: both kinds have brownish black caps, tan undersides, a rich and meaty texture, and wild mushroom flavor. Straw mushrooms, which have a delicate sweetness and a firm, meaty texture, are available peeled or unpeeled, in cans only; drain before using.

Mustard: Dry mustard powder mixed with liquid is a pungent and fiery condiment, adding a clean-tasting hotness to Chinese appetizers and to sauces for Japanese dishes such as teppan-yaki. Chinese, Japanese (karashi), and English-style dry mustards are interchangeable.

Napa cabbage: Both short Chinese and tall Japanese napa cabbage have sweet, creamy stalks with ruffled, pale green edges. Use either kind as you would regular cabbage, but cooking time is less.

Noodles: Bean thread noodles (dried), made from mung bean starch, come in different lengths and thicknesses. Before using, soak in warm water until softened, about 5 minutes. Chinese egg noodles (fresh) come in dozens of widths, sizes, and flavors. Cook according to package directions. Japanese wheat noodles include three of Japan's most popular noodles: soba, udon, and somen. All differ in looks, vary greatly in flavor and texture, and come both dried and fresh. For more details, see page 227. Rice noodles (fresh), made from long-grain rice flour, are soft, pliable, and milky white. For details, see page 97. Wide, flat ones are called kway teow. Dried rice stick noodles are stiff, brittle, and available in varying widths and lengths. For details, see page 141. Thick ones are called lai fun. Yam noodles (shirataki): see Devil's tongue jelly.

Nori: see Seaweed, Japanese.

Okra pods: Tapered green pods, slightly fuzzy, have ridged skin that should be bright green and firm. Choose pods no more than 4 inches long, because larger ones may be tough. If okra is cut, it gives off a mucilaginous substance good for thickening stews and soups; however, for Asian cooking, trim stems without piercing the pods. Chinese okra is similar to common okra but without its thickening qualities.

Oyster-flavored sauce: see Sauce.

Palm sugar: For details on this basic sweetener in Southeast Asian cooking, see page 68.

Palm vinegar: see Vinegar.

Pandan leaf: The fragrant leaves of the screwpine add a distinct flavor and green color to Malaysian dishes, mainly desserts. See page 147.

Panko: see Japanese-style bread crumbs.

Patis: see Shrimp paste.

Peas, edible-pod: This description applies to both snow peas (Chinese pea pods) and sugar snap peas. Snow peas have flat pods with a sweet, sugary flavor and crisp, crunchy texture. Sugar snaps have thicker pods and similar flavor.

Peppers, sweet: Red and green bell peppers have a mild, sweet flavor and juicy flesh. The red kind are the ripe form of green ones. These bell-shaped peppers also come in yellow, orange, purple, and brown.

Pickles, Spanish-style (achara): This is a condiment made from shredded papaya pickled in vinegar with carrots, sweet peppers, onion, and garlic. Also spelled atsara, atchara.

Plum sauce: See Sauce.

Red pepper mix (shichimi togarashi): For a description of this Japanese blend, also called seven-spice, see page 196.

Rice: Glutinous rice, a variety of short-grain rice, is also known as sweet or sticky rice. Grains resemble rice-shaped pearls. When cooked, grains become soft, sticky, and translucent. Long-grain rice is the least starchy of all the kinds of rice; it cooks up dry and fluffy with grains that separate easily. These characteristics make it ideal for fried rice. Medium-grain rice is a daily staple in Japan and Korea; it's also the rice used in sushi; see page 186. For more on rice, see page 204.

Rice cakes, glutinous: Longtong or ketupat are cakes of compressed gluti-

nous rice served with satay and other Malaysian dishes. For instructions on how to make it, see page 72. In Japanese dishes, mochi is cooked glutinous rice formed into balls or cakes; see page 194.

Rice flour: Ground glutinous rice flour is used to create sweet doughs for dim sum and for Chinese and Japanese pastries. Boiled dough forms a smooth, chewy casing; deep-frying yields a lightly crisp exterior with a sweet, sticky inside. Flour made from ground long-grain rice is used to make rice paper, rice noodles, steamed cakes, and other dim sum dishes.

Rice paper: Brittle, semitransparent round or triangular sheets are made from rice flour. Before using, soften between dampened towels. Use to wrap savory bundles of meats and vegetables and eat as is, or deep-fry until golden brown.

Rice stick noodles, dried: see Noodles.

Rice wine: Chinese rice wine is a rich amber liquid made from fermented glutinous rice and millet. It is aged 10 to 100 years to achieve its rich, full-bodied flavor. Shaoxing (Shao Hsing), in eastern China, produces some of the best-quality rice wines. Japanese sweet cooking rice wine (mirin) is also made from glutinous rice; it adds a rich flavor and glossy sheen to cooked dishes. Japanese rice wine (sake), has a clean, lightly sweet, flowery taste. It is also used in cooking and in marinades to tenderize meats or to remove off odors and fishy tastes. For manufacturing and serving information, see page 213.

Sake: see Rice wine.

Sansho: see Japanese pepper.

Sauces (see also Soy sauce): These products are available in Asian markets and some supermarkets. Black bean sauce is made from salted black beans and rice wine; it may contain garlic or hot chilies. Char siu or barbecue sauce is a thick sauce made from fermented soybeans, vinegar, tomato paste, chilies, garlic, honey or sugar, and other spices. Chili sauce is made of fresh and dried chilies and vinegar with seasonings such as garlic, ginger, soybeans, and sesame oil. A sweetened version is popular in Malaysia and Singapore. Filipino fish sauce (patis): see Shrimp paste, Filipino. Curry sauce is a mix of spices used in curry. Fish sauce, an all-purpose flavoring agent used throughout Southeast Asia and southern China, is a thin, amber-colored fermented fish extract. Its distinct pungent aroma, something like soy sauce and fish, mellows with cooking and adds a delicious, slightly salty taste to foods. For descriptions of various kinds, see page 158. Hoisin sauce is a robust combination of fermented soybeans, vinegar, garlic, sugar, and spices. Its spicy-sweet flavor complements many dishes, including mu shu variations and Peking duck. Kung pao sauce contains red chilies, sesame oil, soybeans, sweet potato, ginger, garlic, and other spices. Oyster-flavored sauce is a thick, dark brown all-purpose seasoning made from oyster extracts, sugar, and seasonings. Its distinct sweet-smoky flavor goes well in any meat or vegetable stir-fry. Hot and vegetarian variations are available. Peanut-flavored sauce or satay sauce is best for dipping or barbecuing. Plum sauce is a light, amber-colored sauce made from salted plums, apricots, yams, rice vinegar, chilies, and other spices. The sweet-tart chunky sauce is often served with roast duck, barbecued meats, and deep-fried appetizers. Shrimp sauce, thick and pungent, is made from salted fermented shrimp; it's a staple in Chinese and Southeast Asian cooking. Sweet and sour sauce is simply made from vinegar and sugar. Cantonese versions are fruitier. Popular additions include chili, catsup, and ginger. Teriyaki sauce has a savory, sweet flavor that goes well with any barbecued or grilled meat, poultry, fish, or shellfish. Traditionally, it's made from equal portions of soy sauce and Japanese sweet cooking rice wine; it may include pineapple juice, sake, brown sugar, ginger, and garlic.

Seaweed, dried: In Japan, seaweed is harvested, washed, dried, seasoned, and packaged. Deep green sheets of nori are used to wrap sushi and are shredded for garnishes, and olive-brown giant sea kelp (konbu) is used to make Japanese soup stock (dashi). Chinese-style dried seaweed, sold in round or square bundles in Asian markets, is coarser in texture than the more processed Japanese nori. When reconstituted, the purple, lacy dried leaves look like purple cellophane, and their mild aroma of the sea enhances most seafood dishes.

Sesame oil: Dark amber Asian sesame oil is pressed from toasted white sesame seeds. The best oils are labeled as 100 percent pure. Use just a small amount to add a nutty taste and aroma to marinades, dressings, and stir-fries. Don't confuse Asian sesame oil with the light-colored oil used in salad dressings and for sautéing.

Sesame seeds: Both black and white kinds are used to flavor and garnish dishes. White sesame seeds, hulled and unhulled, has a sweet, nutty flavor. Black sesame seeds are slightly bitter. Toasting, particulary of white seeds, intensifies the flavor and aroma. The Japanese name for sesame seeds is goma.

Shallots: Shallots are familiar enough in Western kitchens that they don't need an introduction. But Asian shallots are generally smaller, so when you are shopping look for bulbs each about the size of a walnut. Fried shallots are used as a garnish; to make them, see page 124.

Shaoxing wine: see Wine.

Shichimi togarashi: see Red pepper mix.

Shrimp: Dried shrimp are tiny shrimp preserved in brine, then dried, creating slightly chewy morsels with a pungent taste. For details, see page 94. Fresh shrimp come in various sizes; when size is important, it is listed in the recipe. See also page 80; for instructions on deveining and butterflying shrimp, see page 129.

Shrimp paste: Malay dried shrimp paste (blachan) is the sun-dried version of shrimp sauce, used as a flavoring in many spice pastes. To make the Malaysian condiment sambal blachan, see page 115. Filipino shrimp paste (bagoong) is similar. This condiment and flavoring agent is made from salted, cured small fish or shrimp that are then fermented for several weeks. The liquid given off, called Filipino fish sauce (patis), is also used as a sauce or condiment.

Shungiku: see Chrysanthemum, garland.

Sichuan peppercorns: The dried reddish brown berries of the prickly ash tree add a woodsy fragrance to foods; for details, see page 42.

Sichuan preserved vegetable: Kohlrabi, mustard greens, napa cabbage, or turnips can be the main ingredient in these spicy preserved vegetables. Chili powder and ground Sichuan peppercorns give them a spicy-salty taste. In traditional Chinese cooking, each vegetable is used in a different way, but for American tastes, all can be used interchangeably.

Somen: see Noodles.

Soybeans, fresh: Even rice doesn't have as many guises in Asian cooking as soybeans do. These rather bland-tasting legumes with very high nutritive value form the base for products as diverse as tofu, soybean oil, soy sauce and other flavorings, soybean paste (miso), bean sprouts, and bean curd sheets.

Soy sauce: The following types of soy sauce are made from naturally fermented soybeans and wheat. Regular soy sauce gives Chinese dishes their characteristic flavor and rich brown color. Dark soy is regular sauce with molasses added. It is thicker, darker, sweeter, and more full-bodied. Use when a richer flavor and deep mahogany color are desired. Reduced-sodium soy contains about 40 percent less sodium than regular soy sauce; it tastes less salty but still has all the rich flavor. Sometimes it's called lite soy sauce. Thick sweet soy sauce (kechap manis) is very dark brown and thick, sweetened with palm sugar, and seasoned with garlic and star anise. Thin soy is lighter in color, saltier, and thinner than regular soy; it is not the same as reduced-sodium soy. Use it in fish, shellfish, and poultry dishes where little or no color change in the food is desired. See also page 225.

Spring roll wrappers: see Wrappers.

Star anise: An inedible 1-inch pod contains eight points, each encasing a shiny mahogany-colored seed. If you can't find a whole pod, use eight broken points. Star anise adds a distinct spiced licorice flavor to rich braising sauces and stews.

Sugarcane: Though you'd think sugarcane would be as sweet as sugar, it contains only about 15 percent sucrose. It is available canned. Fresh sugarcane is sold during the winter in Asian, Caribbean, and Hispanic markets.

Sweet and sour sauce: see Sauce.

Tamarind: The fibrous, sticky pulp around the seeds of the tamarind tree provide the fruity sour flavor characteristic of Southeast Asian curries, chutneys, soups, and stews. The pulp must be mashed in water, then pressed through a sieve; see instructions on page 71.

Tangerine peel, dried: The gnarled, brittle, rust-colored peel adds a light citrus flavor to sauces, soups, and braised dishes. To make your own, see page 53.

Tapioca: A fine, waxy-textured white powder is made from the root of the cassava plant. Tapioca starch is used as a thickener and with other flours to make dim sum doughs. Pearls come in various sizes; small ($\frac{1}{8}$ in.) pearls are used in creamy puddings and sweet desserts.

Taro root: For details on this somewhat hairy, dark-skinned, and rough-textured root, see page 48.

Tobiko: see Flying fish roe.

Tofu: Also called bean curd, tofu is made from soybeans and water. Texture varies: soft tofu is silky smooth and very light; regular-firm and extra-firm tofu has a denser structure and slightly spongy interior. Tofu is also available as sheets, each about 7 by 21 inches. Tofu puffs, a commercial product, each measure about 1½ by 3 inches and come three to the package. Japanese-style puffs are hollow; Chinese ones are more solid in the middle.

Turmeric: This bitter, pungent spice with intense rust color comes from the underground stem of a plant of the ginger family. It is a basic ingredient in many Indian and Southeast Asian spice blends. Look for ground turmeric on super-market spice shelves.

Unagi: see Eel.

Vinegar: Chinese black vinegar comes from the fermentation of a mixture of rice, wheat, and millet or sorghum. For details, see page 47. Palm vinegar is used in Filipino cooking; see page 156. Rice vinegar made from fermented rice, is milder, less pungent, and sweeter than distilled white vinegar. Popular Chinese and Japanese kinds (such as Chinese black vinegar and mirin, respectively range in color from clear or slightly golden to rich amber brown.

Wasabi: Fiery hot Japanese horse-radish is the standard accompaniment to sushi and sashimi. Though its pale green color looks cool and refreshing, it is one of the strongest spices used in Japanese cooking. Asian markets sell fresh wasabi root, but powders and pre-pared pastes are more commonly used.

Water chestnuts: Fresh water chestnuts are 1½-inch pointy-topped tubers with a shiny, inedible brown skin. Inside is the sweet, slightly starchy flesh. Buy fresh ones that are free of wrinkles and mold. Canned water chestnuts have a similar texture, but are not as sweet.

Wheat starch: Wheat flour with all the gluten removed is a fine-textured, off-white powder commonly used to make doughs for dim sum dishes. Steamed dough becomes soft, shiny, and opaque white.

Wine, Chinese rice: see Rice wine.

Wolfberries: Small acidic fruits of a medlar tree are used in Chinese dishes; look for packages of them in the dried foods section of Asian markets.

Wrappers: Egg roll wrappers are made from wheat flour, eggs, and water; the dough is rolled into thin, pliable sheets similar to wonton wrappers. They are filled with savory vegetables or other fillings, then deep-fried until golden brown. Lumpia wrappers are the Filipino version of egg rolls; they are a thin skin made of flour or cornstarch, eggs, and water; the skin is wrapped around a filling of raw or cooked vegetables, seasonings, and sometimes meat or shrimp. Potsticker wrappers are pasta circles made from wheat flour, water, and eggs; they can be used to wrap fillings for gyoza, potstickers, and steamed dumplings (siu mai). Filled wrappers can be deep-fried, pan-fried, or steamed. Spring roll wrappers, made of just wheat flour and water, are square or round and thinner than egg roll wrappers. When fried, they become crisp and smooth with a light texture. Wonton wrappers, made from wheat flour, water, and eggs, are about 3½ inches square and come in two thicknesses. They can hold a variety of fillings, from savory meats to sweet preserves. Thicker ones are used for deep-frying, pan-frying, or steaming; thinner ones in soups.

Yam noodles (shirataki): See devil's tongue noodles.

MAIL-ORDER SOURCES

If you can't find some of the more exotic ingredients in the recipes in this book, don't worry. These mail-order sources can bring the best of Asia to you. Now that's what I call ordering out for Asian food!

All of the companies listed carry a variety of Asian ingredients and offer a catalog, except where noted. Those specializing in cuisine specific ingredients are also noted.

Adriana's Caravan
409 Vanderbilt Street
Brooklyn, NY 11218
Tel: (800)-316-0820
Fax: (718)-436-8565 #9
E-Mail: adricara@aol.com

Anzen Importers
736 NE Union Avenue
Portland, OR 97232
Tel: (503)-233-5111

Central Market
40th & Lamar Streets
Austin, TX 76756
Tel: (800)-360-2552
Fax: (512)-206-1010
E-Mail: cml@centralmarket.com
Website: www.centralmarket.com

China Bowl Trading Company
P.O. Box 454
Westport, CT 06881
Tel: (203)-222-0381
Chinese

CMC Company
P.O. Drawer 322
Avalon, NJ 08202
Tel: (800)-CMC-2780
Fax: (609)-624-8414

Fil-Am Food Mart
685 Newark Avenue
Jersey City, NJ 07306
Tel: (201)-963-0461
Fax: (201)-963-3439
Filipino. Although they are a wholesaler, they will refer you to stores in your area.

Frieda's-By-Mail
P.O. Box 58488
Los Angeles, CA 90058
Tel: (800)-241-1771

House of Spices
8440A Kass Drive
Buena Park, CA 90621
Tel: (714)-739-1455
Fax: (714)-739-5535

House of Spices
127-40 Willets Point Blvd.
Flushing, NY 11368
Tel: (718)-507-4900

Indian Food Mill
460 Persian Drive
Sunnyvale, CA 94089
Tel: (408)-744-0777
Indian

Kam Man Food Products
200 Canal Street
New York, NY 10013
Tel: (212)-571-0330

Lee Kum Kee
304 S. Date Avenue
Alhambra, CA 91803
Tel: (800)-654-5082
Fax: (818)-282-3425
Chinese.

Mo Hotta Mo Betta
P.O. Box 4136
San Luis Obispo, CA 93403
Tel: (800)-462-3220
Fax: 800-618-4454
Website: www.mohotta.com/

Nancy's Specialty Market
P.O. Box 530
New Market, NH 03857
Tel: (800)-462-6291

Oriental Food Market
2801 West Howard Street
Chicago, IL 60645
Tel: (773)-274-2826

Oriental Pantry
423 Great Road
Acton, MA
Tel: (800)-828-0368
E-Mail: oriental@orientlpantry.com
Website: www.orientalpantry.com

Pacific Mercantile Co., Inc.
1925 Lawrence Street
Denver, CO 80202
Tel: (303)-295-0293
no catalog

Penzeys, Ltd.
P.O. Box 933
Muskego, WI 53150
Tel: (414)-574-0277
Fax: (414)-574-0278

Rafal Spice Company
2521 Russell Street
Detroit, MI 48207
Tel: (800)-228-3276
Fax: (313)-259-6220

Spice House
1031 N. Old World 3rd St.
Milwaukee, WI 53203
Tel: (414)-272-0977
Fax: (414)-272-1271

Uwajimaya
519 Sixth Avenue, South
Seattle, WA 98104
Tel: (206)-624-6248
Asian/Japanese

INDEX

ABOUT MARTIN YAN

Martin Yan, celebrated host of more than 1,500 cooking shows, highly respected food and restaurant consultant, and certified Master Chef, enjoys distinction as both teacher and author. His many talents have found unique expression in ten cookbooks, including his recent *Martin Yan's Culinary Journey Through China*.

Born in Guangzhou, China, Yan always possessed a passion for cooking. His formal introduction to the culinary world started at thirteen when he began his first apprenticeship for a well-established Hong Kong restaurant. After earning his diploma from the Overseas Institute of Cookery, Hong Kong, he traveled to Canada and then on to California.

Before receiving his M.S. in Food Science from the University of California, Davis, 1975, Yan taught Chinese cooking for the University of California extension program. He later moved back to Canada and soon became the well-known and much loved host of the syndicated show *Yan Can Cook*. He has been a guest chef/instructor at many professional chef programs, including the California Culinary Academy and Johnson & Wales University (he serves on both schools' advisory committees), the University of San Francisco and Chinese chef training programs across North America. Yan is the founder of the Yan Can International Cooking School in Foster City, California.

Today, Martin Yan enjoys national and international recognition among his peers as a master chef.

Yan Can Cook was twice recognized by the James Beard Foundation with the James Beard Award for Best Television Cooking Show in 1994 and Best Television Food Journalism in 1996. Yan has also been honored with the prestigious Antonin Carême Award by the Chef's Association of the Pacific Coast and the Courvoisier Leadership Award. Along with Paul Prudhomme, he was named Culinary Diplomat for the American Culinary Federation and in recognition of his contribution to the food and hospitality industry he received—along with America's First Lady of cooking, Julia Child—an Honorary Doctorate Degree in Culinary Arts from the leading culinary training mecca, Johnson & Wales University.

Yan has captured the admiration and loyal following of thousands of *Yan Can Cook* fans by combining his cooking artistry and teaching skill with a most personal and unique ingredient: humor. His cooking demonstrations, on television or in person, are as entertaining as they are educational. He is dedicated to dispelling the mysteries of Asian cooking and furthering the understanding and enjoyment of the cuisines of Asia.

"YAN CAN COOK: THE BEST OF ASIA" IS MADE POSSIBLE BY THE GENEROSITY OF THESE PARTNERS.

CIRCULON®

If it doesn't have circles, it's not Circulon.
Introduced in 1986 as the first hard anodized nonstick cookware, Circulon has been the leader in nonstick cookware technology. It offers serious cooks the advantages of hard anodization, superior nonstick coating, heavy-duty riveted handles, and stainless steel lids.

Maker of Oriental sauces since 1888.
Lee Kum Kee, the inventor of oyster-flavored sauce and 60 other Oriental sauces, is proud to be the leader of authentic Oriental sauces since 1888.

VITASOY®
AZUMAYA™ **Nasoya**™

Vitalizing the world for over 50 years.
Vitasoy USA Inc. is North America's largest producer and marketer of soy beverages, water-packed tofu, and fresh Asian pastas. The company markets its products under several well-known brand names, including Vitasoy®, Azumaya®, and Nasoya®.

We shop the world so you can be different.
Cost Plus World Market is a specialty retailer offering customers an ever-changing selection of casual home furnishings and entertaining products from around the world. Emphasizing both quality and value. Cost Plus World Market provides a shopping experience full of discovery in a fun and friendly environment.

The freshest tasting, highest-quality chicken and turkey selections for nearly 60 years.
It's no wonder Foster Farms is the West's largest poultry company. Family-owned Foster Farms has been providing the freshest tasting, highest-quality poultry for nearly 60 years. Foster Farms fresh chicken, fresh turkey, and deli items are always available to meet all your meal-planning needs.

To make a great meal you need the best ingredients, and the same goes for producing a cooking show or writing a cookbook. I'd like to express my deepest gratitude to the companies on these pages, whose generous support has made possible the seventh, eighth, ninth and tenth seasons of "Yan Can Cook: The Best of Asia." They are truly the key ingredients in my recipe for success, and I hope you'll make them yours, too.

ELKAY

Just say Elkay.

Headquartered in Oak Brook, Illinois, the Elkay Manufacturing Company has been bringing the timeless elegance and durability of stainless steel to great cooks everywhere through its extensive line of kitchen sinks, fine faucets, and kitchen accessories.

BRAUN

Designed to perform better.

Braun, a subsidiary of the Gillette Company, manufactures a variety of high-quality, European-designed products including household, oral care and hair care products, electric shavers, and home diagnostic appliances, which are distributed throughout the world.

Monogram.
We bring good things to life.

We bring good things to life.

The new GE Monogram Collection embraces a wide offering of professional, freestanding, built-in appliances that represent the best of European and American design.

Aroma therapy for the kitchen.

A leading manufacturer with a full line of quality kitchenware appliances, dedicated to fulfilling the needs for America's home kitchens.

VINEYARDS

Respect and stewardship of the land are at the heart of the Wente family tradition. My good friends at Wente have taught me the art of pairing Asian food with wine.

MARTIN YAN'S ACKNOWLEDGMENTS

Without the public television series *Yan Can Cook: The Best of Asia*, this book would not be possible. My special thanks to all the people who collaborated on this season of *Yan Can Cook*.

I am grateful to our production partners at KQED-TV, San Francisco, who once again turned our dreams into reality. We didn't just create season 7 of *Yan Can Cook*, but 8, 9, and 10, too! Fifty-two shows in 13 days! Wow! Deanne Hamilton, executive producer; June Ouellette, associate producer; Linda Giannecchini, assistant director; Jolee Hoyt, unit manager; Gigi Lee, production manager; and Larry Reid, director of TV operations. On the *Yan Can Cook* crew, thanks to gayle k. yamada, executive producer and series producer; Linda Brandt, producer; Katherine Russell, director; Ivan Lai, writer; and Tracy McDonough and Helen Soehalim, associate producers.

Thanks also to my international crews. Ivan Lai, writer; and Stephanie Jan, my tireless personal assistant. In Hong Kong, Singapore, the Philippines, and Malaysia: Hal Rifkin, executive producer and director of photography; Ross Babbit, executive producer, director, and editor; Mark Tocher, producer; and Philip Yu, gaffer. In Japan: gayle k. yamada, executive producer and director; and Bill Corona, cinematographer.

During our travels, we were warmly received by many generous, hardworking professionals. Many thanks to our friends at the Hong Kong Tourist Association, Singapore Tourist Promotion Board, Malaysia Tourism Promotion Board, Philippine Department of Tourism, the Ministry of Foreign Affairs of Japan, and the Consulate General of Japan, San Francisco. Without the support of these organizations, we could never have cooked so much in such a short time! I would also like to thank my friends and colleagues at United Airlines, Singapore Airlines, Malaysia Airlines, and Philippine Airlines.

They say behind every good cook there is a great kitchen, and our studio kitchen is truly the greatest. Thanks to Karen Wang and Rhoda Yee, kitchen coordinators; Sandra Rust, culinary coordinator; and the kitchen crew: Julia Lee, Winnie Lee, Vivienne Marsh, Carol Odman, Michael Procopio, and Joseph Strebler. The magnificent set of *Yan Can Cook* is the masterpiece of Bernie Schimbke, set designer and food stylist, and his assistant, my good friend Bernice Chuck Fong. A big thanks to Rieko J. Santana and the rest of the kitchen volunteers: Nick Cheng, Raymond Chew, Andrea Cope, Paul Gallette, Toni Lai, Michael Ng, Nancy J. O'Hearn, Winnie Santos, Dante Sergent, Sudaryanto, and Nancy Taketa. You guys are the best!

We were fortunate to have the support and input of some of the finest Asian restaurants in the San Francisco Bay Area, California. With the help of Rama and Sundri Krishnasamy and Raja Rajasigamoney of Restoran Rasa Sayang in Albany, I now can cook and talk like a Malaysian! My thanks to the Ocampo family from Tito Rey Restaurant in Daly City, where I enjoy wonderful Filipino foods. Thanks also to my dear friend Tokie Onizuka, and the young and talented master sushi chef Victor Onizuka of Tokie's Restaurant in Foster City. I am honored to share my kitchen with these esteemed food professionals.

PRODUCER'S THANKS

Producing a television series is truly a collaborative effort. We are grateful to our outstanding production team. The camera crew: Tim Bellen, Harry Betancourt, and Rob D'Arcy; and technical crew: Walt Bjerke, djovida, Greg King, Dick Schiller, Eric Shackelford, Helen Silvani, Birrell Walsh; and of course the stage managers: Margaret Clarke and Jim Summers. Thanks also to the volunteers: Ellen Berkman, Chien-Yu Chen, Curtis DeMartini, Taj Dhillion, Debbie Guardian, Margo Showers, and Kimberly Stevens.

We also would like to thank those individuals and companies who donated their time, talent, food, furnishings, and equipment in support of *The Best of Asia*, the 7th, 8th, 9th, and 10th series of *Yan Can Cook*.

On-location production
HM Rifkin Productions
New York

Juliet David
Culinary Connections
Singapore

Culinary advisor
Chef Wan Ismail
Culinary Ambassador to
Malaysia and Malaysia Airlines

Technical and culinary support
Clara Lapus and family
Mama Sita's Seasonings
The Philippines

California Asparagus
    Commission
Monterey Mushrooms

Restoran Rasa Sayang
Albany, California

Tito Rey Restaurant
Daly City, California

Tokie's Restaurant
Foster City, California

Tomoye Takahashi
Takahashi Imports
San Francisco, California

99 Ranch Markets
Northern California

Special thanks
Ah Sam Florist
Angray-Fantastico Corp.
BiRite Food Service Distributors
Culture Shock Ethnic Imports
Greenleaf Produce
Man-U, Treasures of China
Oscartielle Equipment USA
OXO International
Royal Hawaiian Seafood
Royal Pacific Foods
Takahashi Home Decor
Whole Foods Markets
Wing Sing Chong Co., Inc.
Wente Vineyards
Wooden Duck Furnishings

gayle k. yamada;
Executive producer and Series producer

MORE TASTE-TEMPTING RECIPES
FROM MARTIN YAN!

Martin Yan introduces readers to the sights, tastes, and techniques of the regional cuisines of China in this companion cookbook to *Yan Can Cook* the series that won the 1996 James Beard Award for Best Television Food Journalism.

Packed with personal anecdotes and mouth-watering photos, this culinary journey brings more than 120 authentic, delicious, and surprisingly easy Chinese dishes to American kitchens.

"He's done more to open China than anyone since Nixon."
Food & Wine

$18.95 at your favorite bookstore.
Or call 1-(800)-647-3600.

THANKS TO OUR INTERNATIONAL FRIENDS

For the gracious reception we received as we traveled the length and breadth of five Asian countries, we are greatly indebted to the following tourist promotion boards and airlines, without whose generous support, *Yan Can Cook: the Best of Asia* could never have become a reality.

Our thanks to the:

Consulate General of Japan, San Francisco

Ministry of Foreign Affairs, Japan

Hong Kong Tourist Association

The original music that so beautifully captures the moods and mysteries of Asia in the public television series, *Yan Can Cook: The Best of Asia*, was composed by Noel Quinlan of The Sound Department, Hong Kong and Australia. For more information on his richly evocative

"Middle Kingdom" CD series, contact Big Sky Music at (e-mail)

bigsky@netvigator.com, or (website) http://www.bigskymusic.com

Thanks, also, to San Jose Taiko for composing and performing the original music that serves as an evocative audio backdrop for the Japan portion of the series.

ALSO FROM MARTIN YAN

If you've enjoyed this book and the public television series, Yan Can Cook: The Best of Asia, wait till you see what else we have in store! For more information about these and other gourmet items from Yan Can Cook, please contact us at: **Yan Can Cook, PO Box 4755, Foster City, CA 94404. (Fax: 650-525-0522) www.yancancook.com**

Books

- *Martin Yan's Culinary Journey Through China*
- *A Wok For All Seasons*
- *Martin Yan, The Chinese Chef*
- *The Yan Can Cook Book*
- *Martin Yan's Simple Guide to Chinese Ingredients and Other Asian Specialties*

This handy guidebook takes the mystery out of shopping for Asian ingredients. It's packed with color photos, cooking tips, and storage information. And best of all, it's small enough to carry with you every time you shop.

Martin Yan's Ultimate Chinese Chef's Knife

I spend so much time slicing, dicing and chopping, that I finally decided to create my very own Chinese Chef's Knife to make cooking easier...and a lot more fun! It was designed with durability and ease of handling in mind and features a high-carbon stainless steel blade, so you can look forward to years of reliable, precision performance.

Yan Can Cook Online

Now you can visit me on the worldwide web at http://www.yancancook.com. It's a place to share our recipes, send us e-mail, and learn about our exciting culinary tours. You'll also find information about the latest trends and specialty items from Asia from my friends and partners on the internet at:

CHANNEL A
www.channelA.com